Amy,
Stay Green!
Beth Fiteni

The Green Wardrobe Guide

Finding Eco-Chic Fashions That Look Great
and Help Save the Planet

Beth Fiteni

∞INFINITY
PUBLISHING

Copyright © 2018 by Beth Fiteni

ISBN 978-1-4958-1217-0 Paperback
ISBN 978-1-4958-1216-3 Hardcover
ISBN 978-1-4958-1218-7 eBook

Published April 2018

INFINITY PUBLISHING
1094 New DeHaven Street, Suite 100
West Conshohocken, PA 19428-2713
Toll-free (877) BUY BOOK
Local Phone (610) 941-9999
Fax (610) 941-9959
Info@buybooksontheweb.com
www.buybooksontheweb.com

This book is dedicated to Joann Elizabeth Tamin (JET), whose little shop Jet's Dream, in Greenport, NY inspired me to write this book; to my Grandma Mary who was a seamstress, and to all the workers who make our clothing – may you and your children always have a healthy and clean environment.

Credits and People to Whom I am Grateful

To my wonderful, brilliant helpers, Rose Schipano, Marisol Maddox, Erica Cirino, Muriel Toussaint, and Leah Kahler, who put up with me and inspired me through this process. This book would not exist without you.

Mary Lee Weir (photographer)
Guzin Potente (model)
Lizbeth Vera (model)
Patrick Kehoe
Katrina Meyer
Karen Joy Miller
Helen Fiteni
Luis Vasquez
Guadalupe Flores
Dominique Drakeford
Lara Spiteri (Cover art, www.facebook.com/lara.spiteri.fashion)

All the experts who spent their time providing interviews: Sass Brown, Jamsin Malik Chua, Anne Gillespie, Amy Hall, and Dan Sanders, and all the ecofashion people/companies mentioned in this book, for their contribution to giving the rest of us greener options.

Table of Contents

SECTION 1
The Fabrics

Introduction

What's Really in Our Clothing
Why Bother Striving for a Green Wardrobe?

"Happiness is when what you think, what you say, and what you do are in harmony." – Mohandas K. Gandhi

Everyone wears clothes (except nudists). Clothing is considered one of the basic necessities of life, in addition to food, water and shelter. It serves the practical purpose of protecting us from the elements, but is also an expression of personal style, status, and even identity. Clothing can also be a form of entertainment, creativity, and reflect our daily mood. Global fiber demand is 60 million tons,[1] with each of us in the US consuming 83.9 lbs. of textiles per person per year on average.[2] Employing about 26 million people worldwide,[3] fashion is big business ($7 trillion/year), and the fashion world creates clothing for ever-changing current trends.

One of the more positive of recent societal trends is the one surrounding environmental awareness and the impacts of our daily activities on the world around us. There is growing awareness that the choices we make every day can end up causing air or water pollution, increased waste in a landfill, or deforestation without us even knowing it. Most people, when made aware of these problems, want to do what they can, within reason, to at least not make the problem worse. While many people are starting to think "green" by saving energy, bringing a reusable bag to the grocery market, recycling, and maybe trying organic or local food, activists haven't yet managed to stir up a widespread mainstream conversation about the impact of our clothing on our environment.

---

1   Fletcher, Kate. *Sustainable Fashion & Textiles: Design Journeys*, 6. London: Earthscan, 2008.
2   Hawley, Jana. "Economic Impact of Textile and Clothing Recycling." *In Sustainable Fashion: Why Now? A Conversation Exploring Issues, Practices, and Possibilities*, 207-232. New York: Fairchild Books, 2008.
3   Fletcher, Kate. *Sustainable Fashion & Textiles: Design Journeys*, 42. London: Earthscan, 2008.

3

As a result, and through no fault of their own, most people who shop at typical malls are likely not aware of the process by which the clothes are made, and most don't consciously question it. So, though many people have become more aware of reading food labels to check ingredients or to see if a food is organic, how many of us read our clothing labels to see what each item is made out of on the basis of its ecological footprint? Even if we did, clothing labels don't exactly announce that a garment was made in sweatshop or dyed with toxic dyes.

This book is here to help move along the slowly growing conversation about the connection between our clothes and the planet.

Whereas native people used to wear animal hide and perhaps a grass skirt depending on the region, nowadays, common fabrics are made from many different raw materials. They are then dyed with synthetic dyes, cut into clothing patterns, sewn according to design, and delivered by plane, train, or truck to stores and boutiques around the world. Right now, the human population is at about 7 billion. Looked at collectively, the production of clothing for that many people has a huge impact on our environment and the health of the workers producing it.

What's Really In Our Clothing

Let's start with polyester. Developed in the 1950s, thankfully polyester slacks went out of fashion after the 1970s, but polyester still holds a big role in today's fashions. About 11 million tons of polyester is produced each year.[4] An ester is "an organic compound formed when an acid and an alcohol combine and release water."[5] The word "poly" derives from Greek and means "more than one; many; much."[6] So polyester is a synthetic plastic polymer made up of many esters, xylene, and ethylene. It can contain purified terephthalic acid (PET), also known as plastic #1, so is technically recyclable, and has many uses, from plastic bottles to the finish on musical instruments. It retains color well, stretches well, eschews wrinkles, and can survive many washes, so, on the positive side, it is durable.

But the key downside is that it is made from petrochemicals. Like most other plastics, it is essentially made from oil. Since there is a concern that plastic #1 water bottles may

---

4   Mcdonough, William, and Michael Braungart. "Eco-Intelligence: Transforming the Textile Industry." green@work, May/June 2002.
5   *The American Heritage Science Dictionary*. Boston: Houghton Mifflin, 2005.
6   Ibid.

Left: Soham Dave, Right: Om Sutra. Both made with natural indigo

leach phthalates, which are hormone-disrupting chemicals into the water especially when the plastic is heated, it makes one wonder if there is the possibility of phthalates being absorbed into our skin, especially if it's a hot summer perspiration-invoking day. One study concluded that polyester underpants might decrease sperm count.[7] The direct cause is not known, but the theory is that the fabric creates an electrostatic field.[8]

Did you know?

Synthetic Fibers pose such a burn risk that US troops in 2006 in Iraq were not allowed to wear them off base.[1]

---

1   Clement, Anna Maria, and Brian R. Clement. *Killer Clothes: How Seemingly Innocent Clothing Choices Endanger Your Health—and How to Protect Yourself!* Summertown, Tennessee: Hippocrates Publications, 2011. 12.

"Most polyester is manufactured using antimony as a catalyst. Along with being a carcinogen, antimony is toxic to the heart, lungs, liver and skin. Long-term inhalation of antimony trioxide, a by-product of polymer production, can cause chronic bronchitis and emphysema. Other by-products include mill wastewater tainted with antimony trioxide, which leaches from polyester fibers during the high-temperature dye process. Recycling polyester, another high-temperature process, creates the same wastewater problems; burning it releases antimony trioxide into the air. Indeed, the conventional manufacture of polyester is so riddled with harmful chemicals a recycling strategy that does not redesign the whole process could not hope to do anything but recapitulate toxic events."[9]

This is echoed in the article "Waste Couture: Environmental Impact of the Clothing Industry," which says,

"The manufacture of polyester and other synthetic fabrics is an energy-intensive process requiring large amounts of crude oil and releasing emissions including volatile organic compounds, particulate matter, and acid gases such as hydrogen chloride, all of which can cause or aggravate respiratory disease. Volatile monomers, solvents, and other by-products of polyester

---

7   Shafik, Ahmed. "Effect of different types of textile fabric on spermatogenesis: an experimental study." *Urological Research* 21, no. 5 (1993): 367–370.
8   Shafik, Ahmed, "Polyester textiles and infertility." *Urol Corr Club Letter.* September 23, 1992. 78.
9   Mcdonough, William, and Michael Braungart. "Eco-Intelligence: Transforming the Textile Industry." *green@work*, May/June 2002.

Top: indigo loom, Bottom Left: Nomi Network (organic cotton tee, recycled bag),
Bottom Right: hand dyed yarn

production are emitted in the wastewater from polyester manufacturing plants. The EPA, under the Resource Conservation and Recovery Act, considers many textile manufacturing facilities to be hazardous waste generators."[10]

Did you know?

The chemical Microban®, which is combined into polyester, nylon, and cotton blends, is an antimicrobial that may contain triclosan, which is currently suspected to be a hormone disruptor. Antimicrobial chemicals kill not only "bad" microbes but good ones as well. The widespread use of antimicrobials is causing concern because germs are becoming resistant to them. Some manufacturers of sportswear are adding the nerve-toxin pesticide permethrin to clothing as insect repellent, which has unknown health effects on the wearer over time.

Nylon is another petroleum-based, and thus nonrenewable, material. It can emit formaldehyde, which is used to make it more elastic. It is considered a polyamide and was originally developed by DuPont® around World War II. It is made of diamine, dicarboxylic acid, and acetic acid.[11] One of its first uses was for women's stockings, or "nylons." It has a nice luster, is stretchable, and was used for many military uses such as parachutes. It resists bacteria and mold, so in other words is slow to biodegrade. In some uses this is a good thing when we need things to last a long time. But when it comes to clothing that we wear a few times and throw away, it means our landfills are full of plastic fabrics that will be there for centuries, slowly off-gassing carbon. That's one reason it's good that styles come back decades later and we can rewear them—less waste. Nylon is energy-intensive to make, and its production creates the greenhouse gas nitrous oxide.[12]

Spandex was introduced in 1959, and was made from cracking petroleum into propylene and ethylene gases.[13]

10   Claudio, Luz. "Waste Couture: Environmental Impact of the Clothing Industry." *Environmental Health Perspectives* 115. no. 9 (2007): 449-454.
11   Clement, Anna Maria, and Brian R. Clement. *Killer Clothes: How Seemingly Innocent Clothing Choices Endanger Your Health—and How to Protect Yourself!* Summertown, Tennessee: Hippocrates Publications, 2011. 34.
12   Fletcher, Kate. *Sustainable Fashion & Textiles: Design Journeys*, 13. London: Earthscan, 2008.
13   Clement, Anna Maria, and Brian R. Clement. *Killer Clothes: How Seemingly Innocent Clothing Choices Endanger Your Health—and How to Protect Yourself!* Summertown, Tennessee: Hippocrates Publications, 2011. 10.

Acrylic is made from acrylic acid,[14] which the Environmental Protection Agency says is a "strong irritant to the skin, eyes, and mucous membranes in humans."[15] It is not known whether acrylic acid causes cancer, but it is a possible mutagen and reproductive toxin, and is toxic to the bladder, brain, upper respiratory tract, eyes, and central nervous system (CNS).[16]

Is synthetic clothing affecting our oceans? For several years, scientists have been finding that plastic particles from clothing may be contributing to the growth of microplastics in our oceans and in the Great Lakes. "Plastic particles less than 1mm, defined as 'microplastics,' have been steadily accumulating in marine environments across the globe. Studies of shoreline debris at eighteen different locations worldwide have identified small, fibrous particles of plastic which are washed up on beaches, embedded in sediments, and even found in cell tissues of marine organisms…. The sources of plastic contamination are numerous, but researchers …have identified synthetic textiles as a primary contributor. When synthetic clothing such as polyester, acrylic, and nylon are washed in conventional washing machines, minute fibrous particles are released from the garments and discharged into the environment through sewage outlets…."[17] In a 2016 study, researchers at the University of California at Santa Barbara found that, "on average, synthetic fleece jackets release 1.7 grams of microfibers each wash. It also found that older jackets shed almost twice as many fibers as new jackets."[18] The study was funded by clothing manufacturer Patagonia.

Aside from the fabrics themselves, there are over 8000 chemicals used with both synthetic and natural fibers to remove oils, break down cellulose, to add color, or to make it stainproof.[19] Some clothing is treated with chemicals postproduction to make it less prone to wrinkling (usually this involves formaldehyde), or more waterproofed

---

14 Clement, Anna Maria, and Brian R. Clement. *Killer Clothes: How Seemingly Innocent Clothing Choices Endanger Your Health—and How to Protect Yourself!* Summertown, Tennessee: Hippocrates Publications, 2011. 34.
15 US Environmental Protection Agency (EPA). "Acrylic Acid: Hazard Summary." EPA Air Toxics Website, April 1992.
16 "Material Safety Data Sheet: Acrylic Acid MSDS." ScienceLab.com: Chemicals & Laboratory Equipment.
17 Eartheasy Blog. "Microscopic Plastic Particles May be Entering Food Chain." 2012.
18 Messinger, Leah. "How your clothes are poisoning our oceans and food supply." The Guardian, June 20, 2016.
19 "Organic Clothes: An Unforgettable Mix of Healthy & Cool." http://www.cool-organic-clothing.com/organic-clothes.html. Cool-Organic-Clothing. 2016.

(using flouropolymers).[20] These features are certainly a convenience, but sometimes the chemicals used can be toxic. Here is an example: "An Ohio woman has launched a lawsuit against Victoria's Secret because of the negative health effects she suffered after wearing one of the company's bras. Several other women have contacted her with similar stories and are hoping to make it a class action lawsuit. Lawyers had the bra tested in a lab and found it contained traces of formaldehyde. It turns out that formaldehyde is a common additive to fabric because of the easy care properties it provides such as preventing wrinkling and static cling among others. What manufacturers seem to have overlooked are the health risks it poses when absorbed by the skin and into the bloodstream."[21]

Did You Know?

Polyvinyl chloride (PVC) is used to make plastisol ink, which is used in some t-shirt and other garment panel printing. It contains phthalates, which are hormone-disrupting chemicals. Thankfully, some companies are starting to use safer alternatives. See www.nontoxicprint.com.

In fact, the "finishing" of fabric to prepare it for dying or printing can be where much of a fabric's environmental impact comes from. "Finishing is the chief cause of environmental impacts in the production phase, using significant quantities of water, energy, and chemicals and producing substantial amounts of effluent. Some of the chemicals used contain toxics, such as heavy metals like copper,[22] chromium, and cobalt, which are known carcinogens, dioxin—also carcinogenic and suspected hormone disruptors—and formaldehyde, a suspected carcinogen."[23] These chemicals are released as waste and are usually treated before being released into the environment, depending on local regulations. But some chemicals are not treatable, so prevention is the best measure.

A group of large companies has gotten together to form the Apparel and Footwear International RSL Management group, or AFIRM. An RSL is a Restricted Substance

20   Clement, Anna Maria, and Brian R. Clement. *Killer Clothes: How Seemingly Innocent Clothing Choices Endanger Your Health—and How to Protect Yourself!* Summertown, Tennessee: Hippocrates Publications, 2011. 44.
21   "I'll Take My Lingerie Without Formaldehyde Thanks..." Beautiful Green. December 4, 2008.
22   Fletcher, Kate. *Sustainable Fashion & Textiles: Design Journeys*, 51. London: Earthscan, 2008.
23   Fletcher, Kate. *Sustainable Fashion & Textiles: Design Journeys*, 49. London: Earthscan, 2008.

Anti-Sandblasting Campaign

Have you ever wondered how brand-new jeans that have a rugged or "distressed" look are made to look that way? Just as it sounds, the jeans are blasted with silica (sand) with blower guns. Workers exposed to this fine sand have suffered health effects in some cases, such as in Turkey, as reported in the New York Times.[1] A study done by doctors at a hospital for thoracic diseases in Istanbul was published in a medical journal for lung specialists called Chest.

"They followed 32 male textile workers who came to their hospital with breathing problems between 2001 and 2009. That year, after news reports of a 'silicosis epidemic,' Turkish health authorities banned sandblasting denim. The men were young, with a mean age of 31. Most were previously healthy…. They had worked a mean of 66 hours a week for a little over two years each, mostly at small sandblasting shops with fewer than 10 workers. Six of the workers died, and 16 others had disabling lung damage from breathing the fine sand. The researchers calculated that a typical worker with silicosis had only a 69 percent chance of surviving five years." The story also states that sandblasting denim jeans has long been banned in Europe and the US.

Workers groups and the Clean Clothes Campaign,[2] an international group focused on improving working conditions in the garment industry, started to campaign against sandblasting in Bangladesh that resulted in numerous media articles. One story reports a worker saying that at one point his mouth and nose started to bleed, while others report effects on their eyes from the dust. The good news is that the media attention is having an effect. "Gucci, Levi's, H&M and Gap have all vowed to stop selling sandblasted products, while Dolce & Gabbana has been targeted in an Internet campaign to take a similar stance."[3] Kalpana Akhter, general secretary of the Bangladesh Center for Workers Solidarity is quoted as saying, "As most Bangladeshi companies have no health insurance, many of those who become sick simply quit their jobs and return to their villages in dreadful health."[4]

---

1   McNeil, Donald G., Jr. "Turkey: Sandblasting Jeans for 'Distressed' Look Proved Harmful for Textile Workers." *The New York Times*, October 31, 2011, New York ed., Health sec.
2   Clean Clothes Campaign. www.cleanclothes.org.
3   Clean Clothes Campaign. "Sandblasting Jeans Comes Under Fire in Bangladesh." Change. org. October 10, 2011.
4   Ibid.

List. The group includes firms such as The Gap, Adidas, Nike, Puma, Timberland, Levi Strauss, Hugo Boss, and H&M. Their website says that substances commonly found in RSLs include:

- Carcinogenic aromatic amines (related to azo dyes, 22–24 banned amines depends on the brand's preference)
- Allergenic disperse dyes
- Heavy metals (e.g. cadmium, chromium, lead, mercury, nickel, etc....)
- Organotins (e.g. MBT, TBT, TPhT, etc....)
- Chlorinated aromatics (chlorinated organic carriers, such as chlorinated benzenes and chlorinated toluenes)
- Flame retardants (e.g. PBBs, pentaBDE, OctaBDE, etc.)
- Formaldehyde
- Phthalates (e.g. DEHP, DINP, etc.)
- Auxiliary chemicals such as PFOS, etc.[24]

Dyes

Synthetic chemical dyes have been known to pollute many a river especially in India and China; 90 percent of wastewater is dumped into rivers.[1] Synthetic dyes are petrochemical-based, can off-gas sulfur dioxide during dying, and contain chemicals such as coal tar, which is made up of many possibly carcinogenic substances. Heavy metals like chromium and cadmium are used to make bright color dyes.[2] Dioxins, which are carcinogens, are also used in the dyeing process and are often discharged into the environment.[3] Azo dyes are commonly used, and are a type of dye made from genotoxic aromatic amines that are damaging to our cells' DNA, and may lead to cancer.

---

1   Egan, Greta. *Wear No Evil*. 2014. 32.
2   Earth Pledge Foundation. *Future Fashion White Papers*. Edited by Leslie Hoffman. New York: Earth Pledge Foundation, 2008. 202.
3   "Synthetic Dyes: A Look at Environmental & Human Risks." Green Cotton. June 18, 2008.

---

24   "AFIRM: Frequently Asked Questions." AFIRM Group. 2014.

The blog Green Cotton writes, "The chemical aniline, the basis for a popular group of dyes known as azo dyes (specifically group III A1 and A2) which are considered deadly poisons (giving off carcinogenic amines) and dangerous to work with, [are] also highly flammable." It goes on to point out the effects on workers: "In the United States, deaths amongst factory workers from several cancers, cerebrovascular disease, lung disease are significantly higher—40 times higher, for some diseases—than in the general population." [4]

The Wall Street Journal reported a case where villagers in Southern China were complaining that their river was turning bright red. Sure enough, an inspection showed that a textile mill, which dyed apparel for companies including Wal-Mart and Nike, was dumping thousands of tons of dye effluent from a pipe under the plant into the river. [5]

Natural dying has been practiced for centuries in many cultures. Fibers can be dyed with natural dyes, often made from plants or minerals. [6] There is a myth that natural dyes are "blah" but one natural dyer writes that she works with about 120 different natural colors. [7] They do last and in some cases even grow brighter with washing. For example, indigo can be made from indigo flowers, and madder plant can make red dye. However, these plant sources need to be grown commercially to make it more affordable vs. petrochemical-based dyes. Though sometimes-toxic mordants (which make the color stick to the fabric) are still even used with natural dyes, there are natural mordants including mineral salts from iron, copper, tin, and alum. [8] One company using natural dyes is Prophetik. "Low-impact" dyes are synthetic but use less water and do not require heavy metals. One company using low-impact dyes is Alternative Apparel, in their Alternative Earth line. [9]

---

4   Ibid.
5   Spencer, Jane. "China Pays Steep Price As Textile Exports Boom." *The Wall Street Journal*, August 22, 2007.
6   Ellis, Catharine. "The Science of Natural Dyes." *Surface Design Journal*, Spring 2013.
7   "In Defense of Truth and Beauty." In Future Fashion White Papers, edited by Leslie Hoffman, by Earth Pledge Foundation, chapter by Cheryl Kolander, 170. New York: Earth Pledge Foundation, 2008.
8   Fletcher, Kate. *Sustainable Fashion & Textiles: Design Journeys*, 54. London: Earthscan, 2008.
9   Egan, Greta. Wear No Evil. 2014. 35.

So, by logical deduction, if these substances are on "restricted" lists, this means some manufacturers are indeed creating clothing and footwear that contain these substances. Most likely these chemicals create ease of production, or enhanced product performance, or are cheaper to use than more natural counterparts. How would a consumer know? We wouldn't, of course, because it's not as though companies advertise this. Not that they're evil, but, as of now, there is no requirement to do so here in the US. However, in the European Union, there is a regulation called REACH (Registration, Evaluation, and Authorisation of Chemicals), in place since 2007, which requires companies to register chemicals in products that are entering their countries in large quantities.

What Having a Green Wardobe Means

First and foremost, let's start with what this book is not about. Let it be said that in no way is this book meant to make people feel badly about their previous choices. It's not as though clothing advertisements would ever lead us to assume the complexity of people and processes working behind the scenes to produce the clothes we buy. We can't feel guilty when we don't know.

This book is meant to inform and empower, since we all "vote with our dollars" and can influence change in the market once we become aware of the pros and cons of products being sold. It is meant to make us savvy consumers see through a new lens, and to get us excited about pursuing planet-friendly alternatives. The book also seeks to bolster people who are intentionally attempting to produce clothing in a sustainable way.

Though I just referred to us as "consumers," this book is also not meant to encourage overconsumption of clothing. An architect I know once said, "The greenest building is the one that doesn't get built." The same goes for clothing. Part of reducing our environmental impact via our closet is simply not purchasing clothing that is not needed. There are many companies nowadays that provide "Fast Fashion," or clothing that is affordably priced and usually not of high quality, so that people can change it out regularly. Often items are worn only a few times, maybe for one season, and then discarded. This is a recent concept, of clothing being "disposable"; in past centuries people tended to have fewer than ten outfits that lasted many years.

"We have lost sight of the true cost of what we buy." - Penelope Cook, Founder and Owner of ecofashion shop Equa, London, UK.

In 2015, director Andrew Morgan created a film on this issue—The True Cost, about the impacts of fast fashion on people and the environment.[25] Many of us have become used to the availability of cheap clothing, which is often poorly made en masse, since it seems to be everywhere. A friend who worked in the fashion industry told me that people would work long hours poring over details of each garment, rushing the order off to China, with everyone along the chain feeling pressured to get items out on store floors faster and faster. China is the largest exporter of fast fashion, accounting for 30 percent of world apparel exports.[26] Part of having a sustainable wardrobe is choosing items we need that will endure the test of time both in terms of style and durability, as well as looking at what material each item is made of.

Steps to a Green Wardrobe

1) Decide if you really need it.
2) Determine if what you need could be found and reused from a thrift store, consignment shop, or sources such as eBay.
3) When you need new clothing, seek fabrics that have the least environmental impact, as described here in the following chapters.
4) Launder clothing using eco-friendly methods described herein.
5) Instead of tossing salvageable clothing, mend or repair it.
6) Donate quality clothing in good condition back to a thrift store so it can potentially be reused. This is still not a perfect solution (see Conclusion chapter). According to the EPA Office of Solid Waste, Americans throw away more than 68 pounds of clothing and textiles per person per year,[1] and 84 percent of discarded clothes winds up in an incinerator or landfill.[2]

---

1   Claudio, Luz. "Waste Couture: Environmental Impact of the Clothing Industry." Environmental Health Perspectives 115. no. 9 (2007): 449-454 and Wallander, Mattias. "Closet Cast-Offs Clogging Landfills." Huffington Post, June 27, 2010. http://www.huffingtonpost.com/mattias-wallander/closet-cast-offs-clogging_b_554400.html.
2   Jacobsen, Jax. Ecowatch. "Fast Fashion: Cheap Clothes = Huge Environmental Cost." September 2016.

---

25   The True Cost movie. http://truecostmovie.com. 2015.
26   Claudio, Luz. "Waste Couture: Environmental Impact of the Clothing Industry." *Environmental Health Perspectives* 115. no. 9 (2007): 449–454.

That is our first step.

A second step is checking first of we can reuse clothing that already exists. This can take two forms. One way to reuse clothing is to shop for previously owned fashions at thrift and consignment shops. While it may take some digging, sometimes these shops will have brand-new items that still have a tag, and even brand name items. As the saying goes, one man's trash can be another's treasure. Websites such as eBay, Craiglist, pre-ownedclothing.com, threadflip.com, buffaloexchange.com, as well as in-person clothing swap "meet-ups" are great resources for buying and selling pre-owned clothing.

Another way to reuse clothing is for designers and even creative home-sewers to "upcycle." This means taking an existing piece (or multiple pieces) of clothing that may be slightly out of style and altering or "repurposing" it/them to make it into something fabulous. (More on this in the concluding chapter.)

So what is this book about?

This book will focus on the good news that there are fashions made with materials that have a lesser impact on the planet than those usually used to make clothes found in common retail stores—in other words, "eco-fashions." So this is the third step—again, we as consumers do have a choice, and we can use the power of our knowledge to create change for the better. It's a matter of our becoming informed of the options and, when possible, making different choices about the types of clothing we opt to wear. A great summation of all the factors that make clothing sustainable is in the book Wear No Evil; author Greta Egan, an inspiring eco-fashionista, lays out what she calls the "Integrity Chart" that lists sixteen criteria that make clothing sustainable and also socially conscious such as organic, fair trade, natural dyes, recycled, low water footprint, etc. The more criteria an item can claim the better.

Just as the planet is facing a big problem with climate change and all its related effects, many believe we do have a window of opportunity to turn things around both through individual action and through policy changes. However, it is human nature for people to tune out when they feel overwhelmed and that there's nothing they can do. So, this book will provide solutions for the regular shopper. It will feature an inspiring and novel message about what types of fabrics are available that have less impact on the planet, where to find them, and will show examples in diverse price ranges.

As an environmentalist of many years, I became interested in this topic while working at Beyond Pesticides in Washington, DC, in the late 1990s.[27] At the time, though I wanted to support sustainable fashions, there was little variety, and what I did find left much to be desired—to be blunt, it was plain ugly. Unless you were a "hippie," no professional would be inclined to wear these clothes to work. Now, as more designers become eco-savvy and want to try new innovative fabrics, more eco-fashion shops are opening and more mainstream styles are available, so even the-not-previously-eco-minded would actually wear them and consider them "cool."

Though I live on a nonprofit salary, currently about 40 percent of my wardrobe consists of clothing made from organic, hemp, or bamboo, and those pieces are some of my favorite clothes. My goal is 100 percent. It is so exciting to find additions to my eco-collection, because I know I'm supporting clothing producers that want to do the right thing. Through this book, I want to share my enthusiasm for this emerging area of fashion by not only telling the story of these fabrics and some of the people who make them available, but also showing pictures of clothing available now at shops and online. I took pictures of my entire eco-wardrobe, so examples of each fabric will be shown along the way!

Rather than focusing on individual designers, since there are hundreds, and new ones emerging every day, this book will describe the types of natural fabrics available today and where to look for them. The first chapter covers organic cotton, an exciting area of growth and interest. The second chapter covers hemp, an old standby of natural fibers. The third chapter covers bamboo, a newly emerging branding of what was known before simply as "rayon." The fourth chapter will cover lyocell and modal, both of which are made from tree fibers. Chapter five will cover a variety of different other alternative fabrics that haven't made it quite as much into the mainstream as the first few.

While most of the book is geared towards illustrating eco-fashions that the average person might be able to find and afford, Chapter 6 focuses on the high-fashion world and which of the most well-known high-end names are incorporating natural fabrics into their lines. A related part of the eco-clothing story is how we care for our clothes. Therefore, Chapter 7 will describe the issues with dry cleaning and what the alternatives are. Chapter 8 will cover natural cosmetics and body products, and Chapter 9 will cover

---

27   Beyond Pesticides: Protecting Health and the Environment with Science, Policy and Action. www.beyondpesticides.org.

furniture and housewares, because there is a natural nexus between what we wear and put on our bodies and the home environment in which we live. Finally you will find resources on where to find all of these wonderful offerings and a listing of places to buy organic/natural clothing, toys, and accessories for babies. The book mostly focuses on the United States, but demonstrates the global economy and how sustainable fabrics and eco-fashion are being produced in countries around the world.

This book hopefully will be a catalyst to bring about the discussion on the connection between our clothes, the planet, and even the lives of those who produce the fabrics. Along the way, you will find fun facts to impress your friends, and some insight and stories from people who grow the fibers, process the fabrics, and design and sell the clothes. Hopefully this will give us a broader, more informed view of what we are choosing when we go to the clothing store.

Most of all, we will have fun in finding out that we have numerous options and that there are beautiful clothes made with good intentions and a broader awareness that will make us look great while saving the planet. Our clothes will come and go, but our planet is the only one we've got.

"It makes no difference where you go, there you are. And it makes no difference what you have, there's always more to want. Until you are happy with who you are, you will never be happy because of what you have."
– Zig Ziglar

Interview: Dan Sanders, Owner, Spiritex, Asheville, NC

Marylou and I had launched a better woman's sportswear line in the 1980s called "ML Marsh Designs." Although our company was successful and Marylou was flourishing as a designer, we were starting to question how things were made, particularly the sourcing and components of the piece goods. Perhaps it grew out of starting a family of our own (by 1989 we had a two-year-old son and a newborn girl) that we started questioning why our wovens reeked of formaldehyde, the lack of naturally dyed piece goods in the marketplace, not to mention wondering about the potentially toxic chemicals used in all aspects of the clothing industry.

The developing eco-consciousness in our personal lives began prompting and leading us toward applying it to our professional lives. We had already shifted to eating organic produce whenever possible, were among the first in our community to recycle our recyclable household waste, and to use unbleached recycled paper (modest shifts by today's standards, but quite proactive back then. At the end of the decade, while perusing a Greenpeace catalog, we were struck by their emphasis on unbleached, dioxin-free paper on the one hand, yet the wide array of branded apparel merchandise they offered was printed on typically bleached, conventional cotton/polyester shirts. The next day I tracked down the merchandise manager of Greenpeace in her Washington, DC office. To my surprise, she was very receptive, "Please, if you can offer something better please do, there is nothing we can find out there that aligns with our mission!" A week later I met her in person. We had a very good rapport and spoke for hours about many possibilities, including the unbleached T-Shirts I had already put into work.

However, there was one potential direction that excited me above all others— the idea of creating the first mass-produced product line from organically grown cotton fiber. It was an idea that kept me awake at night, an idea that with partners Marylou and Eddie Mandeau, was somehow brought to the market in grand scale, within 9 months, through our fledgling company, "Ecosport." Within two years we had established accounts with Greenpeace in virtually every country they had offices, Esprit, Levis, Nike and Patagonia, as we manufactured product for their respective early sustainable merchandise endeavors. Ecosport was sold to a public company in 2000. In 2005, we set out to finish what we started, namely by tightening up the local supply chain. Now our store Spiritex sells clothing made from cotton grown and sewn in North Carolina.

Chapter 1

Organic Cotton
All Cottons Are Not Created Equal

"Isn't all cotton organic?" my aunt asked over Christmas dinner. It took some explaining to get through to her that unfortunately the answer is no. During the course of conversation at our annual holiday family gathering, it came up that the skirt I wore for the occasion was made with organic cotton. Back in the day, all things cotton had been considered "natural," as opposed to clothing made with nylon or polyester, petroleum-based fabrics. And of course, cotton is certainly a natural product since the white puffs that are spun into thread are the protective fiber that surrounds cottonseeds on a cotton plant. It's a wonderful fiber provided by nature that humankind was clever enough to make use of and eventually domesticate.

However, modern cotton crops are grown with the use of many chemicals most people have never even heard of. In fact, the US Environmental Protection Agency considers seven of the top fifteen pesticides[1] used on cotton in the United States as "possible," "likely," "probable," or "known" human carcinogens (causing cancer) such as acephate, dichloropropene, diuron, fluometuron, pendimethalin, tribufos, and trifluralin.

Pendimethalin? What the heck is that, you ask? It's a toxic pesticide that kills the bane of all cotton farmers' existences: the boll weevil. This is the main insect that likes to chew up valuable cotton crops. Due to this weevil, plus many other damaging pests, more insecticides are used on conventionally grown cotton than on any other single crop.

---

[1]   A "pesticide" is anything that kills, mitigates, repels, or destroys a pest. This can include insecticides, which target insects; herbicides, which target weeds; fungicides, which target fungi, and so on.

Cotton crops are sprayed with about 25 percent of all insecticides used on all of the worlds' crops combined, according to the Organic Trade Association, and about 10 percent of all the world's pesticides combined (including herbicides, insecticides, and defoliants).[2] According to the World Health Organization (WHO), 20,000 deaths occur each year from pesticide poisoning in developing countries, many of these from cotton farming. Agrochemical companies make on average $2 billion selling cotton pesticides each year.[3] And, pressure to use chemicals also comes from banks, because they are more likely to offer loans to farmers when they believe that a crop is more secure from the threat of pests.

Sadly, crops sometimes do still fail. Some farmers in India get so in over their heads with debt to chemical companies by buying more and more seed and pesticides that there has been a rash of farmer suicides there over the past few years. In fact, some swallow the pesticides themselves to commit the act. "According to the National Crime Records Bureau (NCRB) data from 2009, more than 216,000 farmers have killed themselves since 1997. Add the figures for 1995, 1996, and 2010 and the total crosses 250,000. That is, two farmers a day for the past fifteen years."[4]

Cotton processing also entails the use of chemicals. Typically sodium hydroxide (a type of salt) and chelating agents are used to increase luster and help the cotton absorb dye better (mercerization)[5], and then acetic acid is used as a neutralizer."[6] Usual salt concentrations in cotton mill wastewater can be 2,000 – 3,000 ppm, far in excess of Federal guidelines for in-stream salt concentrations of 230 ppm, so treatment of effluent is very important."[7] Before it is woven into fabric, cotton may be treated with the biocide pentachlorophenols (PCPs), to protect it from rotting during storage and transport. PCPs are associated with the development of cancers, abnormal reproductive effects and nerve damage, and are thus outlawed from effluents in the US and the European Union.[8] Most conventional cotton is treated with

2   Organic Trade Association. "Textile Exchange Organic Cotton Farm and Fiber Report 2011." 2011.

3   Environmental Justice Foundation. "The Deadly Chemicals in Cotton." In collaboration with Pesticide Action Network. London, UK, 2007.

4   Ghosh, Palash. "India Losing 2,000 Farmers Every Single Day: A Tale of a Rapidly Changing Society." *IBT Media*, May 2, 2013, Politics sec.

5   "What Does Mercerized Cotton Mean?" O Ecotextiles. May 12, 2012.

6   Earth Pledge Foundation. *Future Fashion White Papers*. Edited by Leslie Hoffman. New York: Earth Pledge Foundation, 2008. 209.

7   "What Does Mercerized Cotton Mean?" O Ecotextiles. May 12, 2012.

8   Fletcher, Kate. *Sustainable Fashion & Textiles: Design Journeys*, 48. London: Earthscan, 2008.

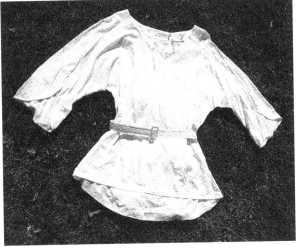

Top Left: Aventura

Top Right: Threads 4 Thought

Bottom: Echo Verde (with vintage lace belt by Nancy's Gone Green)

All on this page: organic cotton

chlorine bleach as well to make it optic white, just for aesthetic reasons, since people associate the whiteness of the fabric with cleanliness. Though sold as a common household cleaner, chlorine bleach is corrosive and is associated with health effects such as eye, skin, and airway irritation at low levels, and "tightness, wheezing, dyspnea, and bronchospasm" at higher levels.[9] It is also highly toxic to fish and other aquatic creatures if it finds its way to waterways.[10]

Did you know?

According to Pesticide Action Network, it takes 2/3 pounds of pesticide to produce enough cotton to make 1 pair of denim jeans, and 1/4 pound to make enough for a regular cotton t-shirt.

The Organic Consumers Association (OCA) points out that despite the large amount of pesticides used, "cotton is farmed on only 3 percent of the world's farmland." In addition to pesticide use, OCA also states that, "94 percent of the US cotton crop is genetically modified."[11] (We'll cover what the problems are with genetic engineering when discussing soy in chapter 4.) For these reasons, they conclude, "Cotton is the most toxic crop in the world." [12]

Not something most people are usually thinking about when buying a pair of jeans.

What does this mean for me?

So this begs the obvious question: Do pesticide residues and other chemicals end up on our skin from our clothing? No research I can find indicates that it's ever been studied. But common sense says probably some small amount of chemicals from the processing, and certainly dyes, would end up being absorbed through our skin if the

---

9   New York State Department of Health. "The Facts About Chlorine." New York State Department of Health: Emergency Preparedness and Response. August 5, 2004.
10   US Environmental Protection Agency (EPA) Office of Pollution Prevention and Toxics. "Chemical Summary for Chlorine." US EPA—Chemicals in the Environment: OPPT Chemical Fact Sheets. August 1994.
11   Genetically modified cotton is highly unlikely to cause any direct health effects to the wearer, but in general, genetically modified fields can cross-pollinate and thereby "contaminate" nearby fields. The effects of these crops on bees and other insects are unknown, so it is still an environmental question mark as to the long-term effects of this practice. In foods, there can be issues of allergies due to mixing the gene of one plant with another, but that is a subject for a different book.... See organicconsumers. org for more information.
12   US Environmental Protection Agency (EPA) Office of Pollution Prevention and Toxics. "Chemical Summary for Chlorine." US EPA—Chemicals in the Environment: OPPT Chemical Fact Sheets. August 1994.

Left: Fir (carbon neutral)

Right: Sita

All on this page: organic cotton

clothing is worn before washing. It is especially likely if, in warm temperatures, the pores are open to allow for perspiration.

Like pesticides, most dyes are petrochemical-based. Dyes are then slowly leached out of our clothing and down the drain when we do our laundry, though hopefully our local treatment plant filters them before they enter surrounding waterways.

Sticking to the jeans example, according to wardrobeadvice.com: "To dye a pair of jeans used to be done with the indigo plant which could be used to create indigo fabric dye. Today, synthetic indigo dye is made with a combination of caustic soda, sodium phenylglycinate and sodamide to form a chemical called indoxyl. The sodium phenylglycinate in the mixture is made from a chemical made in another chemical process by adding ammonia to a chemical called chlorobenzene. This process begins with another chemical that can come from either petroleum or coal. Because petroleum and coal are both inexpensive, many fabric dyes are currently made in a similar fashion."[13]

---

13   "What Are Clothing Fabric Dyes Made Of?" Wardrobe Advice. April 13, 2009.

Color Grown Cotton

Nature is amazing. So amazing that it has produced numerous species of plants and animals, many of which even science has not yet even come to know, nor appreciate. Among these are species of cotton plants that naturally grow in different colors. That's right, not all cotton is white. Again, much white cotton is bleached, using processes that can create dioxin, a carcinogen.

According to cotton researcher James Vreeland, the Mochica people in Peru used to cultivate several colors of cotton 5,000 years ago in the Andes.[1] Some of these cultivars (varieties) can still be found today. He says that modern Egyptian cotton was originally derived from a South American progenitor, and that color-grown varieties reached the US during the colonial period. It has a

---

1   Vreeland, James M., Jr. "The Revival of Colored Cotton." *Scientific American*, April 6, 1999, vol. 280, issue 4. 112.

color range of about eight to twelve shades of brown, red, and green.[2] Color-grown cotton fell out of favor partially because some of the types did not have a long fiber length so were harder to spin on machines, thus making it harder to become commercially viable and compete with white cotton. So, in the early 1980s, Vreeland headed a Native Cotton Project to help try to preserve these varieties. In the 1990s, color-grown cotton made a brief comeback, and brands such as Patagonia, Levi's, and Esprit were making use of it.

In Texas, a woman named Sally Fox was one of the first people in the US to start growing color-grown varieties of cotton on a commercial scale and was considered a cotton innovator. She started growing Foxfibre®,[3] the first color-grown variety that could be spun on machines. She took to color-grown cotton noting that, instead of fading, sometimes the color grows deeper over time, exhibiting deeper green and brown tones. She points out that color-grown varieties can be dyed, and that, for example, if you want to dye a fabric black and it is made of a brown cotton variety, then less dye will be necessary. This saves money for the dyer.

This is also important because dying cotton is large source of environmental pollution. In one essay, Fox wrote that 100 lbs. of cotton dyed with a dye that is considered low-impact, uses about 100 gallons of water and still generates some toxic waste.[4]

It is cheaper to get fabrics from countries such as India and China that do not have as much regulation on disposal of dyes. Fox also points out that in some countries, DDT is still used on cotton, and this can wash into our water during laundering.

Fox continues to sell yarn, fiber, and socks through her business, Vreseis Limited,[5] based in California.

2   Fletcher, Kate. *Sustainable Fashion & Textiles: Design Journeys*, 35. London: Earthscan, 2008.
3   Foxfibre®. http://www.foxfibre.com. 2016
4   Earth Pledge Foundation. *Future Fashion White Papers*. Edited by Leslie Hoffman. New York: Earth Pledge Foundation, 2008. 134.
5   Vreseis Limited. http://www.vreseis.com. 2015.

Again, not something most people are thinking about when at the store trying on a new pair of jeans. According to the article "Your cotton T-shirt may be poisoning you" by Kathleen Barnes,[14] in processing conventional cotton to its final stage as clothing, chemicals are often added at each stage—silicone waxes, petroleum scours, fabric softeners, heavy metals, flame and soil retardants, ammonia, and even the carcinogen formaldehyde. These chemicals might be more of a health issue than the pesticides, which may not last through the cotton processing. On some level we may know these clothes contain chemicals because we can smell them when they bring them home from the store. A colleague in the fashion industry told me that sometimes when samples are shipped to design offices, they are still a bit damp....

So what's a fashionista supposed to do based on little clear scientific evidence? Well, in the world of environmental health, there has been a principle floated since the 1992 Rio Conference called the Precautionary Principle. It states:

"If an action or policy might cause severe or irreversible harm to the public or to the environment, in the absence of a scientific consensus that harm would not ensue, the burden of proof falls on those who would advocate taking the action."

In other words, if a company is about to release a product that might make people sick, they should have to prove that it's safe first, not release it for public consumption and then see if it causes harm. However, this is not the way in which many chemicals are regulated. Pesticides must be registered with the EPA for certain uses, and labels are strictly regulated.[15] Chemical users are supposed to follow the label by law, but of course don't always do that. People may take the label as a suggestion; not understanding it is the law, and that chemical use is serious business.

When the EPA reviews the health effects of chemicals, they consider them one chemical at a time. However, people are exposed to many chemicals in our environment (clothing, water, food), and though these exposures are typically at very low levels, the cumulative and synergistic effects of the mixture of pesticides and other chemicals in our environment is not easily studied, so we don't really know the effects for sure.

---

14   Barnes, Kathleen. "Your Cotton T-Shirt May Be Poisoning You." KathleenBarnes.com. October 16, 2014.
15   US Environmental Protection Agency (EPA). "Pesticide Container and Containment Rule." US EPA—Pesticides: Regulating Pesticides (Storage and Disposal). September 19, 2014.

Top Left: Gaiam

Right: Blue Canoe

Bottom Left: Eco-Centric

All: organic cotton

Ecofashionista Recommendation: We can frame the "Consumer's Precautionary Principle" this way: "If I am about to purchase a product that I am not sure is safe for myself and my family (and I suspect may not be safe for everybody else), then I will choose the safer alternative whenever one is available." A second level of action would be to then petition our government for stricter regulations for such products. Another action would be to contact the company and ask questions about their practices, and write about the response on a blog, social media, or op-ed in the newspaper. Take action for fashion!

Organic Cotton: Why is it Green?

The good news is there is a growing organic cotton industry and market so we can choose an alternative. Organic cotton is grown using natural methods without the use of synthetic pesticides or fertilizers and is not genetically modified. Organically maintained soil helps reduce pollution and sequesters more carbon than conventionally farmed soil. As more farmers start to see the negative health effects of pesticides in their own lives, and as consumers are beginning to demand more and more "green" products, products labeled "organic" from food items to clothing have begun to take off and become rapidly growing economic sectors over the past decade.

According to the Organic Trade Association, organic cotton represents 0.7 percent of global cotton production. It is grown in many countries including India, China, Turkey, the United States, Tanzania, Peru, Egypt and Brazil, and Tajikistan.[16] While still a small percentage, organic cotton has seen stable growth. According to the Textile Exchange "Organic Cotton Market Report 2016," 112,488 metric tons (247,993,590 lbs) of organic cotton were grown globally over the last year. It was grown on 350,033 hectares (864,949 acres) by 194,000 farmers, and has a global market value of $15.7 billion dollars."[17]

Having been vegetarian for over twenty years, I can certainly say it is not only easier now due to the variety of products to choose from, but it is also now more socially acceptable. In this time period, it has also become cool to bring your own bag to the grocery store, to use efficient lighting, and to drive a hybrid car. Similar is the growth of organic cotton—these trends are reflective of an overall market direction. Some great films and other media have helped create the momentum of change in the consumer spirit, and awareness is taking root!

---

16   Organic Trade Association. Organic Cotton Facts. June 29, 2012.
17   Textile Exchange. Organic Cotton Market Report 2016. July 2016.

Aventura (organic cotton)

Cons:

A general downside of cotton is that, depending on where it is grown, cotton can be a water-intensive crop. One kilogram of cotton can require 2114 gallons of water to produce.[18] According to an Ecofashion World article entitled How Thirsty is Your T-shirt? "Growing cotton accounts for 2.6 percent of the world's yearly water usage. One t-shirt made from conventional cotton represents 2700 liters [713 gallons] of water."[19] It takes 1800 gallons of water to make a pair of jeans.[20] About 50% of cotton crops are rain-fed, and 50% are irrigated, sometimes with inefficient watering systems.[21] However, the cotton industry says that cotton is drough-tolerant, and water usage depends on where it is grown. For example, in the US, 64 percent of the cotton crop is produced without irrigation.[22] Over the years, efforts have been made by growers to reduce water used for cotton growing.[23] A benefit of organic production is that organic crops tend to need less water (about 60% less)[24] since soil tends to have more organic matter and biological activity, which increases aeration naturally, helping the soil to hold moisture better.

To address this, organizations like the World Wildfile Federation and others formed the Switzerland-based Better Cotton Initiative, which has helped farmers use different methods to reduce their irrigation use. It incorporates both organic and fair labor standards. "In Pakistan, the Initiative has worked with 75,000 farmers who, as a result, have reduce their water use by 39 percent."[25] Levi's has additionally moved towards using "Better Cotton," and also created a Water<Less line that uses less water in the finishing process.[26] Adidas has committed to making 100% of its apparel from "better cotton" by 2018. H&M has said it will use only better, recycled or organic cotton by 2020.[27]

18   Fletcher, Kate. Sustainable Fashion & Textiles: Design Journeys, 7. London: Earthscan, 2008.
19   Willard, Helen. "How Thirsty is Your T-Shirt?" Eco Fashion World. June 25, 2009.
20   Water Use It Wisely. "It Takes 1,800 Gallons of Water to Make One Pair of Jeans." WaterUseItWisely. com. September 29, 2009.
21   Fletcher, Kate. Sustainable Fashion & Textiles: Design Journeys, 9. London: Earthscan, 2008.
22   Cotton Today. "Water." Cotton Today: Agriculture. 2014.
23   "Cotton Sustainability: Frequently Asked Questions." Cotton Campus. 2015.
24   Egan, Greta. Wear No Evil. 2014. 37.
25   World Wildlife Fund (WWF). "The Impact of a Cotton T-Shirt." WWF. January 16, 2013.
26   Levi Strauss & Co. "Sustainability: Products: Water<Less". levistrauss.com/sustainability/products/waterless/ 2017.
27   Carpenter, Susan. "Cotton That's Kinder than the Planet." LA Times. June 19, 2011.

Top Left:
Giggle

Top Right:
Trinity

Bottom
Left & Right:
Faded Glory

All: organic
cotton

Organic Cotton's Use in Fashion

This spirit is now beginning to show itself in the realm of fashion. After several years of finding organic cotton clothing only in small boutiques where one would often find bongs and other such paraphernalia being sold, I am now finding organic cotton clothing in more and more places, and in more varied styles. In the late 1990s, one could find organic cotton t-shirts and possibly some underwear or an occasional pajama or yoga outfit. I could count the number of companies providing organic cotton clothing on one hand. Though I wanted so much to support the movement, to be slightly critical, these clothes were often ill-fitting and not stylish. They were almost all an off-white "natural" color (not that there's anything wrong with that), and would appeal to the real diehard environmentalists but not to many others. Unfortunately, this perception has lingered and has held back the spread of eco-fashion.

Recent creativity in color and style has expanded the choices significantly. There are now whole shops dedicated to organic cotton and other natural fiber clothes (see appendix at the back of this book). Well-known retailers like Patagonia have been using organic cotton for over fifteen years and throughout more and more of their offerings.

> "In 1996, we converted our entire sportswear line to 100 percent organically grown cotton.... The move didn't compromise quality and it provoked a fundamental change in our attitudes about agriculture. As part of our organic cotton program, hundreds of us took tours of cotton fields, where we could see the dangers of pesticide use and the benefits of organic farming for ourselves. Many of us have since become activists on the issue and have shifted to buying organic foods and clothing for ourselves and our families."[28]

As mentioned, loungewear—including pajamas, nightgowns, and robes—as well as underwear and socks have long been available in organic cotton, but over the years the styles have become more ornate and sophisticated. I remember purchasing such items from Gaiam, which was then called the "Harmony" catalog. In the last few years, however, I have found organic cotton blouses and pants suitable for the workplace, as well as dresses, coats, blazers, and sweaters from such companies as Of the Earth, Sweetgrass Fibers, and ecoSkin, to name a few. Companies offering organic cotton underwear include Pact, Blue Canoe, Rawganique, and Faeries Dance to name a few. Levi's offers a line of organic cotton jeans, as do many of the lesser-known (for

---

28   Patagonia. "Organic Cotton." Patagonia: Materials and Technology. 2015.

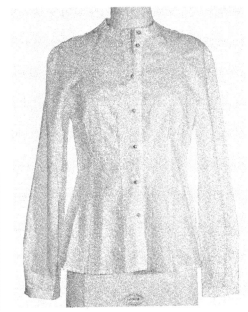

Top Left: Gaiam. Top Right: Fir
Bottom Left: Fisher Henney Naturals
(shirt), Good Society (jeans). Bottom
Right: Sweetgrass (vest), Aventura
(pants). All on this page: organic cotton

now) designers shown here on these pages, such as Loomstate. Shoe companies like zoe&zac and EcoSneaks offer organic cotton footwear.

That's what this book is all about—a celebration of the styles that are just the beginning for this area. As we start to see big names in fashion using organic cotton and these clothes being sold on Fifth Avenue, it's clear that we are at the inception of something big for sustainable fashion. (See chapter 7 for that!)

Left: Yellow 108, Above: Indigenous Designs
Both: organic cotton.

What's the price tag?

"I'd love to wear organic cotton but it's too expensive." That's a common phrase I hear when I talk to people about organic cotton and eco-fashion in general. Many people think it is more expensive just because it's a trendy specialty item, so manufacturers or retailers are just gauging prices. Granted, in some instances that could be the case. But coming back down to the farm level explains some of it too.

It's easier to grow a crop when you can spray chemicals that will kill any type of pest that might come along. However, since many pesticides have not only human health effects but environmental impacts such as toxicity to bees, fish and birds, there is also the downside for nature and surrounding waterways that modern economics doesn't factor in. In other words, there are "hidden costs" that don't necessarily get factored into the price tag, but are paid for by people or wildlife.

Top Left: H&M Conscious (blouse), People Tree (pants)
Top Right: H&M Conscious (blouse), Aventura (pants)
Bottom Left: Ecoskin, Bottom Right: Padhma Creation
All on this page: organic cotton

However, organic farmers are not defenseless. There are "organic" pesticides, made from natural substances, as well as certain farming methods that can be used to deter pests. For example, there are bio-pesticides such as bacillus thuringiensis (BT) that attacks soft-bodied insects, milky spore that is used to kill Japanese beetle grubs, and corn gluten, which is a product made from a protein found in corn that prevents weed seeds from germinating. Sulfur is a mineral-based natural pesticide. These substances are products that might be used by an organic farmer, in addition to good quality compost. Compost is full of living organisms that help healthy soil to flourish, such as a wide a variety of bacteria, fungi, nematodes and micro-arthropods. Crop rotation (more on this below) and avoiding huge fields of single crops (also called monocultures) are two other ways to avoid having a pest devour an entire field.

Under an "organic" program in the United States, a farmer must grow crops on land that was pesticide-free for at least three years prior, and can use a certain amount of these types of natural products to mitigate pests, but some of them can be expensive. And, since nothing is foolproof (not even synthetic chemicals), there is a certain amount of crop loss that can take place. Both of these issues feed into costs. Organic farming requires a lot of extra monitoring for pests, so it can be labor-intensive, and time is money.

One major hindrance to organic farming is that to keep soil productive from one year to the next, farmers need to do crop rotation. This means growing a different crop one growing season on the land they used for cotton the previous growing season. The problem is growing an alternate or rotation crop that can also be sold in the market. Farmers can't usually survive on a crop that is grown only every other season. Some of the large markets incorporating organic cotton fashions into their collections are now starting to make sure there is a market for the rotation crop, which may be a type of vegetable, but more of this needs to happen to really boost the expansion of organic cotton.

One extra financial cost to an organic farmer is the cost of certification. In 1991, the US adopted the National Organic Standards, but it took several years (until the late 1990s) for the United States Department of Agriculture (USDA), which was charged with writing the regulations for this law, to finally come out with the actual rules farmers would have to follow in order to comply with this law. Aside from strict standards to comply with, organic farmers must also then have their operations and

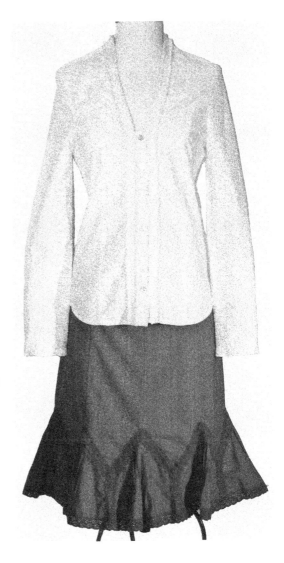

Top Left: Padhma Creation

Right & Bottom: Of the Earth

All on this page: organic cotton

<u>What are "Green" Cotton and "Better" Cotton?</u>

When shopping at eco-boutiques, one will sometimes encounter garment labels saying "green cotton." It might lead you to believe that this is the same as organic cotton. It isn't.

Green cotton simply means that conventionally grown cotton (grown with pesticides) has not since then been treated with formaldehyde, chemical wrinkle-reducers, chlorine bleach, or flame retardants. So after the cotton is harvested, the post-processing has been more natural. Unlike organic cotton, which is certified by the USDA, there are no federal inspection guidelines for green cotton.

Levi Strauss started using organic cotton in its denim in the early '90s but is now shifting away from it in favor of something called "better cotton" to address not only pesticide and fertilizer use but water, soil health and labor standards.

Strauss conducted a life cycle assessment of its 501 jeans and Dockers khakis in 2008 to look into the environmental impact of its most iconic products (jeans were originally created for California miners during the Gold Rush). It found one of its best opportunities for reducing its environmental impact was during cotton production. (The Water Footprint Network, a Dutch conservation group, estimates that it takes nearly 3,000 gallons of water, most of which goes toward growing the cotton, to produce a single pair of blue jeans.) To that end, Levi, along with H&M, Adidas, and the cotton-grower-funded group Cotton Inc., have all embraced the Better Cotton Initiative, which was started in Switzerland in 2009.

The initiative grew out of a movement spearheaded by the World Wildlife Fund, a privately funded international conservation organization that, in the early 2000s, began looking into the environmental impacts of the world's most popular commodities, including cotton. A pilot program in Pakistan led to a 32% reduction in the use of water and pesticides. Pakistan, Brazil, and India are among the countries that participated in the first official crops of better cotton grown during the 2010–11 season." However, one source points out that the Better Cotton initiative does not rule out genetically modified cotton.

(Sustainable Fashion & Textiles, Kate Fletcher, 2008. Pg. 22: http://articles.latimes.com/2011/jun/19/image/la-ig-cotton-20110619)

Top Left: Ocean Pacific (tank top), H&M (blazer), Eileen Fisher (pants)

Right: Patagonia

Bottom: Earth Creations

All on this page: organic cotton

their product certified by a third party agent such as Oregon Tilth, Quality Assurance International (QAI), or the Northeast Organic Farming Association (NOFA), many of whom existed for years when organic standards were self-regulated, predating the federal standards.[29] This costs money. So the farmer must pay annually to be certified organic, usually "a few hundred to several thousand dollars" per year in the US[30] and Canada depending on the size of the operation. This is to verify that when you purchase a product that is labeled "USDA Organic," you can be sure it actually has been raised and processed to strict organic standards.[31]

Most organic farmers I've met wouldn't have it any other way. They put their hearts and souls into their businesses and come from a place of wanting to protect the land. Most organic farmers feel very strongly about not using pesticides despite pressures from pesticide salesmen, financial issues, and reticent family members who try to persuade them otherwise. Some are even mocked by other farmers for making a silly and bad financial decision.

So when I buy a piece of organic cotton clothing, I usually think about the people who made it happen—the farmers, the people who collect the cotton buds in the fields, clean and spin the thread, and the sewers. It's what has always made me feel a bit better about having to open my wallet a bit further in some cases to support this type of business, as opposed to paying $10–20 less for a similar item at a major chain store.

Times are changing though, as both Wal-Mart and Target, two of the world's largest retail department stores, have carried organic cotton clothing and bedding (see chapter 9) and even full organic lines at widely affordable prices. Wal-Mart owns Sam's Clubs, and they both are starting to sell organic foods. (Wal-Mart has been selling organic food since before 2006.)[32] One eco-conscious "buyer," the staff-person at each store who determines what each store will carry and buys it for resale, named Coral Rose, decided to take the risk of offering a line of organic cotton yoga-wear at Sam's Club. The line did so well, that it bolstered the decision to carry even more of

---

29   Organic Trade Association. http://www.ota.com.
30   Baier, Ann H. for the US Department of Agriculture (USDA). "Organic Certification of Farms and Businesses Producing Agricultural Products." USDA. November 2012.
31   US Department of Agriculture (USDA). "Welcome to the National Organic Program." USDA: Agricultural Marketing Service. December 12, 2012.
32   Warner, Melanie. "Wal-Mart Eyes Organic Foods." *The New York Times*, May 12, 2006, New York ed., Business sec.

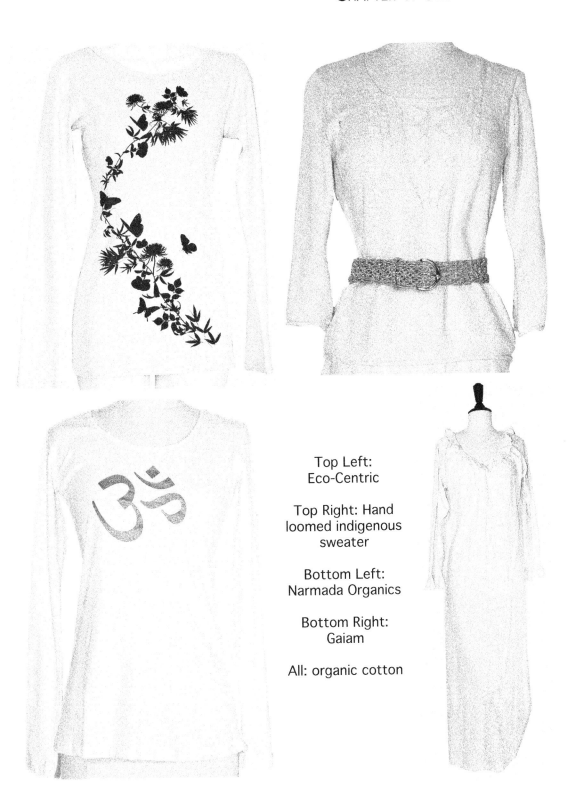

Top Left:
Eco-Centric

Top Right: Hand
loomed indigenous
sweater

Bottom Left:
Narmada Organics

Bottom Right:
Gaiam

All: organic cotton

it. She even took other buyers on farm tours to see the benefits of organic production, and to meet people who had been made sick by pesticide exposure in the fields. Her quote says it all: "The ability to purchase healthy products should not be a privilege determined by income level."[33] A Wal-Mart press release from 2008 stated that, at that time, Wal-Mart was "the largest user of organic cotton in the world, having purchased more than 28 million pounds of organic cotton and an additional 12 million pounds of transitional cotton to date."[34]

Did You Know?

Adidas committed to making 100 percent of its apparel from better cotton by 2018. H&M has said it will use only better, recycled and organic cottons by 2020.[1]

1   Carpenter, Susan. "Cotton That's Kinder to the Planet." *Los Angeles Times*, June 19, 2011, Textiles sec.

I was surprised to learn that H&M and the athletic shoe company Nike were ranked as some of the largest buyers of organic cotton by Textile Exchange several years ago.[35] In fact Nike has a goal of blending more organic and sustainable cotton into their materials, as well as reducing all waste from their manufacturing process, by 2020. More than 26 percent of cotton used was more sustainable (organic, Better Cotton Initiative-certified or recycled) in the 2015 fiscal year, according to their Sustainability Report.[36]

This is clearly a good thing for the planet and creates a huge demand for organically grown cotton. They have made a priority to use "Environmentally Preferred Materials" (EPMs) and have established a metric to determine what meets their criteria, in terms of its chemistry, energy use, water use, and the waste it creates. H&M now carries a Conscious Collection, of clothing made of organic or recycled cotton, and other sustainable fabrics mentioned in this book. They put out an annual Conscious

33   Earth Pledge Foundation. *Future Fashion White Papers*. Edited by Leslie Hoffman. New York: Earth Pledge Foundation, 2008. 257.
34   Wal-Mart. "Wal-Mart's Support for Farmers Adopting Sustainable Practices Yields Earth Month Transitional Cotton T-Shirts." Wal-Mart—News & Views: News Archive. April 7, 2008.
35   Chua, Jasmin Malik. "C&A, H&M Top List of 2012's Biggest Organic Cotton Users." Ecouterre. September 24, 2013.
36   Nike, Inc. "Sustainable Business Report FY 14/15" 2015.

Sita
(organic cotton)

Actions report, which explains their efforts in various sustainability criteria.[37] They also say they are involved in the Better Cotton Initiative (BCI),[38] meaning that the cotton is produced by "a farmer who use less water and chemicals, cares for the soil and natural habitats, and promotes good working conditions on his land."[39]

However, a purist might have mixed feelings about all this. For example, H&M has been highly criticized for labor conditions in the factories where its products are produced. Should we support major corporations who have thus far not cared about the environment or workers and may be doing this just for good press? Is this like going to Burger King and ordering their veggie burger? You would be doing the right thing with your individual choice in making less impact on the planet, but you would still be supporting the overarching company that has negatively impacted people and the environment for so many years.

That decision is up to individual consumers to decide. I tend to fall on the side of expansion so that these products can become more mainstreamed. Because behind each organic cotton t-shirt, pair of jeans, or sneakers we

37   H&M Hennes & Mauritz AB (H&M). "H&M Conscious Actions: Sustainability Report 2012." H&M. March 13, 2013.
38   Better Cotton Initiative. http://www. bettercotton.org.
39   H&M Hennes & Mauritz AB (H&M). "Cotton." H&M—Sustainability > Commitments > Conscious Fashion: More Sustainable Materials. 2015.

buy, there are small farmers and producers who are benefiting, as is our collective environment. Consumers have the power, so should continue to urge retailers to improve their sustainability and ethical efforts.

Why is this important? Because as we seek out clothing that is better for the planet, we should also be aware of the human aspect of our clothing's production. There are about 500,000 people employed in the textile and apparel production industry in the US,[40] but about 35 million people in India,[41] 3.5 million in Bangladesh,[42] and about 15 million in China[43] are employed in this industry where government regulations are more lax. Unfortunately, many of the garments we buy in the United States were produced in "sweatshop" conditions. The term "sweatshop" refers to working conditions that are crowded and extremely demanding, and often dangerous.[44] Workers, mostly women, are often subjected to long hours in rooms lacking ventilation. This has been an issue taken up by international labor organizations for many years in the US and abroad, but the practice still goes on around the world. The report Fashion Victims documents low pay, terrible working conditions, and pushback by employers against unionizing attempts by garment workers across the globe.[45]

In April 2013, the shoddy Rana Plaza garment factory in Bangladesh collapsed. It housed several different manufacturing companies, including Benetton, Mango, and Wal-Mart. Of the 5,000 workers, over 1,000 were killed and over 2, 000 injured. Only a year later after the accident did most people begin to see compensation for their injuries. The incident was cause for widespread criticism of the status quo, and has since resulted in some improvements such as better inspections, but more needs to be done.

---

40   Platzer, Michaela D. "US Textile Manufacturing and the Trans-Pacific Partnership Negotiations." Congressional Research Service. August 28, 2014.
41   Chamberlain, Gethin. "India's Clothing Workers: 'They Slap Us and Call Us Dogs and Donkeys.' " The Guardian, November 24, 2012, World: India sec.
42   Egan, Greta. Wear No Evil. 2014. 20.
43   Domoney, Ruth. "Briefing on the Chinese Garment Industry." Labour Behind the Label. February 2007.
44   The demands and time constraints alone can make an otherwise "safe" workplace dangerous, where minimum wage laws may not always be followed. There are reports of workers' initial wages after hiring being confiscated as some type of fee. That goes around fair wage laws even if minimum wage or some standard is followed after that. China Blue. US: Public Broadcasting Service (PBS), 2007. Film.
45   Alam, Khorshed, and Martin Hearson. "Fashion Victims: The True Cost of Cheap Clothes at Primark, Asda and Tesco." War on Want. December 2006.

Top Left: Padma Creations

Right: Aventura (blouse),
Marika Group (pants)

Bottom: H&M (white top),
Andean Artisan (sweater),
Aventura (pants)

All on this page: organic cotton

This incident was highlighted in the 2015 documentary film *The True Cost* by Andrew Morgan, which delved deeply into the issues of fast fashion and the pressures put on factories to produce cheaper and cheaper clothing, which ends up leading to horrible social injustices, mostly against female garment workers. It is a solemn and moving expose of the subject that illustrates the need for systemwide change. It drives home the point that clothing is not a disposable item, and that human beings in one part of the world work while their children sleep on the floor next to them, just so others in a different part of the world can buy cheap clothes.

A similar program aired on the Planet Green channel in early 2010 called *Blood, Sweat, and T-Shirts*. It featured six young British fashionistas who at first were interviewed saying they just want to look good, and didn't care much about how their clothes were made. They liked being able to buy inexpensive things and then "chuck them away." For the show, they visit India and actually work in the garment production industry for two weeks alongside real garment workers. They worked for several days in an assembly-line type factory, then at a cotton-producing farm, both picking and processing the cotton, and finally in the slums of Mumbai in backstreet sewing sweatshops where they encountered filthy conditions and even child labor. In each location, the work was very challenging and most of them couldn't keep up the expected pace of production. The work was done under difficult conditions and time restraints, and for extremely low wages. The money raised was barely enough to pay for food and some substandard housing for the group. This great expose powerfully illuminated the realities of what garment workers face every day, and the huge disconnect between the workers and the people buying the clothes. (Which is, of course, what product advertisers want. You don't see pictures of sweatshops in store windows.)

Unfortunately, it is even possible for organic cotton to end up being processed in sweatshops. There is some hope, however. According to Sandra Marquardt, On the Mark Public Relations, formerly with the Organic Trade Association (OTA), there is a standard to look for that defines strict environmental and social criteria for organic textile products. She writes:

Top Left: Prana
Bottom Left: Alternative Earth

Top Right: Earth Creations
Bottom Right: Clary Sage

All on this page: organic cotton

Using 95 – 100%
organic fibres:

GOTS
Organic
certified by [certifier's ref.]
Licence no 1234

Using 70 – 94%
organic fibres:

GOTS
Made with (x %)
organic materials
certified by [certifier's ref.]
Licence no 4321

*"There is no guarantee that organic cotton does not make its way into sweatshops. However, to preclude that and to provide standards addressing the post-harvest processing of the organic cotton in the most environmentally sustainable manner, OTA and three international organizations developed the **Global Organic Textile Standard (GOTS)**.[46] GOTS prohibits the use of child and forced labor and includes stringent restrictions on finishing agents and water use. As of December 31, 2009, at least 3,811 facilities globally have already gotten certified to GOTS, which only went into force in 2007, with the logo and additional guidelines only announced in the fall of 2008. These facilities have signed up for this standard despite the fact it is voluntary."*

This is very encouraging, and it is important that we, as consumers, seek out this label. Companies bearing the GOTS label must apply to be considered, and are subject to inspection of their whole process and bookkeeping review. As mentioned, without the GOTS label, it is possible that even organic cotton clothing is produced in sweatshops, so it's best to inquire. Most organic cotton clothing I've seen has been made in the United States which, though not always perfect, tends to have better conditions as set out by the US Department of Labor. However the organic cotton is often grown in other countries such as Egypt and Turkey where standards may differ. If the label doesn't say so, you can (and should) ask the seller or manufacturer. A simple inquiry into the situation could be the necessary force needed for change to occur. Often when the market demands it, the suppliers will respond.

The Problem of Genetic Engineering

Though India is the world leader in organic cotton production, even this segment of the cotton industry has had its problems avoiding genetically modified crops. Genetic modification of crops is becoming an international issue for several reasons. This alone could be the subject of a whole other book, but essentially genetic engineering involves scientists changing the DNA, or genetic material, of plants to make them exhibit traits that are more beneficial for farmers. So crops can be genetically engineered to tolerate different weather conditions, grow larger, or resist pests, for example. This is an innovative area of science that has received support from such

---

46   Global Organic Textile Standard: Ecology & Global Responsibility. 2013. http://www.global-standard.org

All on this page: organic cotton

Top Row (Left to Right): Threads 4 thought, H&M Conscious (with pants by Eileen Fisher), Synergy

Middle Row (Left to Right): Alternative Earth (first three), Faded Glory (far right)

  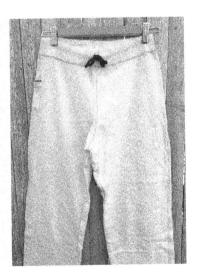

Bottom Row (Left to Right): Eastern Mountain Sports, Hanes, Gaiam

donors such as the Bill and Melinda Gates Foundation.[47] However it is not without controversy.

For example, one measure taken by multinational corporation Monsanto was to create Roundup® ready plants, which are actually *patented*. (Yes, patented life forms are not just the stuff of science fiction.) These plants are genetically altered to be resistant to the herbicide Roundup® (which Monsanto also produces) so when sprayed on fields, the pesticide kills everything except the main crop. Sounds promising, but critics say it conveniently makes farmers dependent on the use of Roundup® so it is a sure way to maintain Roundup® sales. Farmers have experienced genetically altered crops to not always be as successful as they were marketed to be, and there is a fundamental ethical question about spreading altered plants into the environment without knowing much about what the effects will be on pollinators and other wildlife. At this point in time, there is a lot more research to be done to determine the safety of genetically engineered crops in terms of human health, and many believe that there will be downsides to come. Due to this uncertainty, genetic engineering is not allowed for foods labeled "organic."

In the case of cotton, several corporations[48] have created cotton that is resistant to the boll weevil, and have pushed its use in developing countries. This can be a problem for organic farmers because wind and pollinators cross pollen from one field to the other. In January 2010, the online eco-fashion magazine EcoSalon.com reported that a German independent testing lab tested clothing from organic cotton farms in India and found that 30 percent of the cotton had genetically altered DNA.[49] It is believed that the clothing retailer H&M had used some of this cotton, so were caught in this dilemma, as were the international third-party certifying agencies, EcoCert and Control Union. The agencies were fined, and hopefully, by now the problem has been resolved. It is a shame because the story hit the press, and this only serves to feed consumer cynicism. India also has the largest amount of GE cotton in the world, so this situation shows the pressures to use the GE seed that is being heavily pushed by Monsanto in India.

---

47   GM Watch. "Monsanto, Syngenta Cash In on Disaster, No Relief to Farmers." Reader Supported News. September 10, 2012.
48   Including Syngenta and Monsanto; Monsanto's product is called Bollgard ®.
49   DuFault, Amy. "The Ripple Effect of India's Organic Cotton Scandal." EcoSalon. January 25, 2010.

Top: Echo Verde

Middle Left: Pi by Jadie Kadletz

Middle Right: Angel Rox

Bottom Left & Right: Pact

All on this page: organic cotton

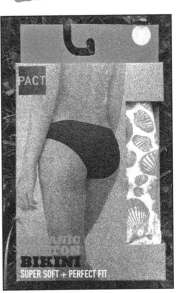

It is not clear whether the farmers were aware of the GMO contamination or not. A follow-up audit of all the farms in question found no genetically modified cotton, so it is believed that the cotton may have become mixed on machinery also used to process conventional cotton. It should be noted, however, that in 2010 the EPA fined Monsanto $2.5 million for selling mislabeled cottonseeds in Texas.[50]

Logo by Fair Trade USA

The Fair Trade Label

With organic cotton, as with any natural fiber discussed in this book, one label to look for is the "Fair Trade" label. Fair Trade means that—when an item is produced by a local grower, sewer, or craftsman—there are fewer middlemen between you and the producer of a fabric or piece of clothing. This benefits producers because the fewer people involved in the chain of selling an item, the more likely the person at the first stages of the production chain will be fairly compensated for their work. There are many organizations that advocate for increased growth in the fair trade market, which not only look at producers being paid fairly but also incorporate social and environmental principles in their definition of Fair Trade, such as TheSupplyChange.org.

One high-end fashion brand that focuses on fair trade standards is EDUN (edun. com), which works specifically with artisans in Africa. Started by U2 frontman Bono and Ali Hewson in 2005, it is sold in stores such as Barneys and Neiman Marcus.

See Chapter 9 for more on organic cotton towels, sateen sheets, and mattresses.

For more info on the sustainability of cotton and wool, check out the USDA Cotton and Wool Yearbook.[51]

---

50   Just-Style.com. "US: Mislabelled Cotton Seeds Cost Monsanto $2.5m Fine." Just-Style.com. July 9, 2010.
51   US Department of Agriculture (USDA). "Cotton and Wool Yearbook." USDA Economic Research Service—Data Products: Cotton, Wool and Textile Data. November 21, 2014.

Chapter 2

Hemp
It's Not Just for Smokin'

Weed. Grass. Ganja. Hash. Pot. Reefer. There are more names for marijuana than there are senators in Congress. So let's get the main question out of the way. We need to distinguish between the type of this plant species that is used as a recreational drug and the kind that is used to make rope, clothing, food items, oil, skin care products, and more (these are considered its "industrial purposes").

There are several species of marijuana plant. The one used for industrial purposes is Cannabis sativa, which grows quite tall. This type contains only minimal amounts (about 0.05 and 1 percent) of the chemical THC (tetrahydrocannabinol). This is the component that creates a high, so therefore Cannabis Sativa is considered "nonpsychoactive." The type of Cannabis grown for its psychotropic effects generally contains 3–20 percent THC by comparison, and this compound is found in the leaves, not the fibrous stems that are used to make hemp thread.[1]

In a paper titled, Hemp and Marijuana: Myths and Realities,[2] which describes the many nuances of each of the various types of Cannabis that exist, author Dr. David P. West writes:

Botanically, the genus Cannabis is composed of several variants. Although there has been a longstanding debate among taxonomists about how to classify these variants into species, applied plant breeders generally embrace a biochemical method to classify variants along utilitarian lines. Cannabis is the only plant genus that contains the unique class of molecular compounds called cannabinoids. Many cannabinoids have been identified, but two preponderate: THC, which is

---

1   North American Industrial Hemp Council. Hemp Facts. 2016.
2   West, David P., Ph.D. "Hemp and Marijuana: Myths & Realities." North American Industrial Hemp Council, Inc.: Industrial Hemp Reports. February 27, 1998.

the psychoactive ingredient of Cannabis, and CBD, which is an antipsychoactive ingredient. One type of Cannabis is high in the psychoactive cannabinoid, THC, and low in the antipsychoactive cannabinoid, CBD. This type is popularly known as marijuana. Another type is high in CBD and low in THC. Variants of this type are called industrial hemp.

So, in simple terms, the answer to the question, "Can you smoke it?" when referring to a skirt made of hemp, is: "No." If you decided to smoke clothes made of hemp, you would have to smoke at least 60 lbs. of them for it to have any effect, and that would be a big waste of clothes if you ask me.

Hemp is also not just for hippies. In fact, industrial hemp and humans go back a long time. According to the North American Industrial Hemp Council (NAIHC)[3] hemp has been grown for at least the last 12,000 years for fiber (textiles and paper) and food. The Italians used to grow hemp, so hemp ropes and hemp sails were what brought Christopher Columbus across the sea to the Americas. Hemp was used for nets, maps, and even the Gutenberg Bible in the fifteenth century.[4] According to the "Marijuana Timeline In The United States"[5] from the Public Broadcasting Service (PBS) Frontline webpage,[6] *"American production of hemp was encouraged by the government in the seventeenth century for the production of rope, sails, and clothing.... In 1619 the Virginia Assembly passed legislation requiring every farmer to grow hemp. Hemp was permitted for exchange as legal tender in Pennsylvania, Virginia, and Maryland."*

George Washington and Thomas Jefferson both cultivated hemp on their farms. Not exactly folks we think of as drug dealers. Benjamin Franklin started the first American paper mill, which made paper exclusively from hemp. The first American flag was made of hemp fibers. The United States Declaration of Independence, signed July 4, 1776, and now on display at the National Archives, was also drafted on paper made from hemp. Covered wagons heading west often used hemp covers.[7]

---

3   North American Industrial Hemp Council, Inc. http://www.naihc.org/. 2016.
4   Electric Emperor. "Uses of Hemp." Electric Emperor. 2009.
5   Public Broadcasting Service (PBS). "Marijuana Timeline." PBS Frontline: Busted—America's War on Marijuana. April 1998.
6   Public Broadcasting Service (PBS) Frontline. http://www.pbs.org/wgbh/pages/frontline/. 2015.
7   Ibid.

Top Left: Two Star Dog
(hemp tencel shirt),
Sweetgrass (hemp skirt)

Top Right: Patagonia (hemp
cotton blouse), Sweetgrass
(organic cotton pants)

Bottom: Earth Creations
(hemp cotton)

Other products made from hemp fiber include: insulation, particleboard, fiberboard, rope, twine, yarn, newsprint, cardboard, paper, horse stable bedding, and compost. Hemp bedding has been found superior to straw and other materials for horse stalls in reducing the smell of ammonia. Just to expand upon hemp's versatility, I'll mention that hemp seed is edible and contains healthy Omega 3 oils, which is a necessary part of the human diet in order to maintain a healthy brain, reduced risk of atherosclerosis, a decrease in symptoms of rheumatoid arthritis, and better mood. Hemp seed is also used to make methanol and heating oil, salad oil, pharmaceuticals, soaps, paint, and ink.[8]

Despite all this, possession of hemp was banned in twenty-nine individual states by 1931 because it became associated with crime and violence. In 1937, Congress passed the Marihuana Tax Act to discourage Cannabis production for marijuana, while still permitting industrial uses of the crop. The government actively encouraged farmers to grow hemp for fiber and oil during World War II. After the war, competition from synthetic fibers, the Marihuana Tax Act, and increasing public anti-drug sentiment resulted in fewer acres of hemp being planted, and none at all after 1958.[9] The Controlled Substances Act of 1970 makes it illegal to grow hemp without a Drug Enforcement Administration (DEA) permit. Approximately thirty countries in Europe, Asia, and North and South America currently permit farmers to grow hemp.[10] Canada legalized hemp with certain restrictions in 1998.[11]

According to the National Organization for the Reform of Marijuana Laws (NORML), there are ten US states that passed legislation in the late 1990s to allow growing industrial hemp for research purposes—Arkansas, California, Hawaii, Illinois, Minnesota, Montana, New Mexico, North Dakota, and Virginia—and several other states have since also passed legislation allowing for the cultivation of industrial hemp. Again, not to be confused with industrial hemp, in 1996 California allowed marijuana to be used for medical purposes, and this is currently under consideration in other states. However, despite the fact that it is not the same as the Cannabis used as a drug, US federal law still prohibits growing industrial hemp. Currently about half of U.S. allow for growing hemp for commercial or research purposes.[12] The North

---

8   Sheppard, Laurel M. "How Products Are Made: Industrial Hemp." Made How, Volume 6. 2015.
9   Johnson, Renée. "Hemp as an Agricultural Commodity." *Congressional Research Service*, February 2, 2015.
10   Ibid.
11   Sheppard, Laurel M. "How Products Are Made: Industrial Hemp." Made How, Volume 6. 2015.
12   National Council of State Legislatures. "State Industrial Hemp Statutes." August 2016.

Top Left: L.O.G.G. (organic cotton top),
Natural High (hemp pants)

Bottom Left: Ecolution (hemp)

Right: Two Star Dog (hemp tencel blouse),
Texture (organic cotton skirt)

American Industrial Hemp Council (http://www.naihc.org) provides more information about the myths and realities of this plant species.

Why is hemp "green"?

Hemp is a very hardy plant that can grow in difficult soil conditions and a wide temperature range. It is grown in countries around the world. It does not require much water or the addition of hazardous pesticides or fertilizers. It grows, as its slang name suggests, like a weed. It has very few natural pest enemies, and grows densely so as to crowd out competing plants, 200 to 300 plants per square meter.[13] It grows back quickly after being harvested—going from seed to harvest takes about ninety days—so is not only considered a sustainable natural product, but also a renewable resource. Hemp produces more fiber per acre than trees, and can be regrown two to three times per year.[14] It takes dye well, so not as much needs to be used. Hemp is also eco-friendly because none of the plant gets wasted. Each part can be used for a different purpose, which is an efficient use of land.[15] Twenty to thirty percent of the plant is fiber,[16] so "On a per acre basis, hemp yields 250 percent more fiber than cotton."[17]

Cons

Like everything else, turning hemp into fabric is not a perfect process. "China, the world's leading producer of hemp fabric, uses chemical methods for processing hemp, while producers in Europe have begun using cleaner biologically-based enzyme technology. Neither method produces fabric with the same whiteness and softness as cotton. As a consequence, hemp clothing is often blended with cotton, which from an environmental perspective consumes far more resources than hemp. To address this concern, Hemptown Clothing and the Canadian federal science organization NRC have collaborated to patent an innovative enzyme process that transforms industrial hemp into a soft, white 'Canadian cotton' product, called Crailar."[18]

---

13   Eco-Handbags.ca. "Hemp Embroidered Passport Front-Zippered Bag with Leaf." Eco-Handbags. ca. 2014.
14   Eartheasy. "Hemp Clothing." Eartheasy—Guides: Wear. 2014.
15   MaryJanesGirl. "Hemp Defined." MaryJanesGirl.com. 2014.
16   Fletcher, Kate. *Sustainable Fashion & Textiles: Design Journeys*, 25. London: Earthscan, 2008.
17   HempSense Natural Skin Care Products. "Ecology of Hemp." HempSense Natural Skin Care Products: Healing Properties of Hemp. 2008.
18   Eartheasy. "Hemp Clothing." Eartheasy—Guides: Wear. 2014.

Top Left: Nada Chair (hemp)

Bottom Left: Ecolution (hemp)

Right: Gramici (hemp)

Also, on a practical level, hemp tends to wrinkle, depending on the material blend, so it will sometimes require ironing. My experience has also been that naturally dyed hemp clothing tends to fade when exposed to sunlight for long periods of time.

The final con I would point out is that I sometimes find hemp clothing being sold not only by eco-fashion retailers but also in places where they sell bongs and other related paraphernalia. I think this needs to change in order for hemp to get the respect it deserves in the higher fashion world. Negative connotations take a long time to overcome. "Sustainable" fashion is now on the cusp of bringing another connotation, another association, and one that can become more mainstreamed.

Use of Hemp in Fashion

Hemp material, depending on how it is processed, can look and feel very similar to linen in terms of its "hand feel" and drape. It is mildew resistant, and not highly permeable by ultraviolet light. It is usually a little coarser than cotton, so for this reason, hemp is sometimes blended with silk to form a smoother, shinier fabric that feels better against your skin. It is sometimes blended with cotton. "The cellulose fiber from hemp is used to make many products, including jeans, shirts, dresses, hats, bags, hair bands, etc. Until the 1920s, 80 percent of clothing was made from hemp textiles.[19]

Heavier versions of hemp fabric can be made into canvas, and can be used for shoes. Modern canvas is usually made of cotton or linen, although historically it was made from hemp.[20] One of my favorite, most comfortable and form-fitting pairs of shoes was a pair of totally hemp clogs made by EcoDragon that could be disposed of by composting when they wore out. The only problem of course was when I got stuck in the rain and the hemp swelled up and hardened (get your mind out of the gutter!), but usually I could wear them back into shape when dry. So I currently have a pair of hemp shoes by Simple that has a natural rubber sole so is more weather tolerant.

The hemp plant produces one of the strongest natural fibers known, after silk. "Hemp fabric is three times stronger than cotton fabric of the same weight; it is also warmer, more absorbent, and longer wearing."[21]

---

19   Id.
20   True Hemp Clothing International. "Hemp History Timeline." True Hemp Clothing International. 2015.
21   Eco-Handbags.ca. http://www.eco-handbags.ca/. 2014.

Left: Texture (hemp & recycled PET)

Top Right: Bring It In A Bag (hemp)

Bottom Right: Green Toe (hemp & natural rubber)

A press release from the Hemp Industries Association (HIA) reported on how hemp was used by high fashion designers for New York Fashion Week in 2008. It says, "Before the official opening of New York Fashion Week, on the evening of January 31 in the elegant sophistication of New York's Gotham Hall, two dozen internationally-recognized designers displayed their latest creations to a waiting high-powered audience at the Earth Pledge eco-fashion show FutureFashion. With fabric supplied by Hemp Industries Association member EnviroTextiles, designers like Donatella Versace, Behnaz Sarafpour, Ralph Lauren, Donna Karan International, Isabel Toledo, and Doo.Ri wove their magic with everything from hemp/organic cotton jersey knits to hemp/silk Carmeuse.... Numerous HIA members, such as Clothing Matters, Dash Hemp, EnviroTextiles, Hemp Elegance, Hemp Traders, Hempy's, Livity

Funfact:

Bathing suits can be made from hemp, usually blended with nylon. Some companies are also producing bathing suits using recycled synthetic fibers.

Outernational, Mountains of the Moon, Satori Movement, Sweetgrass and Two Jupiters, make a varied range of quality hemp clothing and textiles."[22] The release goes on to say that Calvin Klein also used hemp fabrics in some of their designs at the show as well. The "FutureFashion" collection was then put on display in the windows of Barneys New York, which is a very upscale clothing purveyor.

What's the price tag?

As mentioned, with the exception of a few states, it is illegal to grow Cannabis in the United States, and the ban applies to all species of the plant, In fact, taxpayers pay large sums so the Drug Enforcement Administration (DEA) can spray pesticides to eradicate all forms of cannabis in the US, even the "Ditchweed" that is now known as industrial hemp. Therefore, most hemp grown for industrial purposes such as clothing is grown outside the United States. This contributes to a higher cost of hemp items, because the material must be imported. Nonetheless, the US is one of the largest importers of hemp.[23] Most US imports come from China, but also from Canada, England, Romania, and Hungary.[24] Other leading country suppliers include India and

---

22   Hemp Industries Association. "Hemp Fabric Goes High Fashion: Top Couture Designers Use Hemp Eco-Fabrics for New York Fashion Week." Hemp Industries Association—Resources > News & Events: Press Releases. February 11, 2008.
23   Booker, Linda, and Blaire Johnson. "Industrial Hemp." Bringing It Home: Industrial Hemp, Healthy Houses and a Greener Future for America, a Documentary. 2015.
24   US Department of Agriculture (USDA). "Industrial Hemp in the United States: Status and Market Potential." USDA Economic Research Service, 2000.

Top Left & Bottom Right: Earth Divas (hemp)
Bottom Left: Hempmani (hemp)

Top Right: Hemptress (hemp)

other European countries.[25] According to the HIA, China is the largest exporter of hemp textiles. China and Romania tend to use human labor for the processing of hemp, which also adds to cost. This may be a good thing, but for hemp to scale up commercially, better machinery is needed. [26]

There is no official estimate of the value of US sales of hemp-based products. The Hemp Industries Association (HIA) estimates that the total US retail value of hemp products in 2012 was nearly $500 million, which includes food and body products, clothing, auto parts, building materials, and other products. Of this, HIA reports that the value of hemp-based food, supplements, and body care sales in the United States is about $156 million to $171 million annually. The US market for hemp clothing and textiles is estimated at about $100 million annually.[27]

Hopefully the cost of hemp will go down in the future as it gains acceptance. Commercial hemp could provide US agriculturists with an economically viable crop, and it would provide many benefits to consumers and the environment.

Your pets can wear ecofashion, too. Some companies offer hemp and organic cotton collars, leashes, pet beds, and carriers—for example: earthdog. com, organicdogsandcats.com, and thegooddogcompany.com.

Earthdog (hemp collar)
Photo by thegreenlife.com

25   Johnson, Renée. "Hemp as an Agricultural Commodity." *Congressional Research Service,* February 2, 2015.
26   Hemp Industries Association. "Facts." Hemp Industries Association—Resources > Education > FAQs & Facts. 2014.
27   Johnson, Renée. "Hemp as an Agricultural Commodity." *Congressional Research Service,* February 2, 2015.

Ralph Lauren (hemp top), Gaiam (organic cotton pants)

Some companies that make hemp clothing include:
- Patagonia (http://www.patagonia.com/home)
- The Hempest (http://www.hempest.com)
- Rawganique (http://www.rawganique.com)
- Hemp Couture (http://www.hempcouture.ca)
- Hemp Authority (http://hempauthority.com)

Some companies that make hemp shoes and sneakers include:
- EcoDragon (http://www.ecodragon.com/foot.html)
- Sanuk (http://www.sanuk.com)
- Simple Shoes (http://simpleshoes.com)
- Vans (http://www.vans.com)
- Vegetarian Shoes (http://www.vegetarian-shoes.co.uk)

THE BAMBOO PROCESS

Turning Self-Replenishing Bamboo Fields into Crazy-Soft Bamboo Fabrics

First, we cut the seasoned stalks into smaller pieces of raw bamboo.

Next, the bamboo is soaked in a s... approved by the Global Orga... Standard to ensure that this pro... is as environmentally friendly as the bamboo it soaks.

This solution breaks down the bamboo fibers, extracting the bamboo pulp that is then dried into parchment-like sheets.

Once thoroughly dried, these sheets are ready to be milled into a soft, fluffy material referred to as bamboo fiber.

The fiber is then separated and spun into thread that's used to create yarn for weaving.

The end result is a cloth that's twice as soft as cotton and comparable to luxury fabrics like cashmere and silk.

Cariloha store in Florida

Chapter 3

Bamboo
It's Not Just for Panda Bears

It is hard to believe that the soft, almost silky clothing I wear to yoga class was once a tall and hard reed-like perennial tree so favored by panda bears and the inspiration for many a painting in its native Asian countries. A member of the grass familybamboo—one of my favorite fabrics—is considered somewhat of a pest plant when it grows in areas of the US where it is not native due to its tendency to quickly take over large areas. Bamboo grows by an underground system of rhizomes, or roots that send up new shoots, so once a little bit gets established and if there is room, the proper nutrients and enough water, there will soon be a larger stand of bamboo.

This has its benefits, as bamboo has many uses. Bamboo has been used for centuries for building purposes, flooring, food (the soft shoots are found in many Asian dishes), paper, cooking utensils, and of course, its fibers have been made into fabric that is used to make clothing.

According to OrganicClothing.blogs.com,

> "Bamboo is naturally antibacterial and antifungal supposedly because of a bacteriostatic agent unique to bamboo plants called 'bamboo kun,' which also helps bamboo resist harboring odors.... Bamboo is highly absorbent and wicks water away from the body three to four times faster than cotton. In warm, humid and sweaty weather, bamboo clothing helps keep the wearer drier, cooler, and more comfortable and doesn't stick to the skin."

Why is Bamboo Fabric Green?
Bamboo fabric is considered a green product because it is made from a natural, renewable, biodegradable fiber that can be regrown relatively quickly. Bamboo grows through rhizomes or "runners," which are roots that grow beneath the ground and

sprout new trees. It is ready for harvest in four years. Bamboo can grow a yard per day, absorbing much climate-changing carbon dioxide, and is considered the fastest growing grass. Therefore as a fiber source, bamboo is one of the most eco-friendly. Though it is rare to find organic bamboo clothing, growing bamboo does not typically require the use of irrigation, pesticides or fertilizers, so therefore wins out over conventional cotton.

However, there are different shades of green here to be aware of. "Rayon," which most people would not think is a natural product, can be made from bamboo cellulose. Introduced in 1924, it was one of the first artificial textile fibers.[1] Now savvy clothing producers using rayon are starting to label their clothing as made from bamboo to cash in on the products' green cache. Read on…

Bamboo's Use in Fashion

Bamboo clothing is becoming more widely available. Most commonly it is being used to make exercise and leisurewear. Mixed with some stretchy spandex, this sturdy but lightweight and breathable fabric is about as comfortable as you can get. It often has a slight sheen to it, and drapes the body in a flattering way. It can be washed like other laundry and is relatively wrinkle resistant, unlike silk, which usually requires hand washing or dry cleaning.

I own bamboo socks, skirts, and active-wear. I also have bamboo towels and sheets, both of which are remarkably and luxuriously soft. The towels are softer than most cotton towels and the ones I purchased, made by Pure Fiber, almost had a waxy sleekness to them. They almost repelled water, but within one wash they became absorbent and have become my favorite towels. And this company offers many vivid, unique, and attractive colors to brighten up your bathroom. The sheets I bought, also made by Pure Fiber, were similar to sateen sheets made with Egyptian organic cotton, which many of us have come to know and love.

---

1 Clement, Anna Maria, and Brian R. Clement. *Killer Clothes: How Seemingly Innocent Clothing Choices Endanger Your Health—and How to Protect Yourself!* Summertown, Tennessee: Hippocrates Publications, 2011. 9.

Top Left: Bianca Paradis (bamboo)

Bottom Left: Biza (bamboo)

Top Right: Bianca Paradis (bamboo cotton)

Bottom Right: Earth Yoga (bamboo organic cotton)

Cons

The way bamboo cellulose is made into this soft material may require the use of chemicals. Bamboo fiber is made in one of two ways: mechanically or chemically.[2]

The mechanical way involves crushing the woody parts of the bamboo plant and then using natural enzymes to break the bamboo walls into a mushy mass so that the natural fibers can be mechanically combed out and spun into yarn. This is essentially the same eco-friendly manufacturing process used to produce linen fabric from flax or hemp. Bamboo fabric made from this process is sometimes called bamboo linen. Very little bamboo linen is manufactured for clothing because it is more labor intensive and costly. It can cost four to five times more to produce using this method.[3] Bamboo can also be produced using the method used for lyocell, which we will read about in the next chapter, and would also be more environmentally friendly.

However, most bamboo fabric that is the current eco-fashion rage is chemically manufactured in a less eco-friendly way. It starts by "cooking" the bamboo leaves and woody shoots in strong chemical solvents such as sodium hydroxide (NaOH – also known as caustic soda or lye, is strongly alkaline) and carbon disulfide in a process also known as hydrolysis alkalization combined with multiphase bleaching. Both sodium hydroxide and carbon disulfide have been linked to serious health problems. Breathing low levels of carbon disulfide can cause tiredness, headache, and nerve damage. Carbon disulfide has been shown to cause neural disorders in workers at rayon manufacturers. Low levels of exposure to sodium hydroxide can cause irritation of the skin and eyes. Because of the potential health risks and damage to the environment surrounding the manufacturing facilities, textile manufacturing processes for bamboo or other regenerated fibers using hydrolysis alkalization with multiphase bleaching are not considered sustainable or environmentally friendly.

While specifics can vary, the general process for chemically manufacturing bamboo fiber involves the following steps:

---

2   Lackman, Michael. "Bamboo: Facts Behind the Fiber." OrganicClothing.blogs.com. September 18, 2007.
3   Earth Pledge Foundation. *Future Fashion White Papers*. Edited by Leslie Hoffman. New York: Earth Pledge Foundation, 2008. 166.

Top Left: Bamboosa (bamboo), Top Right: Threads for Thought (organic cotton top), Bottom Left: Cariloha (bamboo accessories), Bottom Right: Cariloha (bamboo)

1) <u>Preparation</u>: Bamboo leaves and the soft, inner pith from the hard bamboo trunk are extracted and crushed; the crushed bamboo cellulose is soaked in a solution of 15% to 20% sodium hydroxide at a temperature between 68° Fahrenheit (20° C) to 77° F (25° C) for one to three hours to form alkali cellulose.

2) <u>Pressing and shredding:</u> The bamboo alkali cellulose is squeezed mechanically to remove excess sodium hydroxide solution. The alkali cellulose is mechanically shredded to increase surface area and make the cellulose easier to process.

3) <u>Aging</u>: It is left to dry for 24 hours. During this process, the shredded alkali cellulose is allowed to stand in contact with the oxygen of the ambient air. Because of high alkalinity, the alkali cellulose is partially oxidized and degraded to lower molecular weights. This degradation is to be controlled to produce chain lengths shorter enough to give proper viscosities in the spinning solution.

4) <u>Xanthation</u>: Roughly a third as much carbon disulfide is added to the bamboo alkali cellulose to sulfurize the compound, causing it to gel; any remaining carbon disulfide is removed by evaporation due to decompression, and cellulose sodium xanthate is the result.

5) <u>Dissolving</u>: A diluted solution of sodium hydroxide is added to the cellulose sodium xanthate, dissolving it to create a viscose solution consisting of about 5% sodium hydroxide and 7% to 15% bamboo fiber cellulose.

6) <u>Spinning</u>: After subsequent ripening, filtering and degassing, the viscose bamboo cellulose is forced through spinneret nozzles into a large container of a diluted sulfuric acid solution. This hardens the viscose bamboo cellulose sodium xanthate and reconverts it to cellulose bamboo fiber threads, which are spun into bamboo fiber yarns to be woven into reconstructed and regenerated textile product of bamboo.[4]

---

4   Das, Subrata. "Bamboo—21st Century Eco Fiber: Application in Towel Sector." Fibre2fashion. com. 2007.

Top Left: Biza (bamboo)
Bottom Left: Green Apple (organic cotton tee, bamboo pants)
Right: Arbor (bamboo top), Patagonia (organic cotton skirt)

As mentioned, bamboo fiber is naturally antibacterial. However, this quality may be affected by the processing. The Federal Trade Commission (FTC) says: "There's also no evidence that rayon made from bamboo retains the antimicrobial properties of the bamboo plant, as some sellers and manufacturers claim." [5] In 2009, the FTC charged several bamboo fabric manufacturers with breaking the Commission's Textile Fiber Products Identification Act by making claims about antimicrobial qualities. The companies have since settled and agreed to change labeling.

From a land use perspective, though bamboo of course grows in the wild, Planet Green points out that bamboo plantations can sometimes displace native forests. Also, most bamboo for fiber is grown in China so any fabrics or fibers that are shipped to the US for use in fashions carry a heavy carbon footprint. Bamboo can be grown locally in certain areas of the United States and with some effort, can be grown sustainably. Growers just have to make sure that it remains contained since it is a nonnative species.

So, with this all said, it's up to each consumer to weigh the pros and cons. In my opinion, bamboo is a natural fiber that can be grown and processed sustainably, so is still worth supporting as opposed to petrochemical-based fabrics. As savvy consumers, we should demand that more ecologically sound methods of bamboo processing are used, and that products are labeled clearly so we can tell the difference. Keeping prices fair might also involve some activism on the part of supporters.

What's the price tag?

Bamboo clothing tends to cost about the same or even a little bit less than organic cotton products. Out of the first three fabrics covered here in this book, bamboo is most likely to be affordable. I have found bamboo clothing at Marshall's that is not priced any differently than conventional clothing of a similar style.

Part of the reason for this could be the fact that bamboo does grow so readily. However, the bamboo linen that is processed using the most eco-friendly methods may cost a bit more because this is also more labor intensive as opposed to using chemicals to derive the fibers.

---

5   Federal Trade Commission (FTC). "Bamboo Fabrics." FTC Consumer Information—Money and Credit: Shopping and Saving. August 2009.

Left: Bamboosa (bamboo top),
Aventura (organic cotton)

Top Right: Bianca Paradis (bamboo)

Bottom Right: Jonano (bamboo &
organic cotton)

Companies that make clothing made of bamboo include:[6]

Conventional designers
- Diane von Furstenberg[7]
- Oscar de la Renta[8]
- Agnes B[9]

Eco-designers
- Amanda Shi—Avita[10]
- Linda Loudermilk[11]
- Katharine Hamnett[12]
- Miho Aoki and Thuy Pham at United Bamboo[13]
- Sara Kirsner at Doie Lounge[14]

Clothing manufacturers
- Bamboosa[15]
- Ecodesignz LLC[16]
- Jonäno[17]
- Bambooclothes.com

Fabric manufacturers
- Richfield Tang Knits Ltd.[18]

Switzerland-based Oeko-Tex® Association[19] established the Oeko-Tex® Standard 100[20] testing and certification system in 1992. The system is largely considered the benchmark for fabric testing and standards globally. In order to receive a certain classification, fabrics must meet specific criteria.

---

6   Lackman, Michael. "Bamboo: Facts Behind the Fiber." OrganicClothing.blogs.com. September 18, 2007.

7   Diane von Furstenberg. http://www.dvf.com. Diane von Furstenberg. 2015.

8   Oscar de la Renta. http://www.oscardelarenta.com. Oscar de la Renta. 2014.

9   agnés b. http://www.agnesb.com/dispatch. agnés b. 2015.

10   Avita, Inc. http://avitastyle.com. Avita, Inc. 2008.

11   Linda Loudermilk/luxury eco. http://www.lindaloudermilk.com. Linda Loudermilk/luxury eco. 2015.

12   Katharine Hamnett. http://www.katharinehamnett.com. Katharine Hamnett. 2014.

13   United Bamboo. http://unitedbamboo.com/. United Bamboo. 2015.

14   Doie Lounge. http://www.doielounge.com. Doie Lounge. 2014.

15   Bamboosa. http://bamboosa.com. Bamboosa: Soft on You. Easy on Earth. 2015.

16   EcoDesignz LLC. http://www.bambooclothes.com. BambooClothes.com. 2015.

17   Jonäno. http://www.jonano.com. Jonäno. 2011.

18   RT Knits Limited. http://www.rtknits.com. RT Knits: "...moving towards sustainable textile production." 2010.

19   International Association for Research and testing in the Field of Textile Ecology (OEKO-TEX). http://www.oeko-tex.com. OEKO-TEX Association. 2015.

20   International Association for Research and testing in the Field of Textile Ecology (OEKO-TEX). "OEKO-TEX Standard 100." OEKO-TEX Association. 2015.

Left: Green Label (organic cotton tee), Sweetgrass (bamboo skirt)

Right: Earth Yoga (sustainable bamboo & organic cotton)

Interview: Sass Brown, Former Associate Dean for the School of Art and Design, Fashion Institute of Technology, and Author of "Ecofashion"

1)   What in your background led you get into this movement? What drew you to natural fabrics?

I am a designer by trade, with a great respect for craftsmanship and artisans, which has led me over the years to volunteer, advise and work with, and for, various women's cooperatives, NGOs, governmental agencies and the creative economy in a number of countries around the world. My involvement with sustainable development in the craft sector and a lifelong passion for luxury and cutting-edge fashion grew over the years to incorporate my naturally activistic mindset and a belief that one person can make a difference. As someone who loves and honors craftsmanship, I have always valued tradition and natural fabrics and processes over unnatural.

2)   Tell us about your books and work at FIT and what you have tried to accomplish in raising awareness of ecofashion.

I wrote my first book called Eco Fashion in 2010. At the time I felt that it was important to share and showcase the really great work being done by emerging designers around the world. Everything written till that point had lumped fashion in with design in general, so you'd find a recycled desk and an energy-saving appliance next to an organic t-shirt, with the main focus on the materials and life cycle of the product and very little aesthetic considering. Alternatively there were a number of DIY books on how to upcycle your stained t-shirt into a grocery bag, but nothing that honored the craft of great design in balance with the sustainability of the process.

My second book ReFashioned was an outgrowth of the first, in that I had so much more information on great design work being done with upcycled materials than I could fit into a single chapter on ethical fashion. I learned a lot of lessons from the first book, and had a lot more involvement and fun with the layout of this book than I was able to with my first. I am now working on my third book on artisanship and global craft as the future of the luxury fashion industry, which I intend to be digital, and I'm hoping to partner with a filmmaker to release a documentary to compliment and augment the book.

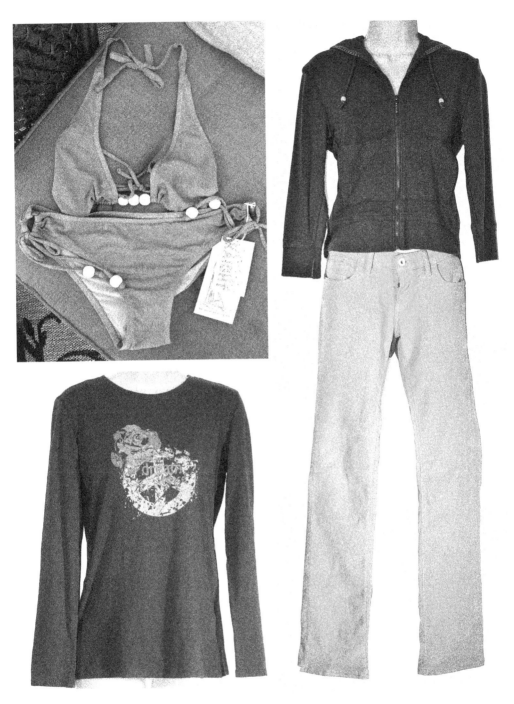

Top Left: Kelly B (bamboo)
Bottom Left: Earth Yoga (bamboo)
Right: Biza (bamboo cotton hoodie), Loomstate (organic cotton pants)

The intent with all my writing, whether my books, articles or blog posts, is to inspire what to consider design at its best. To show there are better options than mainstream fashion. To encourage everyone to consider their dollars as votes, and spend them in support of things they believe in.

3)   What do you think is the most important thing the fashion world needs to keep in mind as we move into the future? That is: what is more important— organic, local, longevity of the product, etc.?

I don't think it's possible to weigh the carbon footprint of a garment against the longevity of the product, or the lessened pollution or chemical use, for example. Everyone has their own moral code that is important to them. Ultimately I think transparency is key to all the issues that the fashion and clothing industry perpetrates on people and planet. I think if clothing came with a warning hang tag, like cigarettes come with a health warning, then no one would be purchasing fast fashion any longer. If the image of the child laborer who sewed the garment, or the stream that was polluted through dying of it, or the carbon emissions racked up as the fiber, fabric and garment were shipped around the world, were emblazoned on the hangtag, I think everyone would have a hard time financing it. I think this t-shirt vending machine in Berlin as part of Fashion Revolution this year highlights that: http://www.trueactivist.com/this-vending-machine-sells-t-shirts-for-2-euros-but-no-one-will-buy-one-see-why

4)   Where do you see the ecofashion/sustainable clothing movement going? That is, is it a fad?

Ethical fashion is not, nor has it ever been, a fad. That doesn't mean it can't be fashionable to care or make a difference through your business or your purchase, because it is. But when we are talking about water crisis in the US, climate change caused in great part by the fashion industry, millions of kilos of textile waste leaching carcinogenic chemicals into the groundwater and soil table from landfill, methane emission from animal agriculture pushing global warming higher, and the physical limitations of fiber growth, oil extraction, and other major ingredients of textiles, this is far from a fad—it is the future of how we consume.

Top Left: Earth Yoga (bamboo & organic cotton)
Top Right: Bianca Paradis (bamboo)
Bottom: Green Apple (bamboo)

5)   What would sustain the eco-fashion movement and help it grow? What must people/consumers and/or designers and manufacturers do to ensure eco-fashion's success?

Publicizing and making available the variety of ethical clothing choices is still paramount, as too many people don't see ethical fashion as a viable alternative to their current shopping habits. We all have to realize there are ramifications for the choices we make whether as a designer purchasing fabric or a consumer purchasing designs, and we should do our due diligence of what those ramifications are and decide whether we choose to fund them or not.

6)   Should it scale up and become more affordable—that is, be available at Wal-Mart?

There is an inevitable dichotomy in upscaling ethical fashion, as the main problem is in fact consumption, meaning that producing more and more ethical fashion is still a problem that strains resources, challenges life cycles, and causes a multitude of problems. A major shift in what and how we consume must happen. Part of that process may well involve mainstreaming ethical fashion and making it accessible, but it is not and cannot be a long-term solution.

7)   What are the best methods to raise awareness about eco-fashion?

It simply has to be better designed, better made, more desirable, and better for the planet, then the mainstream competition simply doesn't measure up.

8)   Who are some of your favorite people involved in eco-fashion, designers or otherwise, that you think deserve more recognition?

Orsola de Castro and Carry Somers, the founders of Fashion Revolution. Livia Firth of Eco Age and founder of the Green Carpet challenge. Artisans around the world struggling to make a living from generations-old crafts. Stella Jean and Dent de Man, both working with the Ethical Fashion Initiative, a joint agency of the United Nations and the WTO. Paul Van Zyl for founding Maiyet, really the first serious luxury ethical fashion house. A host of emerging designers working around the world in partnership with artisans, working with upcycled materials, building better business models, and generally changing our industry.

Chapter 4

Lyocell
Clothing Really Can Grow on Trees

What is lyocell? Wood. Yup, wood. The stuff grown by trees that has been used for housing, building fires, creating art, making paper, and you-name-it over the centuries, can also be made into fabric for clothing. Cellulose can be taken from bleached wood pulp and it indeed makes a lovely fabric.

Lyocell is very closely related to bamboo rayon and can be made from bamboo cellulose. One source says, "Although it is given a separate generic name, the FTC [Federal Trade Commission] classifies Lyocell as a subcategory under "Rayon."[1] However, according to Silk Road Textile Merchants, "The properties and production processes were unique enough for the US Federal Trade Commission to designate Tencel [a brand name of lyocell] as a separate fiber group."[2]

Lyocell is one of the newest fabrics to come along in years. "Fabrics derived from cellulose date back to the middle of the nineteenth century, though no one commercially produced one until 1889. A Swiss chemist, George Audemars, was granted an English patent in 1855 for an artificial silk he derived from mulberry bark."[3] Lyocell was further studied through the 1900s at Courtald's in the UK.[4]

As mentioned, the most popular brand name of lyocell is TENCEL®. It is produced by an Austrian company called Lenzing, with some of it in its Alabama, USA, location. Lenzing has produced cellulosic fibers since the late 1930s and started producing Tencel in the 1990s. The company proudly touts its environmental record and produces a detailed

---

1   FiberSource. "Lyocell Fiber." FiberSource. 2015.
2   Apparel Search Company. "Lyocell Fibers: Apparel Search Fiber Directory." Apparel Search Company. 2015.
3   Made How. "Lyocell." Made How: Volume 5. 2015.
4   Woodings, Calvin. "Introducing Tencel." Tencel at Courtaulds: From Genesis to Exodus and Beyond... 2013.

sustainability report.[5] According to Lenzing.com, "TENCEL® is the first fiber producer awarded with the 'EU-Flower.' The natural origin of the raw material wood as well as high standards for ecologically sound production at all sites enabled Lenzing to receive the EU Eco-Label award." The EU Eco-Label indicates products that have a minimal environmental impact. TENCEL® fabric carries the Oeko Tex 100 certification, an international standard developed in 1992 to certify that it contains no harmful substances.[6] Lenzing is a member of the Textile Exchange, the Hong Kong-based Sustainable Fashion Business Consortium (SFBC), the Sustainable Apparel Coalition, and the RITE Group, a nonprofit organization operating out of London.[7] Lenzing was also granted the Biobased Label of the US Department of Agriculture (USDA).[8] *(Logo by Lenzing)*

Why is lyocell green?

Lyocell is not synthetic, but it is a "regenerated" fiber manufactured from wood pulp. The main ingredient is cellulose, a natural polymer found in plant cells. In the case of Tencel, eucalyptus trees are used - they grow quickly and do not require artificial irrigation, pesticides, or fertilizers. The fiber yield per acre from the trees used in the Lenzing fibers is up to ten times higher than that of cotton.[9]

The lyocell manufacturing process, also used to manufacture TENCEL®, is as follows:
- N-methylmorpholine-N-oxide, a weak alkaline, dissolves the wood pulp from tree farms or bamboo cellulose into a viscose solution. This chemical is a weak alkaline that acts as surfactant to break down the cellulose.
- Hydrogen peroxide is added to stabilize the solution.
- The solution is forced through spinnerets into a hardening bath of water and methanol, ethanol or a similar alcohol.
- This causes the viscose solution to harden into fiber threads, which are then washed in demineralized water.
- Once dried, the regenerated wood or bamboo fiber threads can be spun into yarn for weaving into fabric. [10]

5   The Lenzing Group. "Focus Sustainability: Taking Responsibility for Our Business." Lenzing AG. April 9, 2013.
6   Sympatico Clothing. "What is Tencel® Fabric?" Sympatico Clothing. 2015.
7   The Lenzing Group. "Focus Sustainability: Taking Responsibility for Our Business." Lenzing AG. April 9, 2013.
8   Ibid.
9   Mass, Ed. "Rayon, Modal, and Tencel—Environmental Friends or Foes?" Yes It's Organic: Customer Service > Why Organic? 2014.
10   Made How. "Lyocell." Made How: Volume 5. 2015.

Top: Ann Taylor (lyocell tank), Earth Creations (hemp pants)
Bottom: H&M Conscious (lyocell cardigan), Threads for Thought (organic cotton pants)

Lyocell processing uses a lot of energy. However, it is considered relatively eco-friendly because N-methylmorpholine-N-oxide is an alkaline substance, which, according to tests, is relatively nontoxic to humans[11] and it gets recycled. (One can put their bare hand in the solvent without harm (although it's probably not advisable to leave it there.[12]) The chemical manufacturing processes are "closed-loop," meaning that 99 percent of the chemicals used during the processing are captured and recycled to be used again, so only trace amounts escape into the atmosphere or into waste waters and waste products. This means fewer processing chemicals being released into the environment. The chemical manufacturing process used to produce lyocell from wood cellulose can be modified to use bamboo cellulose.

The remaining wood not used for pulp production is used in thermal plants to generate heat as well as energy for the Lenzing production facility.[13]

Also, since lyocell retains its softness, there is no need for chemical fabric softeners to be used for care during the life of the garment.

How is lyocell used in fashion?

Lyocell can be woven into 100 percent lyocell fabrics (but it still is a bit expensive) or blended with other fibers. Like other natural-based fibers, lyocell is biodegradable. Lyocell can be made into very fine fibers, offering depth and body to fabrics combined with luxurious drape. Short staple length fibers give a cottonlike look to fabrics. Long filament fibers give the finished fabric more silklike qualities, including sheen. Some designers have started to make jeans out of lyocell, and the feedback is that it is very soft.[14]

One of my favorite fabrics due to its smooth feel, lyocell is also strong, absorbent (unlike synthetic fibers), hypoallergenic, and wrinkles a bit less than cotton. It can be dyed into vibrant colors, and has an advantage of managing moisture well, inhibiting the growth of bacteria. "Lyocell prevents the growth of bacteria, which cause odors, naturally without the addition of chemical treatment which may cause allergic reaction and are environmentally unfriendly. Bacterial growth is prevented through the moisture

---

11   Fisher Scientific. "Material Safety Data Sheet: 4-Methylmorpholine N-oxide Monohydrate." Fisher Scientific. April 2, 2008.
12   Mass, Ed. "Rayon, Modal, and Tencel—Environmental Friends or Foes?" Yes It's Organic: Customer Service > Why Organic? 2014.
13   Ibid.
14   Sindelar, Daisy. "As Concerns About Cotton Grow, a Fashionable Alternative Emerges." *Radio Free Europe/Radio Liberty*, September 2, 2013.

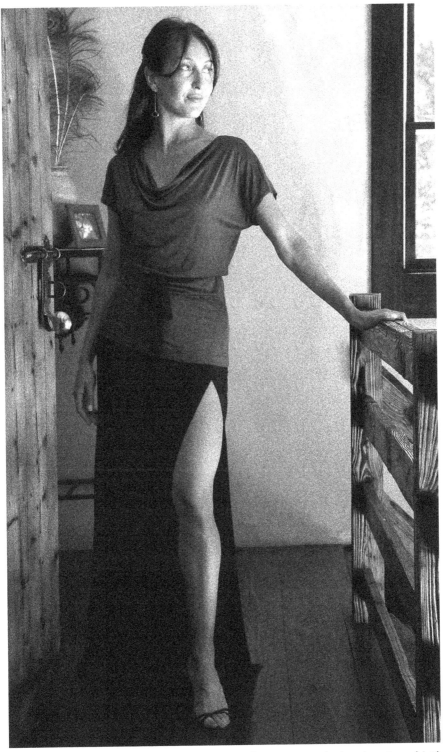

H&M Conscious (lyocell top, recycled polyester skirt)

management of the fiber."[15] This is important because chemical additives are often used on synthetic fabrics and even cotton to reduce growth of bacteria. It therefore also makes a good fill for bedding.

Patagonia uses lyocell, and states on its website that the lyocell they use in their garments comes from eucalyptus tree wood.

> "The trees are grown on sustainably run farms certified by the Forest Stewardship Council (FSC), and the fiber carries the Pan European Forest Council (PEFC) quality seal. It is possible to use bamboo, or other sources of cellulose, but eucalyptus yields the best quality fiber with the least amount of waste. Therefore we think this process is the best available option....[16] The eucalyptus wood pulp is dissolved in a nontoxic organic solvent. The solution is extruded through fine holes to produce fiber and the solvent is recycled in a closed-loop process.... We ensure that the fabric processing of TENCEL® lyocell fiber does not utilize any harmful chemicals (like formaldehyde) sometimes used to finish this type of fabric.

> TENCEL lyocell can be used in place of other regenerated cellulose fibers such as viscose rayon. The benefits of using TENCEL lyocell include the traceable and sustainable origin of the wood pulp and the use of nontoxic chemicals and solvents in the fiber processing. In addition, TENCEL lyocell is a high-tenacity cellulosic fiber, which gives high strength properties to the fabric."[17]

The Flip Side

Lyocell can tend to "pill," forming those tiny little bumps on fabric that make it look less-than-fresh, so must be cared for gently. As mentioned above, some producers use formaldehyde to limit this pilling. In general due to the chemical processing, it may not be the best choice for people with multiple chemical sensitivities (MCS).[18]

The trees Lenzig typically uses for Tencel are grown in South Africa, and the processing takes place elsewhere, so transporting the wood has a carbon impact.[19] "The company

15   Mass, Ed. "Rayon, Modal, and Tencel—Environmental Friends or Foes?" Yes It's Organic: Customer Service > Why Organic? 2014.
16   Patagonia. "The Footprint Chronicles." Patagonia. 2014.
17   Patagonia. "Tencel® Lyocell." Patagonia: Materials & Technology. 2014.
18   Lackman, Michael. "Tencel: Sustainable but Not Necessarily Healthy." OrganicClothing.blogs.com. November 4, 2005.
19   Natural Resources Defense Council (NRDC). "Choosing Between Cotton and Tencel: Which Has the Lighter Environmental Impact?" NRDC—Smarter Living: Stuff. January 23, 2012.

Left: Ann Taylor (lyocell top), Reco Jeans (recycled denim)

Right: Linda Loudermilk (lyocell)

estimates its water use at 154.7 gallons per pound of fiber—considerably more than Brazilian rain-fed cotton, but much less than irrigated organic cotton from California." Lyocell is manufactured, so it does require more energy use than purely natural fibers. "However, Lenzing uses primarily low-carbon biofuels and only 14 percent fossil fuels to keep their carbon emissions down. Tencel's carbon footprint, according to a company-sponsored study, is less than a pound of CO_2 for each pound of fiber. That figure, however, doesn't include shipping impacts."[20]

What's the price tag?

Many mainstream outlets carry clothing made from lyocell and modal, or blends of these with other fabrics, and the price tends to be comparable with conventional fabrics.

Companies that make clothing made of lyocell include:
- Patagonia[21]
- H&M[22]
- Ann Taylor[23]
- Athleta[24]
- J. Jill[25]

According to Silk Road Fabrics, "Tencel is now being used by top designers, DKNY, Calvin Klein, Ann Taylor, and it has gone mainstream, appearing in Lee jeans and even the LL Bean catalog."

Companies using lyocell for bedding:
- Downlite[26]
- Valley Forge Fabrics[27]

Other Forms of Cellulose Fibers

Modal

You may see "modal" listed as the fabric on some of your clothing labels. Modal is another type of cellulosic fiber that is made specifically from the cellulose of beech

20   Ibid.
21   Patagonia. http://www.patagonia.com. Patagonia. 2015.
22   H & M Hennes & Mauritz AB. http://www.hm.com. H & M. 2015.
23   Ann Inc. http://www.anntaylor.com. Ann Taylor. 2015.
24   Athleta. http://www.athleta.com. Athleta. 2015.
25   J. Jill. http://www.jjill.com. J. Jill. 2015.
26   Downlite. "Tencel Lyocell." Downlite: Brands. 2015.
27   Valley Forge Fabrics, Inc. "Sustainable Sleep." Valley Forge Fabrics, Inc.: Bedding. 2012.

Top: H&M Conscious
(tencel)

Bottom: Bella Lux
(modal)

trees. Modal followed after the development of rayon, and can essentially be thought of as a form of lyocell. "No toxic effluent is discharged from the mill, and minimal water is used in the production. Beech trees do not require irrigation or pesticides and are grown on marginal, nonagricultural land."[28]

Modal fabric is light, very soft, and can look quite luxurious. It is sometimes used for undergarments due to its softness. Lenzing also makes some modal fabric. "Modal fibers were developed in Japan in 1951, and Lenzing started selling its version of them in 1964. Lenzing Modal® uses an environmentally friendly bleaching method for pulp."[29] "Lenzing Modal® is made from sustainably harvested beech trees in PEFC (Programme for the Endorsement of Forest Certification schemes) certified European forests."[30]

A great quality of modal is that it tends to hold its color and size even after many washings, and can be machine-washed and dried. "Textiles made from modal are resistant to shrinkage, fading and graying. Modal fibers have found a wide variety of uses in clothing, outerwear, and household furnishings. They are often blended with cotton, wool or synthetic fibers, and take and retain dyes well."[31]

Lenpur

Lenpur is a newer-to-the-scene eco-friendly fabric fabricated from the pulp of sustainable white fir trees.[32] "The main differences in Lenpur compared to other cellulose fibres are its softness, its absorption capacity, its ability to release dampness (as a yarn or fabric), its deodorant properties, and its adsorption characteristics."[33] One company using lenpur says it has "the cosiness of silk, the touch of cashmere, and the freshness of linen all in one fiber" and also resists pilling.[34]

---

28   Baby Bahoonie. "Modal, What Does This Eco-Friendly Fabric Offer?" Baby Bahoonie Blog. June 3, 2011.
29   Mass, Ed. "Eco-Fiber or Fraud? Are Rayon, Modal, and Tencel Environmental Friends or Foes?" Natural Life Magazine. September 2008.
30   Mass, Ed. "Rayon, Modal, and Tencel—Environmental Friends or Foes?" Yes It's Organic: Customer Service > Why Organic? 2014.
31   Ibid.
32   LaMeaux, E.C. "How Are Eco-Friendly Fabrics Made?" GAIAM Life: Your Guide to Better Living. 2014.
33   EcoBioDis SA. "What is Lenpur?" Lenpur.net. 2014.
34   Kim, Hazel. "Otaki Clothing—Night Out Dress." The Skimple Life (blog). March 17, 2014.

Cupro
Made in Italy, Cupro is a "regenerated cellulose fiber derived from cotton linter (the ultrafine, silky fibers that stick to the seeds of the cotton plant after it's been ginned) that has been dissolved in a solution of ammonia and copper oxide. It is similar to rayon, but breathes and regulates body temperature like cotton."[35]

When you see the word "viscose" on a clothing label, this can mean that it was made from the fibers derived from beech trees, or else bamboo. As mentioned in Chapter 3, rayon is a type of viscose, though European mills tend to refer to it simply as "viscose" on the label. It has a nice luster, which gives the material some shine. However, it can tend to shrink when wetted and can also wrinkle, but it irons well. It follows a similar process using sodium hydroxide and carbon disulphide, and other solvents, similar to the chemical processing of bamboo we learned about earlier. So, though it starts from a plant-based, biodegradable and renewable source, viscose still has its issues.

Vital Hemptations (hemp tencel)

---

35   Stewart, Lea. "Cupro: A Cellulose Fiber Made from Recovered Cotton Waste." Ecouterre: Fabrictionary. April 11, 2011.

Chapter 5

Soy, Ingeo, and ... Algae?
Emerging New Fabrics and Whether Animal Fabrics Are Green

Some fabrics are being made from new and innovative sources. Here we will find out that soy and corn are not only good for eating but also for wearing. Fabrics derived from natural sources are sometimes referred to as "azlon." We'll also talk about recycled plastic used for fabric. Finally we will find out more about some familiar fabrics made from animal sources, and the issues surrounding those, so that ecofashionistas can be up on their game.

PART 1

Soy as a Fiber - The "Vegetable Cashmere"

As a health-food enthusiast, I have enjoyed edamame many times over the years (the plain soy beans, served steamed in their pod, that appear on the menus of many Japanese restaurants), as well as tofu, soy milk, tempeh, soy-based veggie burgers, and all sorts of fake-meat concoctions served at offbeat Chinatown restaurants in New York City. It is hard to believe that the soybean can be used for so many things, and now we can add one more item to the list: soy fabric.

I first encountered soy fabric, probably around 2003, at a chic little boutique in lower east side of Manhattan that has since gone out of business. Seeing the rack of clothes including attractive and unique looking sweaters marked "soy" I couldn't believe my eyes. And indeed, the label on this lovely blue-striped garment in my hand read "67% soy." It was nothing short of amazing. Blended with some cotton and a little Lycra, it felt soft and stretchy like any high-end light sweater I've ever had.

Why is it Green?

Like other fabrics featured in this book, soy is derived from a natural source: soybean plants. Soy fabric has made a comeback since 1999 and is made from the scraps left over from processing soybeans (tofu), mostly in China. "Soy protein is liquefied and then extruded through a spinneret into long, continuous fibers that solidify and are then cut and processed like any other spinning fiber. Any protein leftover from the soybean pulp can be used as fertilizer.[1] It's incredibly soft, and is sometimes referred to as the "vegetable cashmere," rivaling silk in its smooth texture.[2] Creating soy fibers is a chemically intensive process, but it is a closed loop process, meaning the chemicals are recycled and used again. Soy fabric is absorbent, warm, resistant to bacteria and UV rays, and when discarded is biodegradable; many fabrics aren't. And it is machine washable.

Soy's Use in Fashion

Right now soy clothing is mainly found as underwear, socks, scarves, sheets, and yoga or exercise apparel. It is also a popular choice for creating soft, comfortable baby clothing. It is also wrinkle and shrink resistant.[3] "Soy can be blended with other textiles…and can be beautifully colored using low-impact dyes."[4] China, the largest textile manufacturer and exporter, has begun mass-producing soy-based yarn. Soy is a very popular crop, so though use of soy in fashion has great potential, it will likely depend on production costs and demands from other uses in the coming years.

One form of soy fabric is called azlon. There is now a trademarked version of soy fabric called Soysilk™. It is produced by the South West Trading Company (SWTC), which claims to be a leading producer of natural fibers and yarns for use by hand-knitters.

Cons

It should be noted that the vast majority of the world's soybean crops now are genetically engineered or "genetically modified organisms" (GMO). In 2014, 82 percent (90.7 million hectares) of the 111 million hectares of the soybean planted globally were biotech.[5] Therefore we can likely assume, unless it's labeled otherwise, that the soy being used for the fabric was genetically altered. Though no studies have been done

---

1   Michigan Soybean Promotion Committee. "How Soy Fabric is Made." Michigan Soybean Promotion Committee. 2013.

2   The EcoMarket. "Soy Fabric." The EcoMarket. 2014.

3   Cool-Organic-Clothing.com. "Soy Clothing Superior Softness Feels Like Your Second Skin." Cool-Organic-Clothing.com. 2008.

4   Barnes, Pamela. "Soy Clothing: The Latest In Eco-Friendly Style." Natural Living for Women. 2012.

5   International Service for the Acquisition of Agri-Biotech Applications (ISSA). "Pocket K No. 16: Global Status of Commercialized Biotech/GM Crops in 2014." ISSA: Biotech Information Resources. 2015.

Top Left: Indigo Apparel (organic cotton & recycled polyester)
Bottom Left: Aventura (recycled polyester)
Right: Blue Fish (linen skirt), hemp scarf

that I could find, it is doubtful this has any direct health consequences on the soy fabric wearer. However, biotechnology presents other issues on an ecosystem level.

The promise of genetic engineering is to be able to create plants that are more resistant to disease or harsh conditions, and thus produce higher yields and feed more people. The intention may be good, but genetically altering plants is highly controversial. First, scientists at private corporations are inserting new genes into the existing gene pool, with unknown consequences on human and environmental health, and on pollinators such as bees and butterflies. One study from December 2009 revealed liver and kidney toxicity in rats that ate GMO corn.[6] Other studies have found tumor growth[7] and fertility issues in lab animals.[8] Secondly, corporations are patenting life, which raises its own ethical questions. This means that a corporation owns the patent to a certain type of bean variety, and if anyone else wants to grow it, they must pay the corporation. To compete in this new industrial era in farming means many farmers feel pressured into producing more by using genetically modified seed, but some farmers have found the yields to not be any better than non-GMO varieties.[9]

There is now a common version of soybean called "Roundup Ready." Roundup is a type of herbicide that kills weeds, commonly sold in the US. The Roundup Ready soy plant has been genetically altered to be immune to the herbicidal effects of the pesticide Roundup, though the chemical will kill most if not all of the plants around it. So therefore farmers are encouraged to not only buy the seed but also the Roundup to spray along with it.

There are things we can do, however. Since we the people vote with our dollar, a major way to make a difference here is by supporting organic farming in terms of our food choices, and eating organic soy products. The Organic Food Production Act, enforced by the US Department of Agriculture (USDA), does not allow organic foods to be genetically modified. Another way would be to call for labeling of GMO crops, which currently is not required in the US, though it is in other countries. Many organizations

---

6   de Vendômois, Joël Spiroux, et al. "A Comparison of the Effects of the Three GM Corn Varieties on Mammalian Health. *International of Biological Sciences (Int. J. Biol. Sci.)* 5, no. 7 (2009): 706–726. doi: 10.7150/ijbs.5.706.
7   Philpott, Tom. "Longest-Running GMO Safety Study Finds Tumors in Rats." Mother Earth News. April/May 2013.
8   Smith, Jeffrey. "Genetically Modified Soy Linked to Sterility, Infant Mortality in Hampsters." The Huffington Post: Huff Post Green: The Blog. August 9, 2010.
9   *Le Monde Selon Monsanto (The World According to Monsanto)*. Arte Video, 2008. Film.

Top Left & Right: H&M Conscious (recycled polyester)
Bottom: H&M Conscious (recycled wool)

such as the Organic Consumers Association[10] actively advocate this. By being informed, we can support a nonpolluted environment for farmers, wildlife, and ourselves.

Since genetic modification is not listed on food items, it also is not identified on clothing labels. The organic food label of the USDA is not typically used for clothing items, though I believe this should change (see last chapter). However, some suppliers may provide information in their marketing materials. For example, The Natural Clothing Company states on its website, "The soybean byproducts for our clothing does not come from US and to our knowledge is not genetically modified. Organic soy fibers are very environmentally friendly and a great choice for the fashion industries for sustainable clothing."[11]

FUN FACT

A big promoter of soy research back in the 1930s was Henry Ford. He used soy to make a wool-like fabric for his car seats, and was said to have the first suit made at least partially of soy. He also promoted soy foods, including soymilk.[1]

---

1   Shurtleff, William, and Akiko Aoyagi. "Henry Ford and His Employees: Work with Soy." SoyInfo Center. 2004.

What's the price tag?
Soy clothing shares a price range with organic cotton and bamboo. It's unlikely to be as affordable as clothing items found at common box stores, but is also not the most expensive in the range of eco-fabrics.

Some Companies Selling Soy Fabric clothing include:
- Faerie's Dance[12]
- Natural Clothing Company[13]
- Hornet Mountain Natural Products[14]
- Climate Clothing[15]

---

10   Organic Consumers Association (OCA). https://www.organicconsumers.org/. OCA. 2015.
11   Natural Clothing Company. "Alternative Fibers." Natural Clothing Company. 2014.
12   Faerie's Dance. http://www.faeriesdance.com/. Faerie's Dance. 2015.
13   Natural Clothing Company. http://www.naturalclothingcompany.com/. Natural Clothing Company. 2014.
14   Hornet Mountain Natural Products. http://www.hornetmountain.com/. Hornet Mountain Natural Products. 2015.
15   Climate Clothing. https://www.facebook.com/climateclothing/. Climate Clothing. 2015.

Top Left: DDC Lab (soy)   Top Right: Texture (soy)
Bottom: Be Present (organic cotton & recycled polyester)

- For babies: Babysoy (website says the company does not use GMO soy)[16]

A Brief Word on Other Unique Fabrics

Sasawashi

Sasawashi[17] is a company that makes clothing and other products with *sasawashi*, a very durable Japanese fabric made from a type of paper called washi (used for Japanese paper doors) and the plant *kumazasa*,[18] which is a hardy plant with antibacterial properties found in the highlands of mainland Japan and Hokkaido. It is a type of bamboo plant, and is slit into thin strands and twisted into a durable yarn. It absorbs moisture, and like other bamboo, it has natural antibacterial and therefore deodorant qualities, so two common uses of it are for socks and towels. The most comparable fabric in terms of look would likely be linen, though it is said to feel as soft as cashmere. It is not "sticky" on the skin even when it is wet. Because it is made of a long smooth fiber, it does not pill or cause skin irritation, and it also keeps out UV rays. It can be washed, but it is recommended not to use bleach.[19] Unlike some of the other natural fabrics, it is made without the use of added chemicals in the process, so is eco-friendly. One company featuring Sasawashi's product line is the Japanese company Kohzo.[20] Earthsake in California offers a sasawashi slipper.[21] Morihata International Ltd. Co. offers sasawashi socks, towels, slippers, body salve, soap, and other items.[22] *(Logo by Sasawashi)*

Ingeo

Ingeo (in-jay-oh) is a synthetic substance made exclusively by NatureWorks LLC and trademarked by Cargill, from corn biopolymers that can be used to make alternatives to plastic, and also for fabric. A polymer is basically a long strand of molecules, and in this case the backbone is carbon that is naturally taken up by plants and made into fiber. It is made of corn sugar to make a polylactide, which is spun into fibers. So from this versatile material, an alternative to polyester can be made that does not derive from petroleum products. It can be made to look like cotton or other fabrics, and can also be blended with other fabrics. I have seen Ingeo dresses and also Ingeo

16   Babysoy. http://www.babysoyusa.com/. Babysoy. 2015.
17   Sasawashi Co. Ltd. http://sasawashi.com/en/. Sasawashi. 2015.
18   Sasawashi Co. Ltd. "About Sasawashi." Sasawashi. 2015.
19   Authentic Goods from Japan. "Characteristics of Sasawashi." Authentic Goods from Japan. 2007.
20   KOhZO DENIM. http://kohzo.ch/. KHoZO Industrial Art. 2015.
21   Earthsake. "Sasawashi House Slipper." Earthsake Store. 2015.
22   Morihata International Ltd. Co. "Sasawashi." Morihata Wholesale Products. 2015.

Top: Eco Malibu (organic cotton, recycled polyester tee), Synergy (low impact dye skirt)

Bottom Left: Be Present (recycled polyester)

Bottom Right: Earth Yoga (organic cotton & recycled polyester)

bathing suits. One aspect of this material that makes it green for those living in the US is that the corn can be grown domestically so does not have to be transported from overseas.

One issue (there always has to be one, right?) is that the corn used, like soy, is likely genetically modified. The NatureWorks website states, "Corn sourced from farmers within a 30-mile radius of our plant Blair, NE, is used to make dextrose (corn sugar). We at NatureWorks purchase this dextrose to make Ingeo biopolymer. The corn used to make the dextrose is a mixed stream of non-GMO and GMO corn grown in the area."[23] This material is not biodegradable under normal conditions, but it is compostable given the right heat and humidity levels. Cargill is one of large multinational corporations that own much of our food supply, which makes me a bit cautious, but I do think it is encouraging to see renewable sources being used to make fabric as long as it does not divert a significant amount of nutrients from the food supply.

Algae

Green stuff growing in our waterways may seem gross, but it may have the potential to provide fiber for the manufacture of fabric. Seacell® Pure is a combination of lyocell and algae fiber from algae grown in Icelandic fjords.[24] Seacell® is made by SeaCell GmbH, a subsidiary of the German company Zimmer AG. The fabric is said to breathe well and is being used mostly for underwear and bedding.[25] It can enhance health by releasing minerals (calcium and magnesium) and vitamins (vitamins C and E) from the algae in the clothing into your skin. Researchers in Sweden confirmed algae fabric's ability to reduce body odor by killing bacteria.[26] A formulation called SeaCell "Active" contains silver ions, which have further antibacterial properties.[27] Seacell Pure has achieved the European Union Eco-Label, indicating that it is eco-friendly.

One of China's leading textile companies, Qingdao Xiyingmen Group, has said it can use the proteins in several types of algae to create fiber that is more durable

23   NatureWorks LLC. "Frequently Asked Questions." NatureWorks: FAQs. 2015.
24   SeaCell. http://seacell.info/. SeaCell. 2015.
25   Fermosa Taffeta Co., Ltd. "SeaCell Yarn—New Material for Green & Health Care: From Nature, for Nature, to Nature." Fermosa Taffeta Co., Ltd. 1997.
26   Dovey, Dana. "Alage-Based Material Takes on Body Odor." Newsweek. Tech & Science sec. October 25, 2014.
27   HEFEL Textil GmbH. "SeaCell Active: Wellness With the Power of the Sea." HEFEL Bed and Sleep. 2015.

Top: Eco Yoga (organic cotton & recycled polyester), Walleska Ecochicc (pop-top belt)
Bottom: Playback (recycled polyester & cotton from watercooler bottles)

than cotton. A spokesman for the company said, "Thanks to its resistance to fire and electromagnetic waves, the fiber can be also used to produce special clothing, such as fireproof gear for firefighters, medical uniforms and other protective clothing."[28]

Algae use for fabric is interesting because it relieves pressure off land-based fiber production, often chemically intensive, by expanding fiber production to include marine plants. Algal blooms can actually be problematic for ecosystems, so perhaps this is a good solution.

Did you know?

"Research to develop biodegradable buttons, zips and spandex elastomeric yarn from corn plastics is ongoing."[1]

1 Fletcher, Kate. *Sustainable Fashion & Textiles: Design Journeys*, 113. London: Earthscan, 2008.

Ramie

Ramie is another plant-based fiber used to make fabrics. It is a member of the nettle family, and is a tall fibrous plant with large heart-shaped leaves that grows in Asia. According to the Natural Fibres website, "Ramie (pronounced Ray-me) is one of the oldest vegetable fibers and has been used for thousands of years. It was used in mummy cloths in Egypt during the period 5000–3000 BC, and has been grown in China for many centuries.... Long before cotton was introduced in the Far East, it was used for Chinese burial shrouds over 2,000 years ago."[29] Ramie is also referred to as China grass and is a hardy perennial grass that is naturally white in color.

Ramie is resistant to bacteria, insects, and stains, is extremely absorbent, making it comfortable to wear, and dyes fairly easily. It has a smooth lustrous appearance that improves with washing, and it does not shrink nor lose its shape. It looks similar to linen and is commonly used to make tablecloths. However, it is also blended with cotton or wool for use in clothing. A downside is that it is not very elastic and tends to wrinkle. Another downside is that, like other plant fiber-derived fabrics, the strands of fiber must be removed from the plant using a chemical process, so this aspect of ramie makes it not totally "green."

Recycled Bottles as a Fiber

Ever heard the word "trashion"? Well, you can now consider yourself one of the few

28 Xinhua. "Algae Menace to be Savior of China's Fabric Industry." China Daily: Green China. August 7, 2010.
29 Natural Fibres. "Ramie." Natural Fibre. 2015.

Top Left: Be Present
(recycled polyester &
organic cotton)

Top Right: Jonano
(peace silk)

Bottom: Compassion
(vegan organic tees)

who have. Yes, clothing fabric can be made from recycled plastic bottles, which are usually made from polyethylene terephthalate (PET). Considering that, as mentioned earlier, nylon and polyester are basically plastic (which is petroleum-based), it actually makes sense that clothing could then be made from recycled plastic. While I am no fan of plastic in general due to its persistence in the environment or non-biodegradability, the reuse of plastic for clothing makes use of an existing resource. Doing so requires less energy and water than creating the same fabric from virgin materials.

One name brand of recycled bottle polyester is RePET. The following diagram shows the basic process for creating spun thread from bottles. Essentially the bottles are picked up, cleaned, and the labels are removed. Then they are sorted by color, crushed, and chopped down into chips. The chips are then melted down in vats and extruded through small holes to create strands. These strands are stretched into thin threads, baled, and sent to manufacturers to be made into clothing.

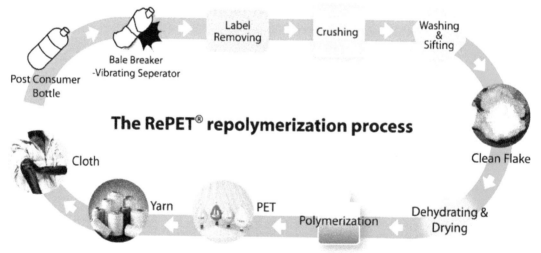

Diagram by RePET®

Another name brand of the recycled bottle fabric developed here in the US is EcoFi, formerly known as EcoSpun, and is made by Foss Manufacturing. "The Ecofi process has the capacity to keep almost 3 billion plastic PET soda bottles out of the world's landfills each year, saving over 1/2 million barrels of oil."[30] Production of recycled polyester is influenced by the price of oil, because polyester is made from oil, and if oil

---

30   Eartheasy. "EcoSpun (Eco-fi)." Eartheasy.com. 2014.

Left: M Marsh Spiritex (recycled polyester jacket), Texture (hemp pants)
Right: Amour Vert (peace silk)

is cheap, polyster is cheap, making recycled polyester less-pricey competitive. But now as there is more awareness and appreciation of this fabric, consumers are more likely to pay a slightly higher price.

A third brand of recycled bottle fabric is Repreve, which is used by Patagonia, Ford (for car seats), The North Face, AquaGreen swimwear, and Chicobags.[31]

Patagonia was a pioneer in this area, making fleece clothing from recycled bottles back in 1993. (Fleece is popular since it is warm, lightweight, and soft. Most people don't even realize that when they're wearing fleece, they are wearing plastic.) Now Patagonia actually recycles polyester clothing back into new clothing, using an "EcoCircle" recycling system through its Common Threads Program.

---

31   Unifi, Inc. "Products Made With Repreve." Repreve. 2013.

Case Study of a Sustainable Apparel Role Model

In the particular case of the clothing brand Nau, a sports clothing company, the owner started out with sustainability in mind. A former employee of Patagonia, he was approached by the cofounder of Marmot to start this whole new brand. All of Nau's clothing is recyclable or compostable, and since recycling blended fabrics is difficult, they don't blend fabrics if recyclability or compostability is prevented. They use only organic cotton and non-GMO corn for their polylactic acid (PLA), a biopolymer that can replace polyester. They use recycled metals whenever possible in zippers and buttons, and also have a take-back program. Working with Japan's Teijin recycled fabric factory, they are attempting to establish a closed loops system. Nothing they produce requires dry cleaning. They hired an auditor to inspect the factories where clothing is being produced to ensure proper practices. — *Future Fashion White Papers pp. 242–248; www.nau.com*

Patagonia launched its Common Threads Recycling program in 2005, and at first was accepting Capilene® Performance Baselayers for recycling. They have since expanded the list of recyclable garments to include worn out Patagonia® fleece, Polartec® fleece clothing (from any maker), Patagonia cotton T-shirts, and some additional polyester and nylon 6 products that come with a Common Threads tag. "We now recycle used soda bottles, unusable manufacturing waste, and worn out garments (including our own) into polyester fibers to produce many of our clothes."[32] Using recycled fibers saves 72 percent on energy versus using virgin fiber.[33]

In addition to Patagonia, other athletic brands using recycled plastic fabric in their clothing and footwear include: Alternative Apparel, Timberland, Teeki, PrAna, and Under Armour. Of note, many of these companies also try to reduce their use of toxic chemicals, use organic cotton or hemp, donate to environmental organizations, and use recycled or biodegradable packaging.[34] In 2014, Nike released a football cleat shoe made from recycled bottles.[35] Some T-shirt manufacturers are also using recycled

---

32   Patagonia. "Recycled Polyester." Patagonia: Materials & Technology. 2014.
33   Egan, Greta. *Wear No Evil*. 2014. 57.
34   English, Nick. "The 14 Athletic Wear Companies That Are Actually Good for the World." Greatist. December 6, 2013.
35   Chua, Jasmin Malik. "Nike Unveils First Football Cleat Made With Recycled Bottles." Ecouterre. December 12, 2014.

bottle fabric, such as Anvil Knitwear.[36] The Florida company clothesmadefromscrap. com makes clothing made from both recycled bottles and reclaimed cotton.

The question is: are there any toxic chemicals in the plastic that can leach into our skin, especially if we perspire? Many people are becoming more aware of hormone-disrupting chemicals called phthalates in plastic products. According to the Mount Sinai School of Medicine, the PET, or "#1" plastic under discussion here, is not one of the plastics considered prone to leaching. However, it is recommended not to reuse even plastic #1 over and over for a long time since eventually it may start to break down. Several studies have found that low levels of the carcinogen antimony exist in PET plastic bottles, because it is used in the production of the bottles.[37] As of right now, research on this subject is limited, so it is unclear how much of any of these chemicals would be reaching your skin and at what level they would start raising concerns. My take on it is that the recycling of fiber is beneficial, because it takes the use of resources from linear to cyclical, so unless you are wearing your recycled PET clothing next to your skin on a daily basis, your exposure level is probably not something to worry about. However, we as consumers do have the power to ask questions, and such inquiries may push researchers to provide the answers.

Did you Know?

The yoga and sportswear company prAna uses recycled polyester, organic cotton, and hemp in some of their clothing, and also has a renewable energy initiative for which they won the EPA's Green Power Leadership award in 2006.[1]

---

1   PrAna. "Sustainability." PrAna. 2015.; Environmental Protection Agency (EPA). "Partner Profile: prAna." EPA: Climate Change > Clean Energy > Green Poer Partnership > Partner List > prAna. May 28, 2015.

Note also that no brand is perfect: A 2016 Greenpeace study of outdoor clothing brands called Leaving Traces showed "widespread use of environmentally-hazardous polyfluorinated chemicals (PFCs)—used to repel water and dirt, in all but four of forty products. Of greater concern, a form of PFC, perfluorooctanoic acid (PFOA), was found in eighteen samples by brands such as Jack Wolfskin, the North Face, Patagonia,

---

36   Gildan Activewear. "About Anvil." Anvil: Company. 2015.
37   Natural Resources Defense Council (NRDC). "Food Storage Containers." NRDC: Smarter Living > Food > Shopping Wise. November 22, 2011.

Mammut, Norrona, and Salewa. PFOA is a cancer-causing substance that persists in the environment, with traces being found in snow on mountaintops and in polar bears' livers."[38] [39]

Did you know?

Using a 3D printer, researchers at the Massachusetts Institute of Technology (MIT) are creating "bio-skin" fabrics embedded with bacillus subtilis natto bacteria that actually responds to heat and moisture—it opens up to ventilate when the wearer perspires.[1]

---

1   Lacey, S., & Arts. (2016, February 16). A living, breathing textile aims to enhance athletic performance. Retrieved August 10, 2016, from http://news.mit.edu/2016/living-breathing-textile-aims-to-enchance-athletic-performance-0216

PART 2

Animal Sources Materials - Are They Green or Not?

Silk

Silk is a loved and luxurious fabric, with its softness and luster, beautiful drapability, and lightweight quality. It has been in use for hundreds of years, dating back 5,000 years in Chinese history, and China remains the largest silk producer today. Silk fibers are natural in that they are made from the cocoon of the silkworm larva. The fiber from each cocoon can stretch out the distance of a mile. However, cultivating silkworms (called "sericulture") does have a downside.

Silkworms live for about thirty-five days—feeding on mulberry leaves—and then spin a cocoon with their filamentous fibers around and around, into what almost looks like a cotton ball. Silk processors take the cocoons and boil them alive until the fibers can be removed, or pierce the cocoon and unravel it. This kills the larvae, except a few from

---

38   Staff. "Greenpeace study reveals hazardous chemicals used by leading outdoor brands." magnifeco.com/greenpeace-leaving-traces-study. Magnifeco. January 31, 2016.
39   Greenpeace Germany. "Leaving Traces: The hidden hazardous chemicals in outdoor gear." http://www.greenpeace.org/international/en/publications/Campaign-reports/Toxics-reports/Leaving-Traces/. Greenpeace. January 25, 2016.

each batch to cultivate the next generation. Animal rights activists have raised this process as an issue.

There is, however, an alternative that does not carry with it as many cruelty accusations. "Peace silk" is made by using silkworm cocoon fiber only after the silkworm larvae hatched inside it has developed into a moth and has left the cocoon, as part of its natural cycle. However, on a silk "farm," the silkworms are usually able to live their full lives, metamorphose, and die naturally. "Raw" or "organic" silk is typically peace silk that also uses no added dyes or chemicals to adulterate it to make it wrinkle-proof or give it other sought-after properties. "Wild" silk can be produced (rather laboriously) by collecting silkworm cocoons from the wild, and then hand-spinning the cocoon fibers into thread. This silk, called Tussah, costs more than conventional silk, but does, of course, provide jobs for local silk-makers, which is not such a bad thing from that perspective.[40]

One downside to producing this type of silk is that when the moth emerges from the cocoon, it breaks through the fiber, so it is no longer one continuous filament, which is better for creating thread. Some say even the Peace Silk process still raises ethical issues. "In India, where the vast majority of Ahimsa [peace] silk is being raised, most silkworm strains are 'multivoltine.' This means that the silkworms do not undergo refrigeration, and the eggs will hatch approximately two weeks after being laid. The ones that are not fed will die within a day of hatching, from a combination of desiccation and starvation."[41] So, clearly, no one method of producing silk is perfect.

Companies producing peace silk clothing:
- Lindee Daniel[42]
- Amour Vert[43]
- René Geneva Design[44]

Leather

Many of us own leather shoes, belts, jackets, or cars with leather seats. Leather is typically made from cowhides, so in its pretreated form is basically a natural, biodegradable product. Its benefits include being very durable and becoming more

---

40   Cool-Organic-Clothing.com. "Guilt Free With Organic Silk." Cool-Organic-Clothing.com. 2008.
41   Cook, Michael. "Ahimsa (Peace) Silk: Why I Think It Doesn't Add Up." WormSpit.com. 2015.
42   Lindee. http://www.lindeedaniel.com/. LindeeDaniel. 2015.
43   Amour Vert. http://www.amourvert.com/. Amour Vert. 2015.
44   René Geneva Design, LLC. http://www.mycorset.com/. René Geneva Design, LLC. 2015.

flexible as it is worn over time. However, like many other products, it comes with its concerns for the eco-conscious consumer. Leather is not only the by-product of the meat industry, but is in itself also a driver of an industry that relies on killing animals (often under cruel circumstances) for profit. One billion animals are killed per year for their skin.[45] People who pursue a vegan (people who consume no animal products) or animal-friendly lifestyle normally eschew leather shoes and accessories. If you've ever met a vegan, thought they were weird, and wondered why they do what they do, you'll understand better after reading this section.

For one thing, many chemicals are used in the processing from the original hide to the final leather product, in order to make it resistant to bacterial decomposition and having the texture and color we desire. First it is soaked, then it is defleshed to remove flesh and fat, then it is limed and sulphuretted to remove hair, and then it is treated with acid and salts. It is treated with tanning agents sometimes for color, but mostly to make it less susceptible to decomposition. It is then dried, cut to the desired thickness, dyed, and greased. The wastewater, containing the fats, acids, sulfur, and tanning chemicals can be foul-smelling and have a significant impact on surrounding waterways.[46] Most tanneries have moved overseas, where regulation is less stringent than here in the US.[47]

Though bark and wood smoke used to be used in the processing, now it is more common for leather to be treated with trivalent and hexavalent chromium, both believed to be carcinogens, along with formaldehyde, sulfuric acid, and bactericides.[48]

Raising animals for meat and slaughter is in itself a very resource-intensive, and often inhumane, endeavor. Under modern factory farm conditions, cattle are raised in several ways. "Beef" cattle usually are allowed to graze out in pastureland, which is typically public land, where they eat, and often trample, local flora. For the last few weeks of their lives they are brought to farms where they are closely confined and fed grain diets laced with antibiotics and growth hormones. Their short lives end after about two years.

45   Katcher, Joshua. "Leather Jacket: The Rebel Icon That Lost Its Gall." The Discerning Brute: Fashion, Food & Etiquette for the Ethically Handsome Man. July 30, 2009.
46   Buljan, J. and I. Kral. Contributions by G. Clonfero, M. Bosnič and F. Schmel. *Introduction to Treatment of Tannery Effluents: What Every Tanner Should Know About Effluent Treatment.* Vienna, Austria. United Nations Industrial Development Organization (UNIDO). 2011.
47   Earth Pledge Foundation. *Future Fashion White Papers.* Edited by Leslie Hoffman. New York: Earth Pledge Foundation, 2008. 53.
48   Earth Pledge Foundation. *Future Fashion White Papers.* Edited by Leslie Hoffman. New York: Earth Pledge Foundation, 2008. 54.

"Dairy" cattle are confined from the start, and are kept pregnant in order to produce milk. Male "dairy" calves often are taken from their mothers on their first day of life and become veal calves, confined in veal crates where they can't move and are fed iron-free food to keep their flesh soft and pink. Many people don't realize that dairy cattle are also slaughtered, and often become grade B beef for hamburger.

Factory farms have been documented to contaminate waterways with excess manure, and also contribute vastly to greenhouse gas emissions. Cattle's digestive systems produce a lot of methane, a potent heat-trapping greenhouse gas, which they release as burps and farts. The processing of meat also requires a lot of energy, which is currently being provided by burning fossil fuels. A 2006 study by the United Nations' Food and Agriculture Organization (FAO) stated that the production, transport, and refrigeration of meat and dairy products is responsible for 18 percent of global greenhouses gases.

Slaughterhouses are often unsanitary places where, by federal law, cattle are supposed to be stunned by a captive bolt to the head before slaughter, but many survive and are conscious as their throats are cut. Meat processing workers have the highest rate of turnover of any other profession in the nation, due to the high numbers of injuries on the cutting floor.

And that's in the United States. Conditions in other countries can sometimes be worse. The 2005 film Earthlings, narrated by Joaquin Phoenix, showed a case of leather producers in India who didn't have trucks to transport their cattle. So they walk them through the streets to the slaughterhouse and if the cow starts to collapse from hunger along the way, salt is rubbed in its eyes to make it get up and run.

In summary, though the meat industry is subject to periodic USDA inspections, this industry is something that people who care about animals, people, and the planet might want to think twice about supporting. Since it is the industry that is supplying the animal skins that become leather, it is difficult to separate the impact of the two.

One redeeming use of leather I have encountered is the reuse of leather, and upcycling of used leather pieces, which I think is a positive extension of the animals' given life. There are companies who reuse and upcycle leather for new purposes. There are also numerous mainstream and boutique shoe stores that offer leather alternatives, such as nonleather canvas shoes, and also "vegan" leather which are commonly made from plastic or natural rubber. Some shops offering alternatives to leather shoes include Mooshoes.com, neuaurashoes.com, and even Payless.

There are some recent innovations in leather alternatives: One promising addition to the leather-alternative options is called Piñatex. It is a close doppelganger for leather, and is made from pineapple leaf.[49] (There is also a more traditional type of silklike fabric used in Southeast Asia called jusi or husi, made of a combination of pineapple or banana leaf fiber.[50]) The most recent non-animal leather option is Muskin. It is made from mushrooms, and looks and feels similar to suede. Developed by an Italian manufacturer, it is non-toxic, biodegradable and breathable so it resists bacterial growth.[51]

Wool

Wool fiber is made from sheep hair and has been used for thousands of years. There are about 1,000 different breeds of sheep, and several main types raised for wool. Most common is the Merino breed of sheep. They produce fine wool, meaning each strand of hair is 20 microns thick. These are raised in Australia, South Africa, South America, and the western US. The Rambouillet is a related breed mostly raised in the western US. There are also long wool sheep raised in Scotland, England, and New Zealand. Sheep are typically shorn once or twice per year. Wool has many benefits for human use in that it is a great insulator, is water resistant, and dyes well. It is also flame resistant, so is sold as a natural alternative to flame retardants in mattresses (see Chapter 9).

The ethical problem with wool starts with a strange biological trait of Merino sheep having wrinkly butts. Yes, you read it right: wrinkly butts. Unfortunately, this leads to a rather disgusting problem: between the folds of skin, dead skin cells, feces, and urine can accumulate, and become a great place for fly maggots to live. This is called "Flystrike." The maggots tunnel into the flesh of the sheep, causing lesions, which can become infected, leading to disease and even death of the animal. Pretty unsavory.

---

49   "Introducing Pinatex." Ananas-anam > pinatex. Ananas Anam. July 15, 2016.
50   McEachran, Rich. "Forget about Cotton, We Could Be Making Textiles from Banana and Pineapple." The Guardian. March 2015. Accessed August 09, 2016.
51   Grade Zero Espace. "Muskin." www.gradozero.eu. August 2016.

So sheep farmers came up with a couple of ideas to deal with this problem. One is to spray sheep areas heavily with insecticides (organic wool is available but very rare and costly). Over time, wool dips have switched from use of highly toxic organophosphate pesticides to pyrethroids,[52] which are less toxic but still can affect the nervous system of the sheep or people exposed to it.

Some companies, such as Vaute Couture, specialize in creating animal-free clothing. See: http://vautecouture.com

The other solution is to simply cut the wrinkly flesh off the sheep and pull it tight; a process called "mulesing." Under Australian law, where much of our wool comes from, there is no requirement for anesthetic to reduce pain during or after this process.

The animal rights group PETA (People for the Ethical Treatment of Animals) called attention to this practice, and many companies are now refusing to use wool made from sheep that endured this cruel practice. PETA claims there are alternatives—such as breeding selectively for the breeds of sheep that do not have the "wrinkly butt" trait.[53] There are also topical treatments for the skin, washing practices, and natural, biological control of flies so as to stop the underlying cause without the use of toxic pesticides.

Finally, wool is also a by-product of the meat industry since it is tied to the production of lamb. So while wool can certainly be considered a natural product, for these reasons, people who do not believe in consuming animal products usually choose not to avoid wearing wool.

Either way, wool tends to be dirty when it is first cut from the sheep, so the pesticides, lanolin (skin oil), and dirt must be removed through a process called scouring, often using either a petrochemical-based detergent or the chemical trichloroethylene.[54] This chemical solvent is considered a likely human carcinogen and can cause damage to the central nervous system, according to the Environmental Protection Agency.[55]

---

52   Fletcher, Kate. *Sustainable Fashion & Textiles: Design Journeys*, 6. London: Earthscan, 2008.
53   People for the Ethical Treatment of Animals (PETA). "Mulesing by the Wool Industry." Peta.org. 2015.
54   Sheep 101. http://www.sheep101.info. Sheep 101. 2014.
55   Environmental Protection Agency (EPA). "Trichloroethylene." EPA.gov: Air and Radiation > TTN Web – Technology Transfer Network > Air Toxics Web Site. January 2000.

As mentioned, there is the alternative of organically raised sheep, which are fed only organic feed and are not treated with chemicals, but meeting all the standards is quite challenging. There is currently small-scale production of organic wool, and it would at least be a step in the right direction to see this option increase. Textile Exchange is currently developing a Responsible Wool Standard.

Similar products to sheep wool include alpaca wool, which is naturally lanolin-free,[56] and mohair, which is made from the fur of Angora goats.[57] Like wool, mohair is also flame resistant. This is distinct from Angora as we know it, which is made from Angora rabbit fur. There is also cashmere, which is combed once a year from the bellies of the cashmere goat. These goats live mostly in the very cold mountains of Tibet, Nepal, and Pakistan.[58] Three to six goats are needed to make just one medium-sized sweater.[59] Now many animals are kept in factory farms, which can be damaging to the environment.[60] It is possible to find organically raised cashmere wool, which has less impact.

Fur

Though fur garments are made from animal skins, I would not categorize fur as an earth-friendly product in the way it is currently produced. Though fur coats are soft and warm, and have long been a symbol of luxury and financial status, I think if people knew how they were made, some of the mystique would be removed. Typically, minks, raccoons, rabbits or other animals are raised in captivity at "fur farms." Then when it's time to use the fur, in order to preserve the animals' coat and not damage it with cuts, the animal is hooked up at the snout and anus with electrodes and electrocuted to death. (Probably not a fun way to make a living for workers either.) Like leather, animal skins will naturally biodegrade if not treated with chemicals.

This is a far cry from the high-fashion, glamorous product it is marketed as, so as many people become more aware, the societal opinion of fur is slowly changing. A recent controversy surrounds the rumor that dog fur from China has been used, especially for trims, but not labeled as such. For example, during a recent winter holiday shopping

56   Rose, Doreen. "Frequently Asked Questions About Alpacas." ShearEleganceAlpacas.com. 2013.
57   Mohair Council of America. "The Story of Mohair." MohairUSA.com. 2015.
58   Natural Fibres. "Cashmere." Binhaitimes.com. 2015.
59   Waight, Emma. "Cashmere and Ethics: The Story of Your Christmas Jumper." Oxfam Fashion Blog. November 23, 2012.
60   Vercillo, Kathryn. "11 Things I Learned About Yarn from AwareKnits." Crochet Concupiscence: Crochet News. August 16, 2011.

season, for example, Neiman Marcus advertised and sold animal fur online as being "faux" on a jacket. "Neiman Marcus has repeatedly sold garments where the animal fur was misrepresented or even described as fake fur," said Pierre Grzybowski, manager of the fur campaign for The HSUS. "How many of these latest jackets were sold to unsuspecting consumers who thought they were buying fake fur?"[61]

Many animal rights groups have taken fur on as an issue, and this has started to challenge the mainstream acceptance fur coats once had. The Humane Society of the United Sates has worked in educating upcoming designers at some fashion schools. In the age of YouTube, you can find out more than you probably want to know. In my opinion, unless you really need fur for survival in harsh elements, it's not glam—it's ghastly.

The next question is whether true faux fur is better for the environment. The answer there is not clear either, because it is usually made from nylon, acrylic, or polyester. All of these are oil-based, which is nonrenewable, and it does take energy to produce. "Producing one kilogram of polyester requires 109 megajoules of energy, with 46 megajoules going toward the raw materials and 63 megajoules used to turn those materials into a finished fiber. Nylon consumes 150 megajoules per kilogram; acrylic, 157."[62] It is unclear how this compares to energy used in the production of real fur because not much study has been done on this. If you do choose to wear fur of any kind, a good route is to shop in vintage thrift stores.

Feathers

People of many cultures have been using bird feathers for centuries, from Native American ceremonies through styles of the 1800s, and they are common in recent years on hats. On the plus side, they are biodegradable, and are naturally a "renewable" product, versus synthetic pillow fillers such as polyester. However, during the 1800s, birds were hunted extensively in many countries for their feathers, and this in fact led to some extinctions. "The nineteenth-century popularity of the feather muff led to the extinction of the Bittern."[63] The Audubon Society was originally formed in the late 1800s to address "murderous millinery" and discourage the trend of plumage for purely

---

61   Viegas, Jennifer. "'Faux' Fur on Clothing May Contain Dog Hair." Discovery News. January 21, 2010.
62   Rastogi, Nina. "A Hairy Situation: Should I Choose Fake Fur Over Real Fur?" Slate: The Green Latern. January 5, 2010.
63   Lowe, Elizabeth D. "Feathers in Fashion." LovetoKnow.com: Beauty and Fashion. 2015.

ornamental purposes. Through the Audubon Society and others, international laws started to be put in place to protect wild birds in the early 1900s.[64]

Pillows have been filled with feathers and down since around AD 400.[65] Many of the feathers used in fashion or bedding today come from farmed birds. If you never thought about where those feathers in your cozy quilt came from, you are probably not alone. The feathers are sometimes plucked from the chest and belly of live geese or ducks, which can be quite painful, or are taken after slaughter (the animals are also used for eggs and meat). Eighty percent of the down and feathers used globally is produced in China; the majority of that—90 percent—come from ducks. Duck meat is an important staple in the Chinese diet, one reason China is the world's leading supplier of down and feathers.[66]

For pillows and comforters this is not an easy decision ecologically, because it is a decision between either farming birds ultimately for slaughter or potentially using more petrochemical-based materials as stuffing. There are, however, pillows filled with organic cotton, buckwheat, and natural latex (see chapter 9). For feathers used for fashion and decoration, some people make quite realistic faux feathers out of plastic or even painted paper. If you really desire down, there are some companies who now follow the Responsible Down Standard (RDS) certification[67] for more ethically raised birds. H&M has agreed to follow this standard as of 2016, and sustainable wool starting in 2018.[68]

Alligator, crocodile, and snake skins

Certain species of crocodiles (often from Australia) and alligators (from the American south) are now farmed in pens for the purpose of their skins. "Exotic animal skins make up almost 10 percent of the total revenue from handbag sales for luxury brands."[69] Alligator and crocodile skin can be quite supple, so product-makers look for pieces with no scratches or scars. One fashion blog points out that the American alligator is the "Rolls Royce of leather richness" and that "the belly usually makes for the most

64   Patchett, Merle. "Murderous Millinery." Fashioning Feathers: Dead Birds, Millinery Crafts and the Plumage Trade. 2011.
65   Ibid.
66   American Down and Feather Council. "Info for Consumers." DownandFeatherCouncil.com. 2014.
67   Textile Exchange. "Responsible Down Standard." www.responsibledown.org. 2016
68   H&M. "Conscious Actions Sustainability Reports." http://sustainability.hm.com/en/sustainability/downloads-resources/reports/sustainability-reports.html. 2015.
69   Kew, Janice and Andrew Roberts. "Crocodile Bites Show Why Your Birkin Bag Is So Expensive." Bloomberg Business. October 16, 2013.

consistent, defect-free leather."[70] Due to any flaws, or just design preferences, it can take several animals to make one bag. Production of these animal skins is subject to the Convention on International Trade in Endangered Species of Wild Flora & Fauna (CITES) to guard against abuse, but of course animal rights' organizations have documented abuses that still do go on. For example, each alligator is supposed to be stunned twice and killed with a swift cut at the throat. But this practice is not always followed and the animals are sometimes bludgeoned to death.[71]

Though snakes shed their skin, this is not the skin that is used for creating fashion. Snakes are farmed as well, or are taken from the wild. One disturbing article described snakeskin production in Indonesia: "The snake is stunned with a blow to the head from the back of a machete and a hose pipe expertly forced between its jaws. Next, the water is turned on and the reptile fills up—swelling like a balloon. It will be left like that for ten minutes or so, a leather cord tied around its neck to prevent the liquid escaping. Then its head is impaled on a meat hook; a couple of quick incisions follow, and the now-loosened skin peeled off with a series of brutal tugs—much like a rubber glove from a hand.... The python's peeled body is simply tossed on a pile of similarly stripped snakes. After a day or two of unimaginable agony it will die from the effects of shock or dehydration."[72]

Similarly to the production of leather, once the snakeskin is removed, it is preserved through salting, pickling in an acidic solution, and tanning (meaning with a tannin solution, not "tanning" as in sitting in the sun) to make the leather more water and bacteria resistant. It is sometimes dyed different colors before being made into shoes and bags.

I had no idea that snakeskin production could be so brutal. People become involved in these industries because there is a market for these products and it is a means of income, often selling from Asia or Australia to fashion houses in Europe. That same fashion blog quoted above writes, "Crocodile skin is a luxurious, supple material that is very much in demand in the fashion industry. With high-fashion crocodile handbags

70   Mendal, Mark. "Learning Exotic Leather: American Alligator." Pan Am Leathers: Exotic Leather Blog. March 19, 2015.
71   People for the Ethical Treatment of Animals (PETA). "Exotic Skins: The Animals." PETA.org. 2015.
72   Reilly, Jill. "From Slaughterhouse to Shop-Shelf: Inside the Factory Where Snakes are Killed, Skinned and Turned Into Handbags." Daily Mail News. February 12, 2013.

selling for tens or even hundreds of thousands of dollars, getting the manufacture of your crocodile skin right is incredibly important for impressing ultra-wealthy clients."[73] If consumers didn't create the demand for this, it would not be lucrative and would be a less attractive option. But the true story is hidden, so unless shoppers investigate snakeskin production before purchasing their handbag or shoes, how would they know?

I'm sure you can guess what I have to conclude about this whole subject. The concept of continuing to cause sentient animals to suffer unnecessarily for shoes and bags, when more humane alternatives exist to make these products, to me, leaves little question as to which choice is best.

---

73   Mendal, Mark. "4 Tips for Making Crocodile Skin Handbags." Pan Am Leathers: Exotic Leather Blog. October 14, 2014.

Interview: Anne Gillespie, Director of Industry Integrity, Textile Exchange

I started in business school and always wanted to create a better word through business. I was passionate about the outdoors and wilderness activities so started working at Mountain Equipment Co-op, which is the Canadian equivalent of REI. I was the buyer for kayaks and technical gear and was offered the opportunity to get into buying apparel. I was not interested at first and even wanted to get rid of all the cotton items, but then through a connection with Patagonia I had the opportunity to visit some organic farms in California. Patagonia was great about sharing their suppliers. Nike was starting to include 3 percent organic cotton into their apparel and wanted to help expand the supply market, so around that time Organic Exchange was formed and I became part of a task force. From there on out my involvement grew and I eventually became an employee. What I like about this field is that the clothing industry is so enormous, so small changes make a big difference. I like being able to leverage the scale of the industry to make meaningful change in the world.

The Organic Exchange became the nonprofit Textile Exchange, which works with industry to help address issues in the supply chain, provide models and case studies, and to create linkages. It serves as a hub for the sustainable textile industry and holds an annual international conference. As my title says, I work towards industry integrity, making sure that actions lead to real and meaningful change, and that suppliers are really supplying the quality of product they say they are. I have helped with various standards including the Responsible Down Standard, and I think that verification is a very important aspect of the chain of custody.

The most important thing people can do is consume less. Buy consignment. Every new item strains the system and means pulling more resources from the earth. There are some great restricted chemical lists being produced to help companies limit their chemical use, but the best thing is to not use them in the first place. Buy great pieces that last a long time so you don't have to replace them, and when you buy, then ask questions—consider the environment, workers, and animals involved in the producing that product.

This is definitely not a fad. There have been countless man-hours put into these efforts and long-term commitments made by clothing companies so it is not going to turn back now. What's exciting is that change is coming from within the industry, not just as a reaction to public pressure. They know they have to deal with quality of water issues in China or will not be able to continue to produce there. They also know that it is likely there will be more chemical regulations in the future so they may as well get a head start and lead the way. The UN has its Global Compact Principles and sustainable development goals and businesses need to be aligned with these in order to succeed. There are also several large companies with a stated commitment to sustainability and a wish to drive change, such as Nike and H&M. North Face has committed to using only down produced under the Responsible Down Standard.

We are now in the age of instant information and social media so it makes a difference when people brag on Twitter about having a jacket made with recycled materials—it adds value to organic products. Transparency and truthfulness accelerate change as information is shared with more people.

I don't like elitism and sustainable being considered a luxury so yes, it should scale up. Wal-Mart creates a huge demand which can change the system. Target has said that all the down it uses will be Responsible Down. However, it is hard to produce organic cotton at the same price as conventional, and to expect it to be at the same price ends up squeezing the people involved in production, which is not fair. It does make a difference when organizations like PETA target big companies. Bed Bath and Beyond is currently a focus of a Change.org campaign.

A person I admire is Adam Mott of the North Face. He went well above and beyond his professional duties and made a personal commitment, spending hours on conference calls to help create the Responsible Down standard.

Consumers should be aware that animal welfare is becoming much higher on the agenda. I may soon be part of an effort to create a standard for rabbit fur production since the angora farms are a big market in China.

SECTION 2
Living La Vida Eco

Chapter 6

Ecofashion on the Runway
Is Ecofashion Going Mainstream—and Upscale?

As mentioned, organic cotton is now widely used by huge apparel retailers, including Nike, H&M, and Wal-Mart.[1] Both Levi's and the Gap have Corporate Sustainability programs. But could it be possible to find sustainable fabrics in the realm of Versace, Prada, and Armani?

To answer this, I did some research. With a few notable exceptions highlighted below, and despite my high hopes, I found out that some high-end designers have dabbled in eco-friendly materials over the past few years but the majority haven't done much at all. For this chapter, I searched the websites of fifty high-end designers for the following search terms: "organic," "hemp," "bamboo," "Tencel," and "sustainability." I also searched the world wide web for an association between each company and the same terms. What I found is that the vast majority of high-end designers have not incoporated natural-based fabrics into their collections, and, with the exception of very few, those that did had very few items.

For example, Calvin Klein used some organic cotton in the 1990s and offered an organic cotton brief a few years ago, but it got discontinued. I loved their description, though: "With all of the eco-friendly advances being made today, Calvin Klein wanted to make sure they kept their customers up-to-date by designing this organic cotton hip brief. This 100 percent cotton hip brief is made of cotton that was grown without toxins or pesticides. This pair of underwear is sustainable and environmentally friendly. With a functional fly and contrast waistband, people may not be able to tell by looking at you that you're green, but they'll be green with envy over how great you'll look!"

---

1   Carpenter, Susan. "Cotton That's Kinder To the Planet." *Los Angeles Times*. June 19, 2011.

They got it, but too bad it didn't stick. And what about everyone else?

In an article in the Guardian newspaper entitled "Luxury brands must wake up to ethical and environmental responsibilities," it was noted that "[m]any of the world's biggest and most elite fashion houses pay virtually no regard to corporate ethics and have yet to take even the first steps on reporting on the social and environmental impact of their operations."[2] Coach was one of the first major companies to move its production out of New York to Chinese factories and labor.[3] From my own research, I found four have produced readily available sustainability reports (Hermes, Louis Vuitton, Ralph Lauren, and Prada), and four mention concerns about sustainability on their websites (Marc Jacobs, Armani, Dolce and Gabbana, and Valentino). Those that do mention sustainability mostly state that they comply with environmental laws and are striving to improve, but don't give much detail.

As for nature-based fabrics, of the fifty designers searched:*

- Fifteen offered at least one item listed as made with organic cotton
- Nineteen offered at least one item listed as made with hemp
- Ten offered at least one item listed as made with bamboo
- Eight offered at least one item listed as made of Tencel

* Some did not offer search functions on their websites; some of the above are part of fabric blends.

In 2012, Greenpeace, which is often on the cutting-edge in calling attention to issues, released a report entitled "Toxic Threads: The Big Fashion Stitch Up."[4] They tested multiple samples from companies including Zara, Calvin Klein, Benetton, Giorgio Armani, Victoria's Secret, Versace, H&M, Levi's, Mango, and Tommy Hilfiger. Specifically looking at phthalates, amines from the use of azo dyes, and nonylphenol ethoxylates (NPE), they found one or more of these chemicals in over 60 percent of the 141 clothing items tested.[5]

Greenpeace has created a whole campaign around this issue, including a Fashion

2   Birch, Simon. "Luxury Brands Must Wake Up to Ethical and Environmental Responsibilities." TheGuardian.com: Environment > Ethical and Green Living – Green Living Blog. September 16, 2011.
3   Eagan, Greta. *Wear No Evil: How to Change the World with Your Wardrobe*. Philadelphia, Pennsylvania: Running Press, 2014. 15.
4   Greenpeace International. "Toxic Threads: The Big Fashion Stitch-Up." Greenpeace International. October 2012.
5   Environmental Leader. "Calvin Klein, Zara Among Worst Chemical Users, Greenpeace Says." EnvironmentalLeader.com: Chemicals. November 21, 2012.

Eileen Fisher (peace silk)

"Duel" that ranks designers,[6] and also a Detox Fashion Manifesto, which designers can sign onto.[7] One result of this pressure is that in 2013 Valentino pledged to remove a full list of toxic chemicals from its production by 2020 and to reduce deforestation.[8] In 2016 Greenpeace released an updated report on those companies who previously signed onto their Detox campaign principles, and showed that several including H&M and Benetton are complying with their pledge to reduce toxic chemicals in their clothing. Others such as Mango, Burberry, Valentino, Adidas, and Puma have made progress but still have work to do, and Esprit and Nike have fallen off track and need to do better.[9] I encourage readers concerned about these issues to become involved and share this information via social media.

Another great resource is called Rankabrand based out of the Netherlands,[10] whereby companies are ranked by sustainability criteria from A to E, like a school report card, with A being the best and E being worst. According to this website, most of the large-name luxury clothing brands on my chart were scored as an E, with a few scoring a D or C.

Some companies at least state on their websites that they do ensure compliance with laws. However, this only shows they are not breaking the law, and does not indicate a commitment to go above and beyond to protect the environment. For example, Versace released such a statement in reaction to its poor ranking by Greenpeace.[11] In the statement below from Marc Jacobs, it is unclear what global laws they are referring to, as one country's laws can certainly differ from another's.

> "At Marc Jacobs International, innovation, creativity, excellence in craftsmanship, and careful consideration for how our work affects the natural environment are all integral to our products. Reflecting this, we maintain stringent requirements for our company and every supplier we

---

6   Greenpeace International. "The Fashion Duel: Let's Clean Up Fashion." TheFashionDuel.com. 2013.

7   Greenpeace International. "A Toxic-Free Future." Greenpeace.org: What We Do > Detox. 2015.

8   Valentino Fashion Group. "Final – Valentino Fashion Group Detox Solution Commitment." Valentino Fashion Group. February 6, 2013.

9   Greenpeace International. "The Detox Catwalk." www.greenpeace.org/international/en/campaigns/detox/fashion/detox-catwalk. 2016.

10   Rank a Brand. "Sustainability: Luxury Brands – Fashion, Clothing & Shoes." RankaBrand.org. 2015.

11   Reuters. "Versace Says Complies with EU Regulations on Textile Chemicals." Reuters.com: Industries. US ed. February 19, 2014.

work with. Our products adhere to every environmental and product safety regulation around the world, and we constantly seek ways to improve our performance. Making clothes that are safe to wear for all our customers is of the highest priority for Marc Jacobs International…. We maintain an ongoing product testing program to ensure compliance with our principles and the regulations that govern our business. We also complete regular, random and unannounced audits and inspections of our suppliers to verify their social performance and working conditions…. We recognize that there is always room to enhance our practices, and we continually assess opportunities to work with our suppliers to further reduce environmental impact. We continue to strive to reach the goal of zero impact on the environment, and while there's more work to do, we pursue that goal aggressively."[12]

It definitely sounds good, though I wish it were a bit less vague.

Similarly, Dolce and Gabbana's page says that its suppliers must comply with environmental laws, and that "[e]mployees are obliged, in the exercise of their daily working activities, to take the greatest care to sustainably consume paper, water and energy, as well as to respect the provisions relative to waste sorting."[13] However, the policy doesn't extend to chemicals used in clothing manufacture. Dolce and Gabbana ranked an E on wwwRankabrand. In fact, the company offered a perfume specifically for babies that potentially exposes young children to phthalates with other chemicals typically used in perfumes.[14] That stinks!

Some Encouraging News

There are some tiny glimmers of hope that large companies are starting to respond to the growing pressure to consider the environment and workers in their production processes. "Ralph Lauren, Oscar de la Renta, and Donatella Versace have experimented with hemp. Oscar de la Renta, Diane von Furstenberg, and Agnes B have tried bamboo. And everyone—from Edun, the label started in 2005 by U2 frontman Bono and his wife Ali Hewson, to mass retailers like H&M, Target, Zara and Wal-Mart—is offering organic cotton."[15]

---

12   Marc Jacobs International, LLC. "Social Responsibilities." MarcJacobs.com. 2015.
13   Dolce & Gabbana. "Code of Ethics." DolceGabbana.com: Corporate. 2015.
14   Fassa, Lynda. "That Stinks: Dolce & Gabbana Launches Fragrance for Babies." Ecouterre.com: The Big Idea. January 31, 2013.
15   Dirksen, Kirsten. "Fashion Guide II: Greenest Fabrics." FairCompanies.com: News. April 2008.

HIGH-END DESIGNERS: USA						
Fabrics/ Philosophy	Organic Cotton	Hemp	Bamboo	Tencel	Sustainability	Rankabrand Rating
Alexander Wang	N/A	N/A	Offers bamboo sweaters and sweatshirts for men.	Offers Tencel-cotton blend knit top for women.	No statement on website.	Not yet rated.
Altuzarra	N/A	N/A	N/A	N/A	No statement on website.	Not yet rated.
Badgley Mischka	N/A	N/A	N/A	N/A	No statement on website.	Not yet rated.
BCBG Max Azria	N/A	N/A	N/A	N/A	No statement on website.	Not yet rated.
Betsey Johnson	N/A	N/A	N/A	N/A	No statement on website.	Not yet rated.
Calvin Klein	Discontinued organic cotton bedding, towels and wool rugs; discontinued organic cotton "Naturals" undergarments for men and women. Hemp: N/A		Offers bamboo and silk blend socks for men.	Offers three Tencel tops and two Tencel dresses for women.	No statement on website.	D: First milestones, should be better.
Carolina Herrera	N/A	Found "Carolina Herrera New York Blue White Textured Silk Hemp Cropped Pant Trousers" on Ebay, September 2014. Bamboo & Tencel: N/A				No statement on website.	Not yet rated.
Cynthia Rowley	N/A	N/A	N/A	N/A	No statement on website.	Not yet rated.
Diane Von Furstenberg	N/A	N/A	N/A	N/A	No statement on website.	Not yet rated.
DKNY	Several skirts, tops & bags, released April 2009.	N/A	N/A	N/A	No statement on website.	E: Don't buy.

Disclaimer: Statistics showed originate from a 2015 study.

HIGH-END DESIGNERS: USA						
Fabrics/ Philosophy	Organic Cotton	Hemp	Bamboo	Tencel	Sustainability	Rankabrand Rating
Donna Karen	"Pure Comfort" bedding sold through Bloomingdales, now discontinued. Hemp: N/A		In 2009, Donna Karan worked with Tonic. com to launch a line of bamboo- and organic cotton-blend T-shirts. Tencel: N/A		No statement on website.	Not yet rated.
Elie Tahari	N/A	N/A	N/A	N/A	No statement on website.	Not yet rated.
Isaac Mizrahi	N/A	N/A	N/A	N/A	No statement on website.	Not yet rated.
Kenneth Cole	N/A	N/A	N/A	N/A	No statement on website.	Not yet rated.
Marc Jacobs	N/A	N/A	N/A	N/A	No statement on website.	E: Don't buy.
Marchesa	N/A	N/A	N/A	N/A	No statement on website.	Not yet rated.
Michael Kors	N/A	N/A	N/A	N/A	No statement on website.	Not yet rated.
Narciso Rodriguez	N/A	N/A	N/A	N/A	No statement on website.	Not yet rated.
Nicole Miller	N/A	N/A	N/A	N/A	No statement on website.	Not yet rated.
Oscar de la Renta	N/A	N/A	N/A	N/A	No statement on website.	Not yet rated.
Pamella Roland	N/A	N/A	N/A	N/A	No statement on website.	Not yet rated.
Ralph Lauren	N/A	N/A	N/A	N/A	No statement on website.	E: Don't buy.
Tommy Hilfiger	N/A	N/A	N/A	N/A	No statement on website.	C: Reasonable, could do better.
Tory Burch	N/A	N/A	N/A	N/A	No statement on website.	Not yet rated.
Tracy Reese	N/A	N/A	N/A	N/A	No statement on website.	Not yet rated.
Vera Wang	N/A	N/A	N/A	N/A	No statement on website.	Not yet rated.
Zac Posen	N/A	N/A	N/A	N/A	No statement on website.	Not yet rated.

Disclaimer: Statistics showed originate from a 2015 study.

Here are some examples of positive steps:

Donna Karan Home offers organic cotton bedding. The website says "Surround yourself with the beauty and comfort of fibers pure and clean. You'll help preserve our air, our water, our soil, and the biodiversity of our planet.... Organic cotton is better for our bodies, our homes, our planet, and our future generations."[16]

Patagonia, Giorgio Armani, Ralph Lauren, Calvin Klein, Disney, Converse, Adidas, J. Crew, J. Jill have all sold products made from hemp.[17] This was even acknowledged in an LA Times articles a few years back: "Hemp, from Hippie to Hip: It's not just for the stoner set. Stella McCartney, Giorgio Armani and Calvin Klein are among the designers incorporating hemp textiles into their fashions."[18]

Again on the hemp theme, in the article, "Organic and Natural Clothing," New York Times journalist Eric Wilson reported on the use of hemp in high fashion. He writes, during the 2008 New York Fashion Week a special runway show was held, "to demonstrate that clothes made from sustainable materials like piña, which is a new fabric derived from pineapples, can be as chic as anything that the world's top designers might create. At the request of Barneys New York, more than two dozen [fashion designers] had designed ensembles using organic fabrics, natural vegetable dyes, and technically advanced fibers derived from soybeans, bamboo, banana leaves, or hemp."[19]

- Versace is one of the first haute couture designer clothing firms that have used Ingeo in their collections.[20]

- In 2006, during the "Future Fashion" show, part of New York's fashion week, popular designers such as Diane von Furstenberg and Oscar de la Renta created clothing from organic cotton and hemp.[21]

---

16   The Donna Karan Company LLC. "Donna Karan Home Collections: Product and Info Care." DonnaKaranHome.com. 2014.
17   Oxford, Nancy. "Hemp, Hemp, Hooray!" TextileFabric.com: Articles. 2009.
18   Carpenter, Susan. "Hemp, From Hippie to Hip." Los Angeles Times. April 18, 2010.
19   Wilson, Eric. "Doing Their Part to Help Save the Planet, in High Style." New York Times. Fashion & Style section. February 1, 2008.
20   Claudio, Luz. "Waste Couture: Environmental Impact of the Clothing Industry." Environmental Health Perspectives, 115(9). A449-A454. September 2007.
21   Fruitwala, Aditi. "The Case for Organic Cotton." The Green American. Sept/Oct 2006.

- In 2011, Gucci created a set of bio-based sunglasses, made from a natural material made from castor oil seeds.[22]

- Brought together by Elle Magazine in July 2010, Diane Von Furstenberg collaborated with others to create solar handbags that were auctioned off for charity. Each purse contained solar collecting technology that can capture the sun's energy and recharge a cell phone. [23]

- In 2014, MaxMara created a collection of clothing made from recycled polyester fibers originally used in bottles.[24]

- Giorgio Armani has been quoted as saying, "The best way to make a contribution in fashion is to promote the idea that a fundamental interest in preserving the environment is itself fashionable."[25]

- Iliana Fendi supports green lifestyle by selling a line of upcycled handbags at her store in Rome, including some that were made by women in Africa.[26]

- DKNY offers a DKNY Pure line made with some of the natural fibers discussed in this book such as linen and lyocell.

- Chanel created software that assist in the creation of more eco-friendly packaging for cosmetics, and at a sustainability conference for the fashion industry, agreed to share the technology with others.[27]

A positive side of putting several large companies under one umbrella is that when that larger company decides to commit to environmental sustainability, it affects the several

---

22   Kering. "Gucci and Safilo Introduce New Sustainable Eyewear Models." Kering.com: Press Releases. May 27, 2011.
23   Liggett, Brit. "Diane von Furstenberg, Vena Cava Design Solar-Powered Bags for Charity." Ecouterre.com: Wearable Technology. July 9, 2010.
24   Edelbaum, Susannah. "Max Mara is the Latest Luxury Brand to Take Sustainability Mainstream." TheHighLow.com: Retail Trends. January 2, 2014.
25   Planet Forward. "BAFTA Stars Wear Sustainable Fashion Inspired by Livia Firth's Green Carpet Challenge." PlanetForward.ca: Sustainable Living. February 14, 2012.
26   Kinosian, Janet. "Ilaria Venturini Fendi Turns Trash Into Treasured Handbags." *Los Angeles Times*. Collections: Design section. November 16, 2012.
27   Mayuri. "Luxury Can Be Sustainable, Chanel, PPR, Giorgio Armani Take Serious Initiatives." EliteChoice.org: Luxury. April 5, 2011.

large brands under this umbrella. Such is the case with Kering group, which owns Gucci, Balenciaga, Stella McCartney, Saint Arent, and Alexander McQueen. Kering anayzes carbon emissions, water use, water pollution, land use, air pollution, and waste as part of their ongoing sustainability efforts, starting with raw materials, all the way through operations and retail.[28] They have committed to ensuring all hazardous chemicals have been phased out and eliminated from production by 2020, and ridding all collections of PVC plastic by 2016.[29] While I tend to be skeptical of large corporations making promises, they are certainly on the right track and putting their money where their mouth is. Dedicating over $10 million per year, the company created a Creative Sustainability Lab and hired fifteen people to carry out the organization's sustainability efforts.[30] I think this is very promising and can make a big difference, and forms a model I hope other large industries will follow.

The Notable Exceptions

Some high-end designers have gone beyond just dabbling to showing a real commitment to eco-friendly practices, or at least using their fashion notoriety to spread the message of concern for planetary causes. I think they are worthy of highlighting:

Eileen Fisher is at the top of the heap when it comes to natural luxury. This New York designer has made a name for herself by consistently trending towards sustainability. A large portion of her garments are made with natural materials, and she offers an "Eco Collection" that features draped cardigans and vests, Tencel cashmere tops, organic cotton jackets, organic linen pants, and organic cotton jeans. Eileeen Fisher has openly stated her commitment to sustainable fashion, and sustainability is a key feature highlighted on the Eileen Fisher website and marketing materials. She has a clothing recycling campaign called Green Eileen with the slogan, "We Want Our Clothes Back," which resells lighltly used pieces for charities that support women and girls, and also holds workshops in several cities to teach people to repurpose fabrics. Eileen Fisher regularly features her clothing line in Earth Day-related events. She gets an "A" in my opinion.

---

28   Kering. "Sustainability." Kering.com. 2012.
29   Kering. "Targets." Kering.com: Sustainability. 2012.
30   Silven, Kirsten E. "Sustainability Project Launched for Gucci, Yves Saint Laurent & Stella McCartney Lines." EarthTimes.org: Business. March 30, 2011.

Eileen Fisher (hemp top), Reco Jeans (recycled fiber)

Stella McCartney is another example of someone who has taken planetary health into considerataion when creating sensational designs that appeal to the vogue-conscious.

"In 2001, Stella McCartney launched her own fashion house under her name in a joint venture with Gucci Group (now PPR's luxury division) and showed her first collection in Paris in October 2001. A lifelong vegetarian, Stella McCartney does not use any leather or fur in her designs." She is the daughter of former Beatle Paul McCartney and photographer and animal rights activist Linda McCartney. [31] She has gained notoriety through a longtime partnership with ADIDAS begun in 2004 and has been able to incorporate hemp and bamboo. Through that work she was asked to be the creative director for the Great Britain team at the Olympics in 2012, and the uniforms incorporated some recycled plastic.[32]

Armani, which has used hemp in denim and in suits, is notable for a policy that is a pleasant surprise. In addition to Valentino, mentioned above, Armani has shown efforts to reduce the toxins associated with its clothing production. Armani has a written commitment to zero discharge, and has stated that the company seeks to go above and beyond minimum required by law, beginning by targeting three specific chemicals.[33] The website says:

- *Alkylphenols (APEs); alkylphenol ethoxylates (APEOs):* By the end of December 2013 we will have supply agreements in place requiring that only APEO-free chemical formulations be utilized.

- *PFCs: perfluorocarbons/polyfluorinated compounds:* We will request our suppliers eliminate 50 percent of any shorter chain PFCs by no later than 31 December 2013, 90 percent of any remaining PFCs by no later than 31 December 2014, and all remaining PFCs by no later than 01 July 2015.

- *Phthalates:* Phthalates banned by Armani's Restricted Substances List will no longer be utilized in products by July 2015.

---

31   Sowray, Bibby. "Who's Who: Stella McCartney." Vogue.co.uk. January 20, 2012.
32   Montealvo, Janet. "2012 Summer Olympics: Stella McCartney Unveils British Team's Uniform." FashioningCircuits.com. March 30, 2012.
33   Giorgio Armani. "Armani Group Corporate Social Responsibility and Sustainability Policy." Alive. Armani.com: Social Responsibility. 2015.

- Our scope is to eliminate the following classes of substances by the year 2020: alkylphenols, phthalates, brominated and chlorinated flame retardants, azo dyes, organotin compounds, perfluorinated chemicals, chlorobenzenes, chlorinated solvents, chlorophenols, short chain chlorinated paraffins, and heavy metals such as cadmium, lead, mercury, and chromium. To this end, by the end of 2015 we will be considering the available alternatives to such substances. [34]

- The company also claims it will publish case studies on the safer substitutes they find for these chemicals, which would be of great use to the entire industry.

This strong and clear commitment is encouraging and shows real leadership. Giorgio Armani's first foray into eco-awareness was in 1995 when the company developed a way to recycle denim into new jeans, which was quite unique at the time. Since then, Armani has also used recycled wool, recycled cotton, and more recently hemp, eco washing (no dry-cleaning, just wash in warm water), and polyester from plastic bottles in their fabrics. They have also worked with fair-trade cotton projects in Peru and Bolivia.[35]

Vivienne Westwood does not use many sustainable fabrics in her lines, but has some notable efforts. She is personally a climate activist and uses her t-shirts to brandish slogans such as "Save the Arctic." She encourages consumers to buy fewer items but ones of quality that last longer, and has several videos encouraging clothing recycling and awareness of climate change.

She made a line of bags inspired by women in Africa as part of an Ethical Fashion Initiative Collection. [36] The Ethical Fashion Initiative is a program of the International Trade Centre, a joint United Nations and World Trade Organization effort that joins top fashion brands with artisans in Africa, and sustainability is a key aspect.[37]

34   Giorgio Armani. "Giorgio Armani commitment to zero discharge." Alive.Armani.com. September 23, 2013.
35   Ethical Fashion Forum. "5 Influential Designers." EthicalFashionForum.com: Fact Cards. 2015.
36   Ethical Fashion Forum. "Vivienne Westwood's Ethical Fashion Africa Collection." Source. EthicalFashionForum.com. December 23, 2011.
37   Ethical Fashion Initiative. ethicalfashioninitiative.org. 2016.

HIGH-END DESIGNERS: EUROPE						
Fabrics/ Philosophy	Organic Cotton	Hemp	Bamboo	Tencel	Sustainability	Rankabrand Rating
Armani	N/A	N/A	N/A	N/A	No statement on website.	E: Don't buy.
Balenciaga	N/A	N/A	N/A	N/A	No statement on website.	D: First milestones, should be better.
Chanel	N/A	N/A	N/A	N/A	No statement on website.	E: Don't buy.
Chloé	N/A	N/A	N/A	N/A	No statement on website.	E: Don't buy.
Dior	N/A	N/A	N/A	N/A	No statement on website.	E: Don't buy.
Dolce & Gabbana	N/A	N/A	N/A	N/A	No statement on website.	E: Don't buy
Fendi	N/A	N/A	N/A	N/A	No statement on website.	E: Don't buy.
Givenchy	N/A	N/A	N/A	N/A	No statement on website.	E: Don't buy.
Gucci	N/A	N/A	N/A	N/A	No statement on website.	D: First milestones, should be better.
Hermés	N/A	N/A	N/A	N/A	No statement on website.	E: Don't buy.
Jean Paul Gaultier	N/A	N/A	N/A	N/A	No statement on website.	E: Don't buy.

Disclaimer: Statistics showed originate from a 2015 study.

HIGH-END DESIGNERS: EUROPE						
Fabrics/ Philosophy	Organic Cotton	Hemp	Bamboo	Tencel	Sustainability	Rankabrand Rating
Louis Vuitton	N/A	N/A	N/A	N/A	No statement on website.	E: Don't buy.
Max Mara	N/A	N/A	N/A	N/A	No statement on website.	E: Don't buy.
Miu Miu	N/A	N/A	N/A	N/A	No statement on website.	E: Don't buy.
Moschino	N/A	N/A	N/A	N/A	No statement on website.	Not yet rated.
Prada	N/A	N/A	N/A	N/A	No statement on website.	E: Don't buy.
Roberto Cavalli	N/A	N/A	N/A	N/A	No statement on website.	Not yet rated.
Stella McCartney	N/A	N/A	N/A	N/A	No statement on website.	C: Reasonable, could do better.
Valentino	N/A	N/A	N/A	N/A	No statement on website.	E: Don't buy.
Versace	N/A	N/A	N/A	N/A	No statement on website.	E: Don't buy.
Victoria Beckham	N/A	N/A	N/A	N/A	No statement on website.	Not yet rated.
Vivienne Westwood	N/A	N/A	N/A	N/A	No statement on website.	E; Don't buy.
Yves Saint Laurent	N/A	N/A	N/A	N/A	No statement on website.	D: First milestones, should be better.

Disclaimer: Statistics showed originate from a 2015 study.

She collaborated with Anvil organic cotton[38] and also with People Tree, a British organic line.She designed uniforms made of recycled plastic for Virgin Atlantic.[39]

Green Fashion Shows

New York, a fashion capital, is home to Merecedes Benz Fashion Week, the biggest exposition of the latest fashions via elaborate runway shows, where top designers vie for the attention of buyers and fashion magazines. Fashion Week is held each September and February, to introduce the fashions for the following season. The tide is starting to turn, however, as several cities are now featuring ecofashion shows on an impressive scale.

Since 2008, Vancouver, Canada has held EcoFashion Week started by Myriam Laroche.[40] Designers there have included Hey Jude, New Oak, and Cherry Blossom.

From 2009 to 2012, there was another event of note in New York—The Green Shows, which were the first of its kind during New York Fashion Week, and featured designers using organic/bio-based and recycled textiles, low-impact dyes, and/or with low carbon footprints, and using fair trade labor. During its four years, The Green Shows produced thirty fashion shows, two pop-up stores, and made a debut at Mercedes-Benz Fashion Week at Lincoln Center, directly bringing ethical fashion to the attention of the luxury fashion industry. They partnered with nonprofit groups such as the Rainforest Alliance, and were fairly exclusive (I remember trying to get in and I was unable), attracting celebrity guests including Russell Simmons. The 2010 Green Shows featured couture gowns by recycled fashion producer Gary Harvey, and partnered with Bloomingdales to feature the gowns in their NYC store windows in April of that year. In September 2010 The GreenShows featured upcycled couture EcoArtFashion designs by Miami artist Luis Valenzuela. The Green Shows describe themselves as: "The GreenShows LLC (TGS) is a leading event, education and consulting company dedicated to promoting the luxury sustainable fashion movement. TGS [highlights] sustainable fashion designers and brands that are leading the fashion industry to accept sustainable practices industrywide as the real future of fashion."[41]

---

38   PR Newswire. "Vivienne Westwood and Anvil Knitwear, Inc. Collaborate on Sustainable T-Shirt to Stop Deforestation." PRNewswire.com. December 16, 2015.
39   Wischhover, Cheryl. "Vivienne Westwood is Designing Sustainable Uniforms for Virgin Atlantic." Fashionista.com. May 2, 2013.
40   Eco Fashion Week. "Eco Fashion Week: April 19-24, Edition 09." www.ecofashion-week.com. 2009.
41   The GreenShows LLC. www.thegreenshows.com. The GreenShows. 2015.

Starting around 2007, Portland, Oregon, began emerging as a hub of ecofashion and hosts an annual fashion show called FashionNXT.[42] I attended Portland Fashion Week in 2010[43] and witnessed a fantastic fashion show featuring solar panels as the runway. Show organizer Tito Chowdhury pointed out that they pioneered this idea, doing it several years before the Mercedes Benz NY Fashion Week did the same. The show is carbon and water-neutral thanks to b-e-f.org. Not all the designers in the shows use sustainable fabrics, but a few who have include: Soham Dave (uses real Indian indigo for dyes),[44] Lenzanita (sustainable, reclaimed materials),[45] and Ethos Paris (uses organic fabrics).[46]

Livia Firth (married to actor Colin Firth) is a big proponent of sustainable fashion. She is the owner of Eco Age,[47] a green branding consultancy based in London, through which she originated the Green Carpet Challenge (GCC) in 2009. This Challenge is an annual high-profile event which encourages high-end designers to show the best of their eco-styles on the runway and offers an award for the best in show. Firth is quoted as saying, "Each award symbolises a beautiful journey from the raw materials to the finished item and is one that the consumer can trust. I hope that in ten years that fashion truly slows down, and that fast-fashion brands start to seriously tackle issues related to social justice, taking care of the garment workers who produce at speed and no cost. We have to reassess the business model as it just can't be sustained at this speed."[48]

This event has been attended by celebrities and none other than Anna Wintour herself, the notorious editor of Vogue magazine. I love this idea of incentivizing designers with an award for doing the right thing. Designers such as Stella McCArthy, Gucci, Victoria Beckham, and Narcisco Rodriguez (2014 winner) have participated. Emma Watson, of Harry Potter fame and an ecofashion supporter herself, has modeled some of the designs from the Challenge. Meryl Streep wore an eco-friendly gown to the event by Lanvin in 2012.

42   FashioNXT Portland. "FashioNXT 2014 Designers." FashioNXT.net. 2015.
43   Portland Fashion Week. "2015 Portland Fashion Week." PortlandFashionWeek.com. 2015.
44   Soham Dave. http://www.sohamdave.com/index.php. Soham Dave. 2011.
45   Dakota by Design. http://www.dakotabydesign.com/Shirts/. Dakota by Design. 2015.
46   Ethos Eco Fashions LLC. http://www.ethosecofashions.com/. Ethos Paris Eco Designers. 2013.
47   Eco-Age Ltd. http://eco-age.com/. Eco Age. 2013.
48   Ojeda, Nelly. "Narciso Rodriguez Awarded for His Ethical Fashion. http://fashionbi.com. May 8, 2014.

Though not a fashion show, Suzy Amis Cameron, wife of filmmaker James Cameron, also supports sustainable fashion, and in 2014 hosted her fifth Red Carpet Green Dress event in Hollywood sponsored by the New York-based company Lux & Eco to help raise awareness.[49] Nonprofit organization Global Green USA has also incorporated green fashion shows into their annual Gorgeous and Green gala in Los Angeles, which attracts green-minded celebrities.

In 2011, a "Runway to Green" fashion show was held at the prestigious auction house Christie's in New York. It attracted Anna Wintour and featured some big names like Stella McCartney, and also Oscar de la Renta who created an organic cotton wedding gown.[50]

Though this book is focusing on ecofashion in the US, I would also point out that there is an Ethical Fashion Show in Berlin, Germany, that has taken place since 2012 during the Berlin Fashion Week.[51] There has been an ecofashion week in New Zealand as of 2013.[52]

As far back as 2008, the nonprofit organization Earthpledge held an ecofashion show in NYC. "With fabric sponsored by EnviroTextiles, designers like Donatella Versace, Behnaz Sarafour, Ralph Lauren, Donna Karan, Isabel Toledo, and Calvin Klein wove their magic with everything from hemp/organic cotton jersey knits to hemp silk/charmeuse."[53]

Celebrity Buy-In

Celebrities are also getting in on the sustainable act.

As mentioned, Emma Watson is a big supporter of ecofashion and collaborated with the British fair trade brand People Tree on a clothing collection in 2011.[54] She wore a lovely gown made of recycled plastic bottles to the Met Gala in 2016.[55]

49   Red Carpet Green Dress. http://redcarpetgreendress.com/home/. 2014.
50   Jenkins, Kestrel. "'Runway to Green' Brings A-List Fashion Designers to Christies' 'A Bid to Save the Earth' Charity Auction Event (Photos)." Ecouterre.com. March 31, 2011.
51   Messe Frankfurt. http://ethicalfashionshowberlin.com/en/. 2015.
52   Edelbaum, Susannah. "New Zealand is Hosting Its First-Ever Eco Fashion Week." TheHighLow.com. July 16, 2013.
53   EnviroTextiles LLC. "Hemp Fashion and Design." EnviroTextile.com: Media. 2012.
54   People Style Watch. "Emma Watson Gets a Royal Showcase for Eco-Chic Clothing Line." StyleNews.PeopleStyleWatch.com. August 18, 2010.
55   Huffington Post. "Emma Watson's Met Gala Dress Was Made Of Recycled Plastic Bottles Because She's Awesome." May 3, 2016

"Kelly Ripa, Cameron Diaz, and Rihanna are fans of Hanky Panky's organic collection of undergarments, made from 100 percent organically grown cotton." [56] Kate Hudson and Jessica Alba were seen wearing 100 percent organic cotton casual tops by Trove.[57]

Celebrities have been known to make a statement by wearing ecofashion on the Oscars red carpet. At the 2013 Oscars, Helen Hunt, Anne Hathaway, and Naomie Harris all wore eco-friendly gowns.[58]

Natalie Portman has been known to wear ecofashion such as vegan footwear. Model Gisele Bündchen also supports ecofashion (and lives in an eco-friendly home).[59]

Emily Blunt wore a sustainable Carolina Herrera gown from the Green Carpet Challenge to the Met Ball event in 2013, joined by John Krasinkski who wore a Tom Ford suit made from OEKOTEX ® certified wool.[60]

High-End Stores Going Green

Barneys, a high-end store based in New York City, was a pioneer in offering sustainable products that were also of high quality and aesthetically appealing. In fact, in a lecture I attended by Julie Gilhart, the store's buyer who first took interest in bringing sustainable items to Barneys, she said that what she observed was that the item in the store had to first attract the customer by the way it looked, it's quality and style. Then, when the customer was informed that it was made with natural materials and/or by hand-crafters in an exotic location, that was often another added layer of appeal. At least at first, the sustainability component was secondary in motivating a sale. However, now as time goes on, Barneys has become known for featuring greener items, and has even given precious window space to eco-friendly fashion window displays in conjunction with the organization Earthpledge. In 2007 it launched an eco-chic label of its own called Barneys Green in conjunction with the New York-based company Loomstate, which makes casual organic cotton apparel sportswear.

56   Freydkin, Donna and Alison Maxwell. "Fashion Forward: Blanchett is Bright in Armani's Black Lace Makeup." USAToday30.USAToday.com: Life > Lifestyle. January 5, 2010.
57   Ibid.
58   Chua, Jasmin Malik. "6 Celebrities Who Wore Eco-Fashion to the 2013 Oscars." Ecouterre.com. February 26, 2013.
59   Ridley, Erin. "Eco-Fashion: Trendy or Timeless?" TheGenteel.com: Society. May 8, 2012.
60   Fashion Compassion. "Emily Blunt and John Krasinkski Join Green Carpet Challenge at 2013 Met Ball." FashionCompassion.co.uk: Blog. May 7, 2013.

Iconic designer Diane von Furstenberg who has been designing since the 1970s, is the current president of the Council of Fashion Designers of America,[61] and is a supporter of sustainability in fashion. She sits alongside big names like Oscar de la Renta and Vera Wang, so she is in a good position to influence many others in the design field.[62]

Conclusion

What is the importance of having high-fashion supporters of sustainable fashion? It is because a lot of ready–to-wear fashion styles you find in stores follow trends from big fashion houses. The influence of big-name designers trickles down even to clothing sold at Wal-Mart. For an industry that attempts to convince us to buy new items every season, it is clearly important for sustainability issues to become more infused in the thinking. Large designers may not typically know the origin of the materials they are working with, but there is more pressure for this to change. In addition to beauty, creativity, and easthetics, designers and all the people involved must realize the impact on the planet and workers of the production, chemical treatments, wash, and disposal of the items they create.

There are planetary and human repurcussions to not being green, so it is not likley that sustainability concerns are just a fad. Designer Michale Kors was onto something when he said: "This generation of teenagers is going to start shopping very differently when they reach their twenties—I think they're going to have an aversion to the idea of disposable fashion," Kors said. "It's a concept that today twenty-somethings grew up on and I have a feeling that today's teenagers with their sophistication aren't going to buy into that. They're likely to rebel because they don't want to be like the generation before them, and will actually want to spend money on things that will last, and [with] versatility and sustainability."[63]

---

61   Council of Fashion Designers of America (CFDA). http://www.cfda.com/. 2015.
62   NY Magazine. "Diane Von Furstenberg." NYMag.com: The Cut > Fashion > Labels and Designers. 2015.
63   Maheshwari, Sapna. "Michael Kors Says Today's Teens Will Reject Fast Fashion in Their Twenties." BuzzFeed.com: Business. October 28, 2013.

Interview: Amy Hall, Director of Social Consciousness, Eileen Fisher

1)   What in your background led you get into this movement? What drew you into using natural fabrics?

I grew up sensing that I wanted to "be of service" somehow, to people, to the world. I didn't have a clear picture of how to make that happen, as "CSR," or corporate social responsibility hadn't been coined yet. So, I emerged from college and grad school with a language degree (Chinese) and an ESL teaching degree. I then fell into nonprofit fundraising and pursued that for the first 9 years of my professional life. Finding EILEEN FISHER was truly a matter of being in the right place at the right time. And I wasn't even hired initially to do this work we now call Social Consciousness. For the first four years of my time with the company, I was helping with PR, events, graphics design coordination. Around 1997, I became the company's first Community Relations Manager, and soon after that was named Manager of Social Accountability, so that I could begin developing our first supply chain human rights program.

Our environmental commitment was articulated a bit later, although it was always present in some way. When Eileen founded the company in 1984, she always had a commitment to natural fabrics. Cotton, linen, wool, silk—these became the foundation of her styles. In addition, because of her vision for "timeless" styles that were not driven by seasonal trends, the EILEEN FISHER line was inherently sustainable in terms of its longevity. Buy a piece one year and it will work with your wardrobe years later.

2)   Tell us about your company and what makes it unique, both the products themselves and also any extra efforts you'd like to highlight—(I love your Green Eileen efforts and No Excuses campaign, for example.)

EILEEN FISHER is a highly unconventional company. We are 40 percent employee-owned (through an ESOP, or Employee Stock Ownership Program); we have amazing benefits, like profit-sharing and a wellness benefit. Our workplace culture is one of collaboration and connection; we really love being together and treat our coworkers as family members. And we are known for trying new approaches. For example: when Eileen became disheartened by the amount of waste generated by clothing, she championed the launch of our Green Eileen initiative. It began by having our employees bring back gently used EILEEN FISHER clothing, in return for a $5 gift card redeemable at our stores. The clothing was cleaned and resold, with the resulting profits donated to women's and girls' programs via the Eileen Fisher Community Foundation. The initiative was so successful that we expanded it to our customers; we now receive hundreds of items a week from customers at all of our stores in the US. In our dedicated Green Eileen stores (Yonkers and Seattle) and our EF Lab store (Irvington, NY), we offer upcycling workshops, teaching people how to make rugs, lampshades, bags, and new wearable art from the previously worn product. Not only is the Green Eileen program fully self-sustaining, but it provides new life for old clothing while teaching people about principles of sustainability in a fun environment.

3)   How do you source your fabrics/designers?

We have a very talented and dedicated Design team, most of whom have been with the company for many years. Not only do they have long-term relationships with many of the mills that develop our fabrics, but they also attend international fabric shows—like Pitti Vilati—to gain inspiration and look for new iterations of our tried-and-true favorites. Some of our designers travel to far-flung places to seek out artisanal specialties that could complement our regular line in the form of a gorgeous wrap or scarf.

4)   What is the most important thing the fashion world needs to keep in mind as we move into the future? That is, what is most important—organic, local, longevity of the product, etc.?

To me, the most important thing to keep in mind is where we're headed as a planet. We have heard multiple times that by the year 2030, the world's demand for water will exceed supply by 40 percent. That's not just drinking water, but clean water that feeds our farm fields and supplies our dye houses. As a company that depends on farms for 90 percent of its products (think cotton, flax, wool, silk, hemp), the future viability of our business depends on a healthy planet. If we are facing a future (only 15 years away) of many fewer resources that directly impact our supply chain, we need to rethink how we make our clothes and how much clothing we produce. The apparel industry as a whole needs to take action, too. There simply won't be enough for all of us to thrive in the same way we are currently running our businesses.

5)   Where do you see the ecofashion/sustainable clothing movement going? That is, is it a fad?

We see "ecofashion" as a business imperative. For all the reasons cited above (question 4), there truly is no choice but to do things differently.

6)   What would sustain the ecofashion movement and help it grow? What must people/consumers and/or designers and manufacturers do to ensure ecofashion's success?

We need to rethink what it means to buy and wear clothes. How many t-shirts does one person need? How many pairs of jeans? How many sweaters or fancy dresses? The issue of consumption is not addressed seriously enough. Not only are we depleting the world's resources through mass production of clothing, but we are also disposing of clothes in a careless, horrific manner. If we don't run out of water, we will drown in the waste produced by discarded apparel and related waste.

7)   Should it scale up and become more affordable?

Ecofashion should become more affordable AND conventional clothing (i.e., those products made with toxic dyes, chemical pesticides, and cheap labor) should become more expensive to the consumer. I'm not sure how realistic that is, but until "eco" fashion becomes the norm, we have no hope of changing people's behavior.

8)   What are the best methods to raise awareness about ecofashion?

Every individual responds to different triggers, which I call "light bulb moments." For many, we become more eco-minded when we become pregnant for the first time. We want to give our children the cleanest start to their lives, so we begin eating organic food—and feeding them organic food as they grow up. That transfers to household cleaners, use of pesticides, and other "clean" products. Since ecofashion is more about connecting to the health of the earth rather than personal health (unless people make the connection to farm workers), there is a visceral link to the state of the planet I'm leaving my children. That, for me, is a powerful argument. Do I want to leave my children a world full of toxic waste, depleted farm fields, insufficient water, and rampant poverty? Or do I want to leave my children a world that is better than the one we currently live in? I don't know anyone who would the former.

9)   Who are some of your favorite people involved in ecofashion that you think deserve more recognition?

Livia Firth, Stella McCartney, Stacy Flynn (Evrnu), LaRhea Pepper.

Eileen Fisher (organic cotton)

Chapter 7

Dirty Laundry
Greener Ways to Care for Your Clothes

Though this is book mainly focuses on sustainable fabrics, I learned about a year ago that there is another surprising aspect to clothing's impact. If you look at an organic garment's environmental impact from "cradle to grave," meaning from the processing of the material, production of a garment, transportation, use, and final disposal, there is one area that stands out. Believe it or not, the worst impact any garment will have on the Earth during its lifecycle is the way it is laundered after you buy it. "The biggest gains in environmental performance for many fashion and textile pieces can be made by tackling the impact arising from their washing and drying."[1] Between 75 and 80 percent of our clothing's lifecycle impact comes from washing and drying.[2]

The Dirty Side of Dry Cleaning

I'll discuss home detergents below, but let's start with dry cleaning: if you use a dry cleaner to clean your garments, you are likely paying for a highly toxic chemical called perchloroethylene (also referred to as tetrachloroethylene, or "Perc" for short) to be used to clean them. When you wash with soap or detergent, the product serves to alkalinize the water and also to saponify (make soapy) and dislodge dirt and oils. Perc, however, is a chemical solvent, so it is able to remove dirt and oil-based stains without water. It has been used since after World War II and is a very effective cleaner, which can also degrease metals. However, it also has a downside.

There are about 35,000 dry cleaners in the United States and Canada.[3] The majority (~85 percent) of dry cleaning businesses use Perc, a chlorinated hydrocarbon.[4] In

---

1   Fletcher, Kate. *Sustainable Fashion & Textiles: Design Journeys*, 76. London: Earthscan, 2008.
2   TreeHugger. "11 Ways to Green Your Laundry." TreeHugger.com. July 10, 2014.
3   Mastny, Lisa. "Dry Cleaning." Worldwatch Institute. 2013.
4   Office of Pollution Prevention and Toxics: US Environmental Protection Agency (EPA). "Chemicals in the Environment: Perchloroethylene." EPA.gov. August 1994.

regular use by dry cleaners starting in the 1930s as an alternative to kerosene being used as a cleaner, Perc became the chosen cleaning fluid since it had minimal odor and was nonflammable.

However, by the 1990s, the United States government recognized that this chemical could pose health effects such as cancer in humans.[5] The International Agency for Research in Cancer classifies Perc as a "probable human carcinogen."[6] Perc volatilizes into the air (becomes a vapor), and exposure through inhalation can cause neurological effects such as dizziness, headache, nausea, or even death, depending on the dose.[7] It is also associated with reproductive harm and sperm abnormalities. According to the Agency for Toxic Substances and Disease Registry (ATSDR),

> "The Department of Health and Human Services (DHHS) has determined that tetrachloroethylene may reasonably be anticipated to be a carcinogen. Tetrachloroethylene has been shown to cause liver tumors in mice and kidney tumors in male rats."

In 1994 the National Institute for Occupational Safety and Health and the National Institute of Environmental Safety and Health conducted a study involving more than 600 dry cleaning workers with five or more years of working in the industry in the US. The study found a sevenfold increase between the risk of tongue cancer and regular exposure to Perc.

The US Environmental Protection Agency (EPA) lists Perc as a hazardous waste.[8] It can also exist in a liquid form, and has been detected at several hundred Superfund sites across the US. Superfund sites are locations contaminated with harmful toxins that the federal government has designated for cleanup.[9] Cleanup can be an expensive proposition for responsible parties, and if those responsible can't be found, the government (taxpayers) foots the bill. There is a multistate Coalition for

---

5   US Environmental Protection Agency (EPA). "Tetrachloroethylene (Perchloroethylene)." EPA.gov: Air and Radiation > TTN Web – Technology Transfer Network > Air Toxics Web site > Tetrachloroethylene (Perchloroethylene). December 2012.

6   Mastny, Lisa. "Dry Cleaning." Worldwatch Institute. 2013.

7   Public Health Service Agency for Toxic Substances and Disease Registry: US Department of Health and Human Services (HHS). "ToxGuide™ for Tetrachloroethylene C_2Cl_4: CAS# 127-18-4." October 2014.

8   US Environmental Protection Agency (EPA). "Fact Sheet on Perchloroethylene, also known as Tetrachloroethylene." EPA.gov: Chemical Safety and Pollution Prevention > Pollution Prevention and Toxics > Existing Chemicals. February 2012.

9   US Environmental Protection Agency (EPA). "Cleaning Up the Nation's Hazardous Waste Sites." EPA.gov: Superfund. June 17, 2015.

Remediation of Dry Cleaners to make sure cleanups are done right.[10]

Because of these concerns, Perc is regulated under many laws.[11] In 2007, California became the first state to ban both the use of Perc and the purchase of new Perc machines, which will go into full effect by the year 2023. Because Perc vapors can waft into apartments above, the EPA required that no new Perc dry cleaning machines could be installed in residential buildings after July 13, 2006. Under the National Emissions Standards for Hazardous Air Pollutants, the EPA has called for the removal of dry cleaners that use Perc from residential buildings by 2020 nationwide.[12]

So what is an eco-conscious fashionista/o to do?

What Consumers Can Do

1) The clothing manufacturer is required to tell you how to care for a garment. Try to avoid purchasing clothing that says: "Dry clean only" on its label. Some clothes bearing this label may be hand-washable, so use your best sense on this or ask your dry cleaner. However, there still may be occasions when we need to bring clothing to a professional cleaner.

2) Clothing used to go through a cylinder through which Perc was pumped and filtered, and then clothing was moved to a dryer, allowing Perc to escape into the air. Today, due to federal rules adopted in 2006 requiring only "fourth generation" standards, clothing is dried within the same unit, removing most remaining vapors. So to be extra safe, if you use a dry cleaner that uses Perc, be sure to air out bags outdoors before bringing them inside your home so as to avoid off-gassing (releasing)

---

10   State Coalition for Remediation of Drycleaners. http://www.drycleancoalition.org. 2015.
11   Toxic Substances Control Act, October 11, 1976; Clean Air Act, December 17, 1963; Comprehensive Environmental Response, Compensation, and Liability (Superfund) Act, December 11, 1980; Resource Conservation and Recovery Act, October 21, 1976; Clean Water Act, October 18, 1972; Safe Drinking Water Act, December 17, 1974.
12   40 CFR 63.322(o)(5). 58 FR 49376, September 22, 1993, as amended at 61 FR 49265, September 1996; 71 FR 42744, July 27, 2006.

the Perc into indoor air.[13] A skeptical colleague of mine who does home energy and safety inspections told me that he decided to put the concern about Perc to the test. He took a gas meter he uses for work into his closet after bringing home dry-cleaned clothes, and found the meter reading at its maximum, so he is a skeptic no more!

3) Until legislation requires that dry cleaners tell us what they're using, the best we can do is choose a dry cleaner that advertises itself as "green," "nontoxic," or "eco-friendly" and ask them to identify which type of solvent is used. We'll discuss the different types below.

4) Write to your state legislators and ask them to require all professional cleaners to publicly disclose their cleaning fluid. All dry cleaners should be mandated to disclose the type of cleaning agent being used in an obvious location visible to customers. Non-Perc cleaners should be required to list their solvents and detergents, and the government (federal and/or local) should provide a webpage explaining any safety information consumers should know. Any dry cleaner that is advertising itself as "green," "nontoxic," "sustainable," "eco-friendly," etc. should be inspected periodically to verify that the company is indeed using an alternative to Perc, since these terms are meant to distinguish their system from the industry standard.

Note that the term "organic" in the dry cleaning context should be prohibited due to the confusion amongst the general public about the meaning of the term—it does not mean the same thing as it does with food. (See below.)

5) If your dry cleaner offers hanger recycling (reusing), bring your hangers back, and if they accept reusable garment bags, use those. (See below)

Alternative Cleaning Methods

The good news is that there are several alternatives to Perc now in use by professional cleaners. None are 100 percent perfect, but certainly all are a better alternative to Perc. I have ranked them below, starting with the most eco-friendly first.

---

13   US Environmental Protection Agency (EPA). "An Introduction to Indoor Air Quality (IAQ): Volatile Organic Compounds." EPA.gov: Air > Introduction to IAQ. July 9, 2012.

1) Wet Cleaning: This is a nontoxic method using water and mild detergents in an advanced system of computer-controlled machines that mildly agitate clothes, reducing wear and tear. It can be used for "dry-clean" only clothing. (In truth, except for CO_2, no "dry" cleaning solvents are dry; all chemical solvents are liquid, and then clothing is put through a dryer. The "dry" is in reference to lack of water.) Several environmental and government organizations consider this method the safest and most eco-friendly option.

2) Liquid Carbon dioxide: As it sounds, this method uses highly pressurized liquid carbon dioxide, usually from industrial byproducts, as well as detergents, to clean clothing. The EPA Design for the Environment (DFE) Programs recognize the liquid carbon dioxide (CO_2) cleaning process as one example of an environmentally preferable technology that can effectively clean garments.[14] One problem is that this method requires a different type of equipment than that used for Perc cleaning, which can cost three times as much by comparison. The main health concern stated on the Material Safety Data Sheet (MSDS) is inhalation of large doses, which can cause dizziness, asphyxiation, and stinging of the nose and throat. Critics say that it doesn't get clothes as clean as other options unless other chemical solvents, such as Solvair (which contains propylene glycol, a mildly toxic agent when used in high concentrations), are added to help lift off stains.

3) Liquid silicone (siloxane D5): Sold under the brand name GreenEarth, this is a colorless, odorless substance that acts as a carrier for detergents. The EPA does not regulate D5 silicone or recognize it as a potential carcinogen or toxic air contaminant. According to GreenEarth Cleaning,[15] D5 silicone is used in personal care products and degrades into silica (sand), water, and carbon dioxide. However, according to Consumer Reports, "Some studies have shown siloxane can cause cancer in laboratory animals."[16] The Material Safety Data Sheet (MSDS) states that repeated inhalation led to enlarged livers in rats, but under normal usage it should not be a risk to consumers.

---

14   US Environmental Protection Agency (EPA). "Design for the Environment Programs, Initiatives, and Projects." EPA.gov: Safer Choice. July 2, 2015.

15   GreenEarth Cleaning. http://www.greenearthcleaning.com. 2015.

16   Watson, Tom. "Dry Cleaning is Getting Greener, But Some Efforts Are Spotty." *The Seattle Times.* September 6, 2008.

4) Rynex: Made from an aliphatic propylene glycol ether. The MSDS says it is mildly irritating to skin, a moderate to severe eye irritant, and a respiratory irritant.[17] It is not listed as a carcinogen, or as a hazardous waste.

5) K4 System (Butoxymethoxy/butylal): Not yet widely used in the US, a promising German solvent technology similar to cyclosiloxane D5, marketed as "neither a hazardous material nor a hazardous substance in Europe."[18] The MSDS does not show acute toxicity concerns, but says "do not allow undiluted product or large quantities of it to reach ground water, water course or sewage system."[19] It has not been reviewed by IARC [International Agency for Research on Cancer] for carcinogenicity.[20]

6) Hydrocarbon: Petroleum-based solvents including DF-2000 and Eco-Solv. They are flammable but are currently the most popular Perc alternative because they are affordable and, being petroleum-based, the industry is more familiar with how they work. Hydrocarbon solvent is classified as a VOC, and is a likely contributor to smog formation. Like Perc, hydrocarbon is also a neurotoxin and skin and eye irritant for workers.[21] Hydrocarbons have not been classified as to their carcinogenicity by the IARC.[22]

Resources: To find a dry cleaner that is using an alternative to Perc, see <u>nodryclean. com</u>.[23]

Be a Smart Consumer

- Many dry cleaners are using the words "green," "organic," "eco-friendly," or "natural" in their window advertisements. Though these terms often mean that

---

17   Rynex Technologies LLC. "Material Safety Data Sheet: Rynex-3 Dry Cleaning Solvent." Equinox Chemicals. August 11, 2011.
18   SystemK4. "SolvonK4—the halogen-free solvent." Kreussler Textile Care. 2015.
19   Vogel, Herr. "Material Safety Data Sheet acc. to ISO/DIS 11014." Abteilung TQM. October 18, 2010.
20   Toxics Use Reduction Institute (TURI) at UMass—Lowell. "Assessment of Alternatives to Perchloroethylene for the Dry Cleaning Industry: Methods and Policy Report No. 27." TURI. June 2012.
21   San Francisco Department of the Environment. "Dry Cleaning: How to Green Your Cleaning." SFEnvironment.org. 2009.
22   World Health Organization (WHO) International Agency for Research on Cancer (IARC). "IARC Monographs on the Evaluation of Carcinogenic Risks to Humans—Volume 92: Some Non-heterocyclic Polycyclic Aromatic Hydrocarbons and Some Related Exposures." WHO IARC. 2010.
23   NoDryClean.com. http://nodryclean.com. 2015.

the business is using one of the above named alternatives to Perc, there is no verification of that, so be sure to ask.

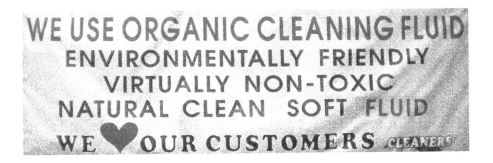

- Don't Get "Greenwashed": I believe many shop owners are trying to do the right thing and are not trying to be misleading. However, typically if a dry cleaner is using hydrocarbon solvent, the term chosen will be "organic." However, this does <u>not</u> mean the same thing as it does on a food item. The term "organic" on food is a highly regulated definition that means food has met strict US Department of Agriculture standards that do not allow the use of pesticides or genetic modification. However, the term "organic" in terms of dry cleaning fluid is totally different. It is referring to the chemical makeup of the substance being carbon-based. For example, the study of carbon-based molecules is referred to as "organic chemistry," the often dreaded class in high school. Therefore Perc is also "organic" in that it contains carbon (its molecular formula is C_2HCl_3).[24]

Other Ways Dry Cleaners Can Be Green

Other ways dry cleaners can reduce their environmental impacts include:

1) Recycling (reusing) metal hangers or using cardboard recyclable ones (which can also be printed with advertising).

2) Reducing the usage of standard plastic bags. Standard dry cleaning bags are petroleum-based, thus taking hundreds of years to decompose. They are usually #4 plastic, which are recyclable along with plastic grocery bags, but unfortunately most end up in the garbage. Dry cleaners can reduce plastic bag use by using biodegradable

---

24   Greensleeves: The Green Dry Cleaner. "Consumer Alert: Dry Cleaning Services Misleadingly Branded as Natural and Organic." http://www.thegreendrycleaner.com. 2015.

plastic bags. One brand of biodegradable bags is "Eco Green" made in Canada, which is made from a polymer said to break down in two years.

A great way to reduce standard plastic bag use is by bringing your own reusable garment bags. These are sturdier garment bags that you can put your name on and use over and over, instead of disposable plastic bags. Some dry cleaners offer their own reusable garment bags for sale. There are several brands of reusable garment bags available for the public to purchase online:

- Reuseniks: cotton[25]
- Green Garmento: polypropelyne[26]
- It's My Bag: plastic[27]

What About Regular Laundry That I Wash Myself?

Any time it is possible to wash your own laundry, it is advisable to do so. This way you can have control over your laundry detergents and, in some cases, also the amount and temperature of the water used.

Detergents

When shopping for laundry detergents, you want to look for products that do not contain certain ingredients like the following:

Phosphates

Though phosphates help remove grease and reduce residues, when they go down the drain, unless they are well filtered by sewage treatment plants, they can act as fertilizer and cause algal blooms in nearby lakes or bays. Most modern detergents do not contain this ingredient.

Fragrance

Though we may like the way certain detergents smell, and we want to have a "clean" soapy scent, those scents are made from chemicals. Many fragrances contain chemicals called phthalates, which help the scent to last longer. However, numerous studies have found phthalates to be hormone disruptors. In fact phthalates were first discovered to be a health concern by breast cancer researcher Dr. Ana Soto at Tufts

---

25   Reuseniks. http://www.reuseniks.com. 2015.
26   The Green Garmento. http://www.thegreengarmento.com. 2015.
27   It's My B. http://www.ItsmyB.com. 2015.

University in Boston in the 1990s. She put breast cancer samples in plastic test tubes one day and came back to find the cancer cells had multiplied rapidly by the next day. She asked her colleagues if anyone had accidentally added anything to the test tubes, but they had not. She eventually realized it was chemicals in the plastic test tubes themselves. Phthalates are also found commonly in cosmetics (see chapter 8), and have been implicated in such health effects as breast cancer, reproductive disorders, feminization of male fetuses, and even obesity.

Bleach

Many extol the virtues of bleach because not only is it a powerful disinfectant, but it also gets white clothing very white, and television commercials tend to play up these qualities. However, bleach may not be as benign as we think. Bleach, or sodium hypochlorite, is toxic to fish if released into waterways. What happens when you wash something down the drain depends on your local treatment plant. Bleach can also be caustic to human skin, and hazardous if directly inhaled. The combination of bleach and ammonia is very dangerous—it forms the toxic substance chloramine, which can cause acute respiratory problems. If you need to whiten your clothing, a natural alternative to bleach is hydrogen peroxide. It whitens and is not toxic; it decomposes into water and oxygen. However, you should note that excessive use of peroxide eventually erodes fabrics.

Detergent Alternatives

So what should we use instead? Look for detergents that are bio-based and do not contain synthetic fragrances. The best bet when buying detergents is to shop at health food stores. Places like Whole Foods, local organic food shops, and even Trader Joe's or Fairway are more likely to carry eco-friendly detergents that do not contain harmful ingredients than standard grocery or chain stores, though thankfully this is changing. If you are not sure and you open the container to a very strong scent, precautionary sense would suggest choosing another. To reduce waste, EPA also recommends: when possible, "buy items, such as laundry detergent and fabric softener, with minimal packaging. Buy items in bulk or in concentrated form (e.g., concentrated laundry detergent)."[28]

---

28   US Environmental Protection Agency (EPA). "Laundry Room & Basement." EPA.gov: Green Building > Green Homes. December 19, 2012.

One of my favorite eco-friendly items that I discovered in the past few years is the laundry wash ball. As mentioned, detergents work by making water more alkaline to loosen soil molecules. Laundry balls do the same thing through the use of small ceramic balls contained within a perforated rubber ball—the ceramic orbs make the water alkaline. I was a skeptic myself, but I have found that it really does get your clothes clean, though you may need some extra care for heavy stains. There is no scent, so clothes come out smelling fresh but not perfumed. Laundry balls have been around since the 1990s, and there are several versions of laundry balls on the market including the SmartKlean Laundry Ball, the Greenwash Ball, and the Eco-Friendly Laundry Ball.

Similarly, there are dryer balls that help make clothing soft without chemicals. Typical fabric softener dryer sheets coat clothing with a thin layer of surfactant, which often contains numerous chemicals and fragrances containing phthalates. Chemicals found in fabric softeners and dryer sheets include alpha-terpineol, benzyl acetate, benzyl alcohol, camphor, chloroform, ethyl acetate, and others. "These chemicals have been found to cause various health problems including central nervous system disorders, irritation to mucous membranes, pancreatic cancer, irritation to upper respiratory tract, headaches, nausea, vomiting, [and] dizziness."[29] Many companies now make

---

29   Romero, Vanessa. "7 Toxic Reasons to Ditch Dryer Sheets." HealthyLivingHowTo.com. April 3, 2013.

natural fabric softeners that can be purchased at health food stores. Or even better (and cheaper), try adding half a cup of baking soda to your laundry which makes the water alkaline, softening fabrics. One study analyzing dryer vent emissions found twenty-five different volatile compounds being released into the air, and "of those, two chemicals—acetaldehyde and benzene—are classified by the Environmental Protection Agency as carcinogens, for which the agency has established no safe exposure level."[30]

Water Use

Want to know your water footprint? Find out at H2OConserve.org

Most people know by now that wasting clean water is not a good thing, especially since it is a resource from nature that not everyone on earth has easy access to these days. Some areas of the United States more than others must really pay attention to their water usage due to dwindling sources. Water use in the United States is increasing every year, and in recent years nearly every region of the country has experienced water shortages.[31] Be mindful of water usage when choosing your washing machine: front loading clothes washing machines use about 1/3 to 1/2 the water used by top loading machines.[32]

Studies show that using less water does not negatively affect how clean the clothes get.[33] Front loading machines also spin rapidly, removing most of the water, so they reduce the amount of energy needed to dry your clothing as well.

It also makes the most sense to make sure the laundry machine is full when you turn it on, rather than washing one pair of jeans at a time, since the machine must fill up with water just for one garment. Some machines have settings for small, medium, and large loads, so this is another option for controlling how much water is used.

Energy use

There is one aspect of water use that many people don't think about: it also takes energy to pump and heat water. Every time we turn on a tap or shower, pumps must

---

30   University of Washington. "Scented Laundry Products Emit Hazardous Chemicals Through Dryer Vents." ScienceDaily.com: Science News from Research Organizations. August 24, 2011.

31   US Environmental Protection Agency (EPA). "Water Supply in the US" EPA.gov: WaterSense. June 25, 2015.

32   Consumer Energy Center: California Energy Commission. "Clothes Washers." ConsumerEnergy Center.org: Residential. 2015

33   Earth Pledge Foundation. *Future Fashion White Papers*. Edited by Leslie Hoffman. New York: Earth Pledge Foundation, 2008. 101.

move the water through pipes, which takes energy. Also, heating water is very energy intensive, and often involves burning oil or natural gas. Warm water cleans better than cold, but rinsing in cold water can safely be recommended for all clothing. Warm or hot rinses are not necessary and could possibly damage your clothes, especially anything with elastic in it. Therefore, using temperature settings on your machine can save energy and money.[34]

Logo by U.S. Environmental Protection Agency

According to the EPA, about 90 percent of the energy used for washing clothes in a conventional top-load washer is for heating the water.[35] A key thing to look for when purchasing clothes washers (or any appliance) is the Energy Star symbol. This is a designation by the EPA that rates an appliance as more energy efficient than a standard equivalent. "The average washing machine uses about forty-one gallons of water per load. High-efficiency washing machines use 35 to 50 percent less water, as well as 50 percent less energy per load."[36] Both top- and front-loading washing machines can be Energy Star-rated by the EPA.[37] However, since front-loading washers use less water, they also save on energy use. Look for the best model for you at the Energy Star website.[38]

Similarly, drying clothing at high temperatures uses more energy and also reduces the lifespan of the clothing. If your dryer gives you options, choose a cooler temperature.

Wash and care

One way to honor your clothing and help it last longer is to always check the tag for wash and care instructions. You can even check the tag in the store and decide if that's a garment you want to buy based on these instructions. The Federal Trade Commission (FTC) regulates these labels. Washing instructions must include several elements: washing by hand or by machine, bleaching, drying, ironing, and any warnings to prevent damage. The FTC care labeling clarifies the definitions of "hot," "warm," and "cold" water, and is in alignment with the definitions used by the American Association

---

34 US Environmental Protection Agency (EPA). "Pollution Prevention (P2)." EPA.gov/P2. June 29, 2015.
35 US Environmental Protection Agency (EPA). "Laundry Room & Basement." EPA.gov: Green Building > Green Homes. December 19, 2012.
36 Ibid.
37 Energy Star (EPA; DOE). "Clothes Washers for Consumers." EnergyStar.gov: Certified Products. 2015.
38 Energy Star (EPA; DOE). http://www.energystar.gov. Energy Star. 2015.

of Textile Chemists and Colorists. This is important because the wrong temperature could set stains instead of getting rid of them.

Temperatures used in Washing Machines[1]
Designation: Wash Temperature ± Rinse Temperature

Top-Loading Machines	Front-Loading Machines
Cold: 80 ± 5°F Warm: 105 ± 5°F Hot: 120 ± 5°F	Cold: 68 ± 5°F Warm: 90 ± 5°F Hot: 120 ± 5°F

Washing machines may have temperature control settings.
If you are not sure about wash and care instruction symbols,
see: http://www.textileaffairs.com/c-common.htm

---

1 Association of Textile, Apparel & Materials Professionals (AATCC). "AATCC Monograph M6: Standardization of Home Laundry Test Conditions." AATCC.org. July 31, 2013.

Drying Tips

The most eco-friendly option for drying your clothing is using a "solar dryer." In other words: a clothesline. Yup, the way our grandparents used to dry their clothes was actually far greener than using an electric clothes dryer, and it saves money, too. Using a tumble drier when you launder adds 7 kilograms on average to a shirt's carbon footprint.[39] Pegging up clothes may take a few extra minutes of your time, but it pays off. The average American home could save about 6 percent on its annual electric bills by using a clothesline instead of drying clothes in a machine.[40] However, some areas forbid it because they consider it an eyesore, so indoor drying racks are another option. If you choose to use a dryer, look for energy efficient models, and make sure to clean lint filters often to encourage proper air circulation.

---

39 McLaren, Warren. "Want Greener Clothes? Try Our 8 Tips for Less Laundry." TreeHugger.com: Living > Sustainable Fashion. November 12, 2009.
40 US Energy Information Administration. "Residential Energy Consumption Survey (RECS)." EIA.gov: Consumption & Efficiency. 2015.

Innovative design to reduce environmental and health impacts

Some green-minded designers are starting to think outside the box for ways to reduce the environmental and health impacts of laundering clothing. One idea is to make modular clothing so you only wash the part that's dirty. There are also designers making clothing with ventilated armpits so the need for washing is further minimized. Some clothing used for medical purposes is being infused with silver ions, since silver has antimicrobial qualities. This reduces the need for washing since it reduces odors created by bacteria found on the skin.

In summary, part of having a "green" wardrobe is caring for it in a green way. Common sense steps like proper washing, sorting darks from lights, using quality hangers, and using the right iron temperature help preserve clothing longer, which equals less money spent on new garments and more sustainability. Reducing dry cleaning, or choosing less toxic dry cleaning options, using reusable dry cleaning bags, using eco-friendly detergents or laundry balls, avoiding bleach, and being conscious of hot water usage are more ways to reduce our clothing's impact on the planet.

Natural Treatments for Clothing's Natural Enemies

Moths

Pesticides are chemicals that kill, mitigate, or repel pests. We may not think of them this way, but mothballs repel moths, so they are a pesticide. Mothballs often contain the chemicals naphthalene or p-dichlorobenzene, which are nerve toxins. Granted, it can be upsetting to look in the closet and find that moths ate our clothes, such as wool sweaters. The good news is that there are safer alternatives to mothballs. Usually larvae can come in on the fabric itself, so good cleaning before storage helps reduce the problem. Some natural alternative repellents include cedar chips, dried lavender flowers, rosemary, mint, white peppercorns, and clove.[1]

Mold

If your home has poor air circulation, mold can actually grow on clothing. The key to mold control is moisture control. If there is mold growth in your home, you must clean up the mold and fix the water problem so the mold does not return. This may involve fixing leaking pipes or walls. Always store garments in a well-ventilated area. The EPA offers suggestions as to mold prevention and cleanup.[2]

---

1   US Environmental Protection Agency (EPA). "Sure, Your Home is Clean...But Is It Safe For Your Family? Be Smart About Using Household Produts!" EPA.gov. October 2006. and Colvey, Anne. "Natural Moth Protection." GreenLivingOnline.com: Homes. 2015.
2   US Environmental Protection Agency (EPA). "A Brief Guide to Mold, Moisture, and Your Home: Moisture and Mold Prevention and Control Tips." EPA.gov: Air > Indoor Air > Mold and Moisture. March 5, 2012.

Chapter 8

Eco-Cosmetics to Match Your Eco-Wardrobe
Know the Ugly Side of Beauty

While the lovely scents wafting out of mall department store cosmetics counters and their beautiful pictures of gorgeous faces may entice us, there is a stinky story behind the products being sold at such outlets. We all want to look our best, and it is certainly alluring to keep trying the next best product that will remove wrinkles in our skin or add just the right shade of rosiness to our cheeks. However, if we truly want to be green, we must think about what's in all those pinks, blues, and brown hues we use every day.

There are numerous contaminants that are found in commonly sold personal care products. Several books have been written about this topic, including Drop Dead Gorgeous[1] by Kim Erickson (2002), Not Just a Pretty Face: The Ugly Side of the Beauty Industry[2] by Stacy Malkan (2007), and Toxic Beauty[3] by Dr. Samuel Epstein (2009). There are organizations that now exist to raise awareness about the issue of toxic ingredients in cosmetics and body products, which are mentioned below. Therefore, here I will just offer an overview of the main issues and review a few of the ingredients that we should be aware of.

There are 10,500 personal care products in the US. However, in its more than thirty-year history, the cosmetic industry's safety panel (the Cosmetic Ingredient Review, or CIR) has assessed fewer than 20 percent of cosmetics ingredients, and found only eleven ingredients or chemical groups to be unsafe.[4] Most cosmetic ingredients have been is use for many years, so are generally considered safe by the test of time.

---

1   Erickson, Kim. *Drop Dead Gorgeous: Protecting Yourself from the Hidden Dangers of Cosmetics.* 1st ed. New York: McGraw-Hill, 2002.
2   Malkan, Stacy. "3 Lessons from Walmart's New Chemicals Initiative." NotJustaPrettyFace.org. September 12, 2013.
3   Epstein, Samuel S., and Randall Fitzgerald. *Toxic Beauty: How Cosmetics and Personal-Care Products Endanger Your Health and What You Can Do About It.* 1st ed. Dallas, TX: BenBella Books, 2009.
4   Environmental Working Group (EWG). "Myths on Cosmetics Safety." EWG.org. 2015.

However, here are some of the concerns to be aware of:

Cancer: When the Washington, DC-based health and safety advocacy organization Environmental Working Group (EWG)[5] conducted an investigative report in 2005 called "Skin Deep,"[6] they found that one-third of personal care products they looked at contained at least one chemical linked to cancer. Follow-up work in 2007 found 22 percent of all personal care products might be contaminated with the cancer-causing impurity 1,4-dioxane, including many children's products.[7]

What's the Deal with Pink-Ribbon Cosmetic Campaigns?

Be aware of "Pinkwashing," or marketing by major companies that position themselves as leaders in the fight against breast cancer while engaging in practices that may be contributing to rising rates of the disease. "The Campaign for Safe Cosmetics has repeatedly asked Avon, Revlon, and Estee Lauder— the three largest users of the pink ribbon in the cosmetics industry—to sign the Compact for Safe Cosmetics, a pledge to remove chemicals linked to cancer, birth defects, learning disabilities, and other harmful health impacts from their products. The companies have been unwilling to make this public commitment to eliminate carcinogens and other chemicals of concern from their products."[1]

---

1   Campaign for Safe Cosmetics. "Action Alerts." SafeCosmetics.org: Take Action. 2015.

Hormone Disruption: Some cosmetics and body care products may contain chemicals that disrupt the endocrine, or hormone, system. Hormone disruption is when chemicals act as if they are hormones in our bodies, so they either block our normal hormones from attaching to their receptors, or they attach to receptors and act as hormones themselves. This can lead to early onset of puberty, reproductive and genital defects, interfering with the male reproductive tract development, lower testosterone levels in adolescent males, and lower sperm count in adult males.[8] The concern with hormone-disrupting chemicals is the long-term exposure over time, which we experience when using these products on a daily basis.

---

5   Environmental Working Group (EWG). http://www.ewg.org. EWG. 2015.
6   Environmental Working Group (EWG). "Why This Matters – Cosmetics and Your Health." EWG. org: EWG Research. 2015.
7   Ibid.
8   Zero Breast Cancer. "Phthalates (THAL-ates) – The Everywhere Chemical." NIEHS.NIH.gov: Research Funded by NIEHS – Division of Extramural Research and Training. 2015.

As smart, eco-conscious consumers, we can make choices to better protect ourselves. When shopping for body care products, here are a few ingredients to avoid when possible:

Phthalates

Phthalates are used in lotions, perfumes, and nail polish to make them last longer and stick to the skin or mail better. Phthalates are associated with hormone disruption. Diethyl phthalate (DEP) or di-2-ethylhexyl phthalate (DEHP) are common ingredients you may see on labels. They have been found to cause reproductive birth defects in lab animals, particularly in males.[9]

Parabens

Parabens are used as antimicrobial preservatives. They can be absorbed through the skin and are associated with hormone disruption, developmental and reproductive toxicity. "Parabens may be found in a wide variety of products including shampoos, lotions, deodorants, scrubs and eye makeup, and are found in nearly all urine samples from US adults regardless of ethnic, socioeconomic, or geographic backgrounds."[10] There is a concern about association with breast cancer because parabens have been found in breast tumor tissue. Methylparaben and propylparaben are the most common types of parabens you might see on a label.

Formaldehyde

Formaldehyde is a known carcinogen (recognized by several government agencies) used as a preservative in nail polish and hair products such as dyes and keratin treatments. Brazilian hair straightening products often used in salons contain high levels of formaldehyde.[11] An additional concern is with formaldehyde-releasing preservatives (FRPs), which release small amounts of formaldehyde over time. "Quaternium-15 is the most sensitizing of these FRPs. Other formaldehyde-releasing preservatives include imidazolidinyl urea, diazolidinyl urea, sodium hydroxymethylglycinate, dimethyl-dimethyl (DMDM) hydantoin, and 2-bromo-2-nitropropane-1,3-diol (bronopol)."[12] The US government's Occupational Safety and

9   Natural Resources Defense Council (NRDC). "Pthalates." NRDC.org: Smart Living > Chemical Index. December 28, 2011.
10   Ye, Xiaoyun, et al. "Parabens as Urinary Biomarkers of Exposure in Humans." *Environmental Health Perspectives*, Vol. 114, 1996, 1843-1846.
11   Andrews, David, et al. "Flat-Out Risky – Executive Summary: Obama Administration Moves to Curb Toxic Hair Straighteners." EWG.org. April 2011.
12   Campaign for Safe Cosmetics. "Formaldehyde and Formaldehyde-Releasing Preservatives." SafeCosmetics.org: Get the Facts > Chemicals of Concern. 2015.

Health Administration has set limits for safe levels of formaldehyde in salons to protect workers.[13]

Triclosan
If you have washed your hands with antibacterial soap, you have probably been exposed to triclosan. It is a registered germ-killing pesticide that is commonly used in soaps and toothpaste. "Triclosan is an antibacterial agent and preservative used in personal care and home-cleaning products; it is persistent in the environment and may be associated with endocrine (hormonal) toxicity."[14] A problem associated with widespread use of triclosan is that some microbes are becoming resistant to it anyway, so it's wiser to use warm water and regular soap. Efforts to have this chemical banned are ongoing, and some companies, such as Proctor and Gamble, have taken the proactive step of removing it from their products.[15]

> Avoid using products containing *microbeads* - these are tiny plastic beads (5mm or less) often used in exfoliants or even in toothpastes. Clearly it's advisable not to swallow them, but the tiny beads are small enough to pass through sewage treatment plants. They end up polluting our waterways and can be eaten by fish. Some products include biodegradable alternatives which are equally effective, such as pulverized almond, walnut or pecan shells.

Lead
Lead is a metal that is toxic to the nervous system. In 2007, the organization Campaign for Safe Cosmetics tested thirty-three popular brands of lipsticks for lead content at an independent lab. They found that "61 percent of lipsticks contained lead, with levels ranging up to 0.65 parts per million."[16] Unfortunately, these findings were confirmed, as lead was found in hundreds of brands of lipstick; findings published in 2009 and 2012 by the US Food and Drug Administration (FDA). The FDA found the highest lead levels

---

13   US Department of Labor: Occupational Safety & Health Administration (OSHA). "Hair Salons: Facts About Formaldehyde in Hair Products." OSHA.gov: Safety and Health Topics. 2015.
14   Environmental Working Group (EWG). "Triclosan." EWG.org: EWG's Skin Deep Cosmetics Database. 2015.
15   Beyond Pesticides. "Proctor and Gamble to Eliminate Triclosan from Its Products by 2014." BeyondPesticides.org: Daily News Blog. September 20, 2013.
16   Campaign for Safe Cosmetics. "Lead in Lipstick." SafeCosmetics.org: Get the Facts > Regulations > US Laws. 2015.

in lipsticks made by three manufacturers: Procter & Gamble (Cover Girl brand), L'Oreal (L'Oreal, Body Shop, and Maybelline brands), and Revlon.[17]

Fragrance
Fragrances are used in perfumes, lotions, soaps, and also in washing detergents. They are considered a trade secret, so companies don't have to tell us what's in them. They can contain dozens or even hundreds of synthetic chemical compounds, including phthalates, which are used to extend the life of the scent after applied.[18] Fragrances can be irritants and also sensitizers, meaning that people can become sensitive to future exposure to fragrances for the long term.[19] One group of fragrances that is of concern is synthetic musks, because they tend to accumulate in body tissue. They have been found in the "cord blood of newborn babies, as well as in blood, breast milk, and body fat."[20]

Hair Dyes and Shampoos
Coal tar, a known human carcinogen that is banned from cosmetics in European Union, is found in some popular dandruff shampoos such as Neutrogena T-Gel Shampoo.[21] It is also found in some dark (black) hair dyes. "The National Cancer Institute has discovered a connection between hair dyes, especially dark ones, and the group of cancers that impact blood and lymph nodes, such as non-Hodgkin's lymphoma and multiple myeloma.... The most problematic hair dye ingredient is a family of chemicals called arylamines. Arylamines are a known risk factor for bladder cancer and have been found to cause cancer in experimental animals. One of these is para-phenylene diamine (PPD)."[22] Also, the following ethanolamines (DEA, MEA, TEA, ETA), which are used as foaming agents in shampoos have been banned in Europe because they may form carcinogenic compounds called nitrosamines on the skin or in the body.[23]

17   Ibid.
18   Breast Cancer Fund. "Choose Safe Cosmetics." BreastCancerFund.org: Reduce Your Risk > Tips for Prevention > Choose Safe Cosmetics. 2015.
19   Sarantis, Heather, et al. (Campaign for Safe Cosmetics and Environmental Working Group (EWG). "Not So Sexy: The Health Risks of Secret Chemicals in Fragrance." EWG.org. May 12, 2010.
20   Campaign for Safe Cosmetics. "Synthetic Musks." SafeCosmetics.org: Get the Facts > Chemicals of Concern. 2015.
21   Campaign for Safe Cosmetics. "Coal Tar." SafeCosmetics.org: Get the Facts > Chemicals of Concern. 2015.
22   Sherman, Cathy. "The Dangers in Hair Coloring and Safer Alternatives." NaturalNews.com. February 1, 2008.
23   Morse, Jessica. "This Isn't Pretty." BareBeauty.com. 2015.

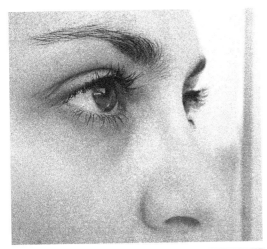

Men's Products

I would note that while some men may think that none of this applies to them, unfortunately some of the chemicals in question are in men's products, too. For example, "diethyl phthalate (DEP) has been found in fragrance-containing products such as cologne, aftershave, shaving cream, shampoos, and deodorants."[24]

Why is this allowed?

You may reasonably ask why the government allows these chemicals to be used. The US Food and Drug Administration (FDA) regulates cosmetic and body care product ingredients, and there are so many products the agency can't review each one. As the law currently stands, the agency encourages but does not require companies to submit testing data on ingredients before they can be used in a product. "Under the Federal Food, Drug, and Cosmetic Act, cosmetic products and ingredients do not require FDA approval before they go on the market."[25] There is a Cosmetic Ingredient Review medical expert panel that meets quarterly to assess the safety of cosmetic ingredients, but that is all. Often, only if there is a complaint registered about a product or ingredient, and many people report a negative reaction, does the government investigate and consider pulling a product from the market. "That's why FDA is trying to increase consumer awareness about the importance of reporting cosmetic-related problems."[26] FDA cannot require recalls of cosmetics, but they can "request that a company recall a product."[27]

For the sake of comparison, pesticide manufacturers must test their pesticides in studies, and then the Environmental Protection Agency (EPA) must review the manufacturers' studies. The EPA then decides whether or not to register the chemical for use in the United States and how it should be used, and thus labeled. As you read in chapter one about organic cotton and why it's important to reduce the use of pesticides, even this level of protection is considered not enough by many health advocates.

The reason for this is that scientists have a difficult time determining the level of risk. Risk is a factor of how toxic a chemical is, the amount of exposure a person may get,

---

24   Ibid.
25   US Food and Drug Administration. "How FDA Evaluates Regulated Products: Cosmetics." FDA. gov: About FDA > Transparency > FDA Basics. June 25, 2015.
26   Ibid.
27   Ibid.

and how susceptible that person may be to that exposure, e.g. children, elderly, and people with compromised immune systems are considered more vulnerable than a healthy adult. In order to determine if a product is safe, assumptions must be made about what level of exposure people are exposed to, on average. It is also easier to determine the impact of one chemical at a time using scientific methods, but very difficult to determine how chemicals behave when in concert with each other in our bodies.

Therefore, most people probably assume that more protection is offered by government regulations than might be the case. We would all like to trust that products on store shelves are safe, but it comes down to consumers taking responsibility for being informed and taking action. We can speak up about issues on social media, in groups we belong to, and write to companies and to elected officials to push for a more precautionary approach where needed.

Skeptics will rightly point out that it's not as though a person will apply a lotion or wash their hair and suddenly drop dead from exposure to these chemical ingredients. I'm sure if that were the case, something would have been done about it by now. However, as of now, scientists are still discovering those interactive or "synergistic" effects of accumulating small amounts of these chemicals in our bodies over time. Considering that we daily apply lotions, shampoos, and makeup directly to our skin, or spray perfume that we end up inhaling, the goal is to determine whether this can cause health effects and if so, which effects. For example, if a chemical happens to be a hormone disruptor, which either blocks or mimics estrogen in the body, how much of it can accumulate in the body before it triggers breast cancer? This is yet uncertain, but according to the American Cancer Society, it is known that the female hormones estrogen and progesterone can promote breast cancer cell growth.[28]

As mentioned, one consolation is that most cosmetics producers pull their ingredients from a common list that has been used for years. So by now, at least most acute problems have been detected. One of the latest concerns is regarding nanotechnology, which makes ingredients into extremely fine particles, which then have an increased ability to penetrate the skin. The FDA can do inspections of cosmetic manufacturers,

---

28   American Cancer Society. "What Are the Risk Factors for Breast Cancer?" Cancer.org: Learn About Cancer > Breast Cancer > Detailed Guide. June 10, 2015.

and occasionally does its own analysis of products if it believes there is a potential problem.

How Do I Find Better Options?

Thankfully, even popular magazines are starting to cover this issue of what's in our cosmetics, though it's often a conflict since cosmetics companies advertise in their pages. But what if you're at the store and you can't remember if an ingredient in a product you want to purchase is on this list? Well, you have several options.

- With the Internet at our fingertips via smartphones, we can easily access more information about ingredients. There is a terrific website called safecosmetics.org that is run by a group called the Campaign for Safe Cosmetics (led by the author and toxics activist Stacy Malkan, mentioned above) that rates individual products in terms of their toxicity level. If you have a phone with Internet access, you can stop and check it on the spot. Another resource is http://nomoredirtylooks.com.

- The most thorough resource I've found to know what is safe and what isn't is Environmental Working Group's (EWG's) Cosmetics Database found at: http://www.ewg.org/skindeep/. This is a searchable cosmetic safety database matching the ingredients in 60,000 products with fifty reputable toxicity and regulatory databases. EWG provides extensive information on product-specific health and safety concerns.[29] For example, EWG offers a Sunscreen Guide, because there are concerns about hormone disruption with the common ingredient oxybenzone in suntan lotions. It absorbs into skin and may cause changes at the cellular level. It is recommended to use lotions that contain sun barriers such as titanium dioxide or zinc oxide.[30]

- The Campaign for Safe Cosmetics and Environmental Working Group offer pocket guides that you can slip into your purse or wallet so you can do a quick check if you are not the smartphone type.

- Another option—and personally what I think is the easiest way to approach this issue—is to seek out the right places to buy cosmetics. You can buy eco-friendly

---

29   Environmental Working Group (EWG). "EWG's Skin Deep Cosmetics Database." EWG.org/skindeep. 2015.
30   Environmental Working Group (EWG). "EWG's Guide to Sunscreens." EWG.org/2015/sunscreen. 2015.

cosmetics online, and at most health food stores/natural food stores such as Whole Foods. These stores carry lines of cosmetics and shampoos that do not contain harmful chemicals and will often say so right on the label.

- It may seem strange to buy your mascara in the same place where you buy your organic apples, but you have a far higher chance of finding less toxic body products there than you do in department stores or drug stores, and you'll be supporting companies that are sincerely trying to do the right thing. However, be smart and don't assume these stores have screened the healthiest options for you. Some brands are "greener" than others. Always read the labels. Look for products containing natural and organic ingredients. For example, grapeseed oil is sometimes used as a preservative instead of parabens. You may see "paraben-free" on lotions and "Free of toluene and DBP" (dibutyl phthalate) right on the packaging.

- Speak Up: Support groups that are raising awareness, write letters, and sign petitions. Share your action on social media. And best of all, vote with your dollars, because the more we support companies doing the right thing, the sooner other companies will catch on.

The question of cost

Do less toxic cosmetics and body products generally cost more than the standard options? Not necessarily. Many are on par with the cost of products found in department stores. Physician's Formula, which sells in common drugstores, has developed a line of cosmetics called Organic Wear that is much more affordable than department store prices. It would be a good brand for teenagers who wish to experiment in terms of blushes, bronzing powders, and eye shadows.

Renowned author Naomi Wolf wrote the piece The Beauty Myth originally in 1991 (reissued in 2002) and pointed out that people, mostly women, spend $20 billion on cosmetics and body products every year. Some people would say women don't even really need makeup and it is an unnecessary and unfair cultural pressure that does not equally apply to men. So, I would say that this opinion is something to consider when evaluating what we really "need." If we do choose to wear makeup, then we can try to consider the environment and our health in the selection process. And this does apply to men as well—in the selection of shaving lotions, hair gels, colognes, and shampoos.

What are the safest, most eco-friendly alternatives?

Years ago, I went for a professional photo shoot with my work colleagues for a brochure about our organization. While sitting in the chair having makeup done by the photography studio aesthetician, I chatted with her about the natural makeup I usually wear. Her comment, as she brushed my eyelids from a large palette of colorful eye shadows, was that it sounded interesting but it seemed limiting. "They don't offer too many colors, do they?" she asked. I responded with an honest "No," and she shrugged it off as if to say, Oh, well, then forget it. Similarly, a guy cutting my hair at the local haircutting chain was offering me products from his shelf and when I explained why I'd rather use my natural products, he just said, "Oh, those natural products don't work."

In response to the two skeptics, I am happy to say that now more and more companies are providing natural products, including some high-end versions, and as the competition grows, the products keep improving. Now there is a larger selection to choose from and each successful brand keeps expanding its wares. Many small companies are emerging so there may be an opportunity for you to support a local business.

List of natural and organic cosmetic companies
Here are a few accessible brands available at the time of writing that take care to be as natural as possible, and even including organic ingredients. Note that many more are becoming available all the time at stores and online:

- Aubrey Organics – http://www.aubrey-organics.com
- Burt's Bees – http://www.burtsbees.com
- Dr. Hauschka – http://www.dr.hauschka.com/en_US
- Jane Iredale – https://janeiredale.com

- Jurlique – http://www.jurlique.com
- Kiss My Face – http://www.kissmyface.com
- Mineral Fusion – http://www.mineralfusion.com
- Sanre Organic Skinfood – https://www.sanreorganic.com
- Weleda – http://usa.weleda.com/index.aspx

Other resources: A full list of companies who signed the Compact for Safe Cosmetics, a standard for nontoxic ingredients established by the Campaign for Safe Cosmetics, by the year 2011 can be found here in the group's Market Shift report: http://safecosmetics.org/downloads/MarketShift_CSC_June15_2012.pdf

The Green Beauty Guide (2008) and Green Beauty Recipes (2013) both by Julie Gabriel.

Eco-Jewelry

Gia Machlin, President & CEO, EcoPlum

When it comes to eco-friendly jewelry, there are tons of options. It's a matter of paying attention to what jewelry is made of, and also finding trustworthy jewelry makers. As described in *Style, Naturally*, sustainable jewelry can be made from "recycled glass, recycled metal, sustainably harvested wood, bowling balls, and other crazy materials."[31] I have seen beautiful jewelry made from glazed paper beads, often made in Africa, by women who use old calendars or magazine pages and roll them into colorful beads. I own jewelry and a handbag made from repurposed soda can pop-tops, and a wristwatch made from tagua nut.

Tagua has a lovely cream luster, and has been used as an alternative to ivory (often made from illegally poached elephant tusks). Tagua is grown in South America and can be dyed to different colors. Thankfully in many boutiques around the country and certainly online, you can find all of these alternatives made by artisans who are very proud of their craft, and it feels good to support them.

---

31   Oakes, Summer Rayne. Style, Naturally: The Savvy Shopping Guide to Sustainable Fashion and Beauty. San Francisco: Chronicle Books, 2009, p.82.

Beware of Conflict Diamonds

While gold and diamond jewelry is beautiful, it comes with a dark side that they don't show us on commercials. Before looking in the jewelry case, consider this:

"In Sierra Leone, Angola, the Republic of Congo, Liberia and the Ivory Coast, the sale of conflict diamonds continues to thrive for many reasons. Rebels make large profits because they use free labor–they threaten villagers at gunpoint, forcing them to dig for diamonds. If villagers refuse to follow soldiers' orders, their limbs are amputated as punishment. Rebels sell the diamonds on the black market for less than other diamonds. Therefore, wholesalers make a bigger profit. The rebels use the money gained from the diamonds to fund wars."[32]— CNN

The UN has established the Kimberley Process to identify conflict-free diamonds that were obtained legitimately, but unfortunately it still does not prevent sale of unethical diamonds. And mining the earth for gold is equally perilous, for the environment and surrounding communities. The Smithsonian has reported:

- The majority of the world's gold is extracted from open pit mines, where huge volumes of earth are scoured away and processed for trace elements.

- To produce enough raw gold to make a single ring, 20 tons of rock and soil are dislodged and discarded.

- Much of this waste contains mercury and cyanide used to extract the gold from the rock, and the contaminated soil runs off clogging rivers.

- Air quality is also compromised by gold mining, which releases hundreds of tons of airborne elemental mercury every year, as well as sulfur dioxide.[33]

There is a No Dirty Gold campaign[34] to raise awareness, and fortunately there are companies making jewelry from recycled gold and diamonds. One such company is Brilliant Earth—they make wedding rings and high-end jewelry from sustainably and ethically sourced gold and silver, and diamonds from Canada, South Africa, Botswana, and Russia. Its stated mission is to cultivate a more ethical, transparent,

---

32   CNN ireport. Conflict Diamonds, The Uncut Truth. http://ireport.cnn.com/docs/DOC-881410.
33   Bland, Alsatair. Smithsonian.com. The Environmental Disaster That is the Gold Industry.
February 14, 2014.
34   No Dirty Gold. http://nodirtygold.earthworksaction.org/

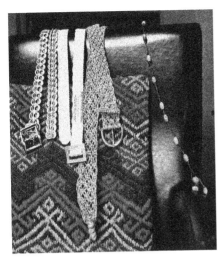

Eco-friendly accessories, including:
Belts: Walleska Ecochicc (soda can tabs), Nancy's Gone Green (vintage lace), Earth Divas (hemp)
Necklace: Handmade hemp wooden bead
Handbag: Plasticbagbag.com (upcycled plastic bags)
Flip flops (recycled or biodegradeable rubber), left to right: Planet Flops, Simple Shoes, Feelgoodz

and sustainable jewelry industry and to go above and beyond the Kimberley Process. Suppliers adhere to strict labor and environmental standards and can demonstrate a complete chain of custody for their gemstones. This company also uses recycled gold and platinum. The precious metals come from secondary sources and are refined. The company has funded a mobile school in a mining community in Congo to offset the negative effects of the mining and offer hope of other economic opportunity for students.

Everyone has a choice—we can purchase some of our jewelry from the nearest jeweler without asking important questions about the impacts each piece has caused, or we can choose to seek out companies that strive to make the effort to do right by people and the planet.

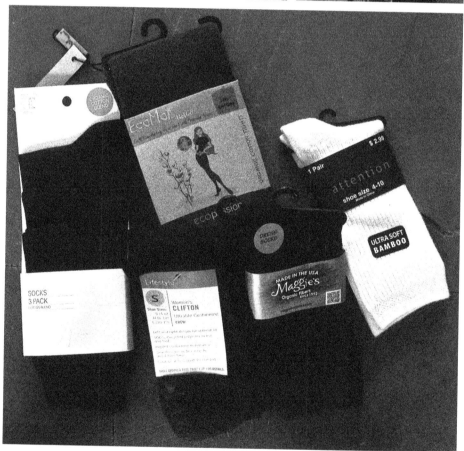

Top Left: bamboo frame sunglasses, Top Right: carbon neutral frames
Bottom: variety of bamboo and organic cotton socks

Chapter 9

Eco-Housewares
Don't Let the Bed Bite

By now you may be convinced that surrounding yourself in the delectable delights of eco-fabrics is a good way to go. Perhaps, does the thought of being surrounded by plastic-based fabrics now bring a slight wrinkle to your nose? If so, then you may want to think about where you spend about one third of the day (or night)—your bedroom.

What's wrong with your bedroom, you ask? Well, let's start with the bed. Since the dawn of our homo sapienhood, humans have used fire for both good and bad. It can be used to cook, but also to burn a house down. Because of the chance of fires in our homes either by arson or acts of nature, for many years the United States federal government has required fire retardants to be used in the manufacturing of mattresses and other furniture and appliances as part of its fire codes, according to the international nonprofit National Fire Protection Association (NFPA) 701 standards which have been in place for decades.[1]

The NFPA was established in 1896 to reduce the hazards of fire by providing and advocating codes and standards.[2] NFPA has tests that measure the flammability of a fabric when it is exposed to flame, to see how long it burns, and how much ash it leaves behind. Flame "resistant" means it will not melt or drop when exposed to extreme heat. Fabric certified as flame "retardant" is chemically treated to self-extinguish, and certified to have passed the relevant NFPA test.[3]

NFPA has various standards for fabrics depending on how they will be used. The standards apply to textile materials used extensively in interior furnishing for public buildings such as schools, churches, and theaters. In these places, curtains, window

1   National Fire Protection Association (NFPA). "NFPA 701: Standard Methods of Fire Tests for Flame Propagation of Textiles and Films, Current Edition: 2015." NFPA.org: Codes and Standards. 2015; National Fire Protection Association (NFPA). "About NFPA." NFPA.org. 2015.
2   Sew What? Inc. "Flame Retardancy: Navigating Flame Retardancy Regulations in the United States." SewWhatInc.com. 2015.
3   Sew What? Inc. "Facts on Flame Retardancy." SewWhatInc.com. 2015.

shades, table linens, textile wall hangings, as well as fabrics used in awnings, tents, tarps, and other similar architectural fabric structures must be certified flame retardant. This is a good thing on the one hand—in order to minimize the spread of fire—should your house be going up in flames.

The Triangle Waist Company fire of 1911 in Manhattan highlights the need for fire safety around fabrics.[4] A garment factory on the eighth through tenth floors, it is believed that the fire started there from a cigarette. Unfortunately, 146 people died because doors were locked to prevent stealing.

However, since the late 1990s, scientists have been finding that the chemicals used to retard the spread of fire might be bad for our health. The most commonly used fire retardants are PBDEs (polybrominated diphenyl ethers). They are mixed into textiles for curtains, foams, such as in cushions, and also into plastics, such as those used to make televisions and computer monitors, as well as hair blow dryers. According to the Alliance for a Clean and Healthy Maine, "Children and adults in the United States have ten to forty times more PBDEs in their bodies than people living in Europe or Japan, because the US is the largest consumer of PBDE flame retardants in the world."[5]

Interestingly, the ATSDR suggests, "Children living near hazardous waste sites should be discouraged from playing in the dirt near these sites. Children should also be discouraged from eating dirt and should wash their hands frequently." But what about the fact that they are sleeping in beds treated with chemicals?

That said, it is far more likely for people who work in an industry using these chemicals to be exposed to them than we are in our homes (depending on how far we live from any toxic waste sites), but as furniture and appliances age, particles can end up in dust that we (and our pets) breathe. This has been found to be a major route of exposure to people in their homes. PBDEs are persistent in the environment and tend to bioaccumulate in body tissues.

---

4   Cornell University: ILR School & Kheel Center. "Remembering: The 1911 Triangle Factory Fire." http://www.ilr.cornell.edu/trianglefire/. 2011.
5   Alliance for a Clean and Healthy Maine. "PBDEs – The Toxic Flame Retardants." CleanAndHealthyME.org. 2013.

Earthsake

Heart of Vermont
(organic cotton)

Sources say that fire retardants are linked to thyroid disorders and reproductive problems in animals and humans.[6] Studies in laboratory animals and humans have also linked PBDEs to memory and learning problems, delayed mental and physical development, lower IQ, advanced puberty, and reduced fertility.[7] However, according to the US Agency for Toxic Substances and Disease Registry (ATSDR), "There is no definite information on health effects of PBDEs in people. Rats and mice that ate food with moderate amounts of PBDEs for a few days had effects on the thyroid gland. Those that ate smaller amounts for weeks or months had effects on the thyroid and the liver."[8]

Studies have found PBDEs in women's breast tissue, as they tend to reside in fat tissue. They therefore also have been detected in breast milk and in the umbilical cords that link mother to baby. Though there is no proof of connection with breast cancer as of yet, as of 2004 the European Union and the US placed a ban on two of the major commercially used brominated flame retardants, called penta- and octa-BDEs as a precautionary measure.[9] As a result of growing awareness, there is a grassroots organization that has formed just to address this issue, called People for Clean Beds (See peopleforcleanbeds.org).

What about Other Furniture?

The issue of chemicals in our furniture goes beyond beds and beyond fire retardants. Furniture such as couches can contain other chemicals as well.

- Fabric may be dyed with chemical dyes (as we read about earlier) such as the carcinogenic chemical hydrazine, and also treated with formaldehyde.
- Polyurethane foam and adhesives may contain ethylene oxide, a probable carcinogen that can also cause brain and nerve malfunctions
- Resins, paints, and dyes may contain the solvent benzene, a carcinogen.
- Lacquers and the adhesives in pressed wood can off-gas VOCs (volatile organic compounds) that the American Lung Association reports can irritate

---

6   Williams, Florence. "My Ikea Couch Reeks of Chemicals: Why Are Flame Retardants Required in Furniture, Anyway?" Slate.com: DoubleX Health. June 21, 2010.
7   Gross, Liza. "Flame Retardants in Consumer Products Are Linked to Health and Cognitive Problems." The Washington Post, April 15, 2013. Health & Science section.
8   Agency for Toxic Substances and Disease Registry (ATSDR). "ToxFAQs™for Polybrominated Diphenyl Ethers (PBDEs)." ATSDR.CDC.gov. September 2004.
9   Gross, Liza. "Flame Retardants in Consumer Products Are Linked to Health and Cognitive Problems." The Washington Post, April 15, 2013. Health & Science section.

eyes, skin, and lungs and cause headaches, nausea, and even liver and kidney damage.

- Regular vinyl, or polyvinyl chloride (PVC), used in the making of some furniture, is a carcinogen that can cause liver damage with chronic exposure."[10]

Carpets—Hazards Beneath Our Feet?

Carpet is another source of indoor contamination. From the production of synthetic carpet to its installation, there are toxins and hazardous chemicals used at nearly every step of the process. Most carpets are made from fibers derived from petroleum. Synthetic fibers are usually made up of nylon, polypropylene or polyester. All three are created by similar chemical processes using oil and natural gas. They are bonded to their backings with adhesive, and may be treated with bleaches, dyes, stain protectants, and antistatic solutions. Add to this mixture antibacterial and antifungal agents, as well as chemical baths containing substances like chlorine and bromine to render the carpet nonflammable. That "new carpet" smell is therefore volatile organic compounds (VOCs).[11]

Carpet can be a repository for chemicals such as pesticides tracked in on shoes, and can harbor dust and dust mites. Cigarette smoke and chemicals like those released from air deodorizers typically settle in carpeting so become part of your indoor environment.[12] Once there, they can stick to carpeting for quite a while, until released over time.[13]

So what are better options?

Luckily, as more awareness of these issues grows, entrepreneurial companies are ready to provide alternatives.

Beds

A simple search on the Internet can provide a list of mattress options that do not incorporate PBDE flame retardants. Instead, they use borate as the fire retardant,

---

10   Fornoff, Susan. "What's in Furniture? It's Enough To Make You Sick: Labels, Certification Could Bring a Breath of Fresh Air to Consumers Who Can't Tolerate the Toxic Emissions." SFGate.com. October 24, 2007.

11   Keith, Cristie. "Carpet of Chemicals: Is There an Alternative?" PurelyPets.com: Wellness Center – Health Alerts. 2002.

12   US Consumer Product Safety Commission (CPSC). "The Inside Story: A Guide to Indoor Air Quality." CSPC.gov: Safety Education > Safety Guides. 2015.

13   Corsi, Richard. "Chemicals in Carpet Can Linger Long After Exposure." ScienceBlog.com/community. October 4, 2000.

which is not harmful when used in this way since it is not volatile. Wool can also be used as alternative because it is naturally flame resistant. Due to its particular chemical composition, it has a high ignition temperature.[14] Wool, however, would not be as appealing to vegans (read the deal on wool production in chapter 5). Also, some wool is also treated with chemicals if it is not organic. Note that some states require a doctor's note stating a health requirement to allow for the exemption from standard chemical fire retardants.

One exciting alternative being made by several companies is a wide range of mattresses made with organic cotton. They come in various types and sizes, from single to king. You can also find futons stuffed with organic cotton. I have one in my own house.

An organic mattress should be certified by the Global Organic Textile Standard (GOTS). GOTS certification requires that all processing stages through manufacturing of the finished product take place in GOTS-certified facilities, and all traders involved in the supply chain be certified to GOTS as well. "Manufacturers may not claim that their products are GOTS-certified if only certain components (such as batting or fabric) are certified to the standard."[15]

Various companies make organic cotton mattresses and futons, including:

- A Happy Planet (www.ahappyplanet.com)
- Earthsake (www.earthsake.com)
- EcoChoices (www.ecochoices.com)
- EcoMattress Store (www.eco-mattress-store.com)
- Lifekind (www.lifekind.com)
- Mountain Air Organic Beds (www.mountainairorganicbeds.com)
- Rawganique (www.rawganique.com)
- White Lotus Home (www.whitelotushome.com)

There are also variations of organic cotton mattresses that include mixtures of organic cotton with other natural materials or fibers, such as wool, and natural rubber.

---

14   International Wool Textile Organisation (IWTO). "Wool and Flame Resistance: Fact Sheet." IWTO.org. 2013.
15   Organic Trade Association (OTA). "What is an Organic Mattress?" OTA.com. 2011.

Natural rubber is derived from latex, which is produced by several species of trees in response to a cut in the bark. This is as opposed to synthetic rubber, which is made from petroleum. (As a side note, spandex is also synthetically made.) There are even memory foam mattresses made of natural rubber.[16]

You can also find fully natural rubber mattresses and bed toppers, and mattresses made of mixtures including rubber or wool. Some of the companies making natural rubber mattresses include the above list as well as:

- A Happy Planet (www.ahappyplanet.com)
- Eco Sleep Solutions (www.ecosleepsolutions.com)
- Good Night Naturals (www.goodnightnaturals.com)
- Natural Mattress World (www.naturalmattressworld.com)
- Pure Rest Organics (www.purerest.com)
- Savvy Rest (www.savvyrest.com)
- The Natural Sleep Store (www.thenaturalsleepstore.com)

While not yet using organic materials, Swedish home furnishings company IKEA says it aims to use more sustainably sourced materials, including 100 percent recycled polyester fibers within five years, and is also modifying its fiber material blends to ensure easier fiber separation at a product's end-of-life.[17]

> **NOTE:** Reducing chemical exposures is especially important for babies. Flame retardants are used in nursing pillows, cribs, changing pads, and stroller seats, especially in anything containing polyurethane foam.[18] "Scientists have found evidence suggesting that chemicals designed to prevent fires are getting into your children's blood and rewiring their brains, leading to attention deficit disorder, hyperactivity, hearing problems, slow mental development and, possibly, cancer. They're not great for adults either—men with high blood levels of flame retardants had a decreased sperm count, and women took longer to conceive—but because children's nervous systems are still

---

16   Essentia. http://www.myessentia.com. 2013.
17   Ikea. "Energy and Resources: We're creating positive changes." 2016. http://www.ikea.com/ms/en_US/this-is-ikea/people-and-planet/energy-and-resources/#waste
18   Sohn, Emily. "Baby Products Loaded With Toxins." News.Discovery.com: Human > Life. May 18, 2011.

developing, they are even more vulnerable."[19]

See the Appendix B for green baby solutions and resources.

Eco-Bedding and Towels

Currently, it is not difficult to find organic cotton sheets and bathroom towels, as well as pillows stuffed with organic cotton, buckwheat, or natural rubber. An internet search will turn up numerous sources for organic cotton bedding and towels from green-oriented companies. They can be found through some of the same online sources listed above, at specialty boutiques, and online through websites such as:

- Coyuchi (https://www.coyuchi.com/)
- Earth Linens (http://www.earthlinens.com/)
- In2Green (https://www.in2green.com/)
- Boll & Branch (https://www.bollandbranch.com/)
- Under the Canopy (http://underthecanopy.com/)

However the least expensive, most mainstream place I have found to obtain them is at Target. They intermittently sell sets of organic sheets in appealing colors that have a sateen finish, and also full sets of bath towels of varying colors and good quality. Bed Bath and Beyond and Macy's carry organic cotton bedding by Under the Canopy.

Since it is still much more common to find towels and sheets that are not organic, you may wonder whether it's worth it to bother with such items. When it comes to sheets and pillows, remember that you are sleeping on them and both the material and the chemical dyes and treatments come in contact with your skin, face, and respiratory system. Most common pillows are filled with synthetic materials such as polyester or polyurethane foam, sometimes as pellets.[20] Many common sheets are treated with formaldehyde to alleviate wrinkles.

You use towels to dry your skin off after a shower. While this may not be a huge route of exposure to chemicals in the grand scheme of things, I see this as a great way to support organic farming. It's also a great conversation piece when you have guests.

---

19   Kaplan, Sheila. "The Posion Crib: When Protective Chemicals Harm." Salon.com. June 10, 2010.

20   Boys, Jami. "Understanding Filler Materials: Polyfil, Pellets, Mircobeads, Beanbag Filler, Foam & More." Sew4Home.com: Tips & Resources > Buying Guide. September 3, 2009.

In addition to organic cotton, towels can be made from hemp. Sheets and bathroom towels can also be made from bamboo (see chapters 2 and 3). I own some of each. The bamboo sheets I have seen have had a lovely satin-like sheen to them and a soft flowing texture, not quite, but almost, like silk sheets. The one drawback I have found is that since they do not contain chemicals to deter wrinkles, they may require some time with your iron, if you are the type to worry about such things. (Yes, I have a friend who does indeed iron her sheets.)

Remember that down pillows and comforters, as comfy and insulating as they may be, come with an ethical price. Down feathers come from ducks and geese, and are the soft layer of feathers closest to the bird's skin. Depending on the country the birds are raised in, the feathers are either plucked after slaughter, or sometimes while the animal is still alive, causing considerable pain and open wounds.[1]

1   Hickman, Matt. "Down Comforters: Animal Cruelty Dependent Upon Where You Buy." HuffingtonPost.com: Huff Post Green. January 23, 2012.

Bamboo sheets can be purchased online from:
- Cariloha (http://www.cariloha.com)
- Greenearthbamboo (http://greenearthbamboo.com)
- Greener Country (http://www.greenercountry.com)
- Luxury Bamboo Bedding (https://luxurybamboobedding.com)

The company Looolo, based out of Canada, makes textiles that are made to be fully biodegrade at the end of their useful life. They use certified organic materials and only dyes that are free of toxic chemicals.[21]

Eco-Furniture
Numerous companies sell eco-friendly furniture that does not include the chemicals mentioned above. For example, some companies make sofas using organic materials and natural latex. Many of these sell in boutique furniture stores while some are more mainstream. A list of over 200 of such companies can be found on the Sustainable Furnishings Council website (http://www.sustainablefurnishings.org). The LEED

21   Fletcher, Kate. *Sustainable Fashion & Textiles: Design Journeys*, 96. London: Earthscan, 2008. http://www.looolo.ca/truesustainability.html.

(Leadership in Energy and Environmental Design) certification program established by the US Green Building Council is helping to advance the market and availability of less toxic furnishings. One label to look for on products is Greenguard, which is a certification system ranking products' eco-friendliness.[22]

ECO-TIP: While not the focus of this book, it should be mentioned that there are numerous companies that sell furniture made from repurposed materials of all kinds, which can be very creative. Many artisans make furniture of reclaimed wood from barns, for example. You can also find furniture made of recycled materials such as recycled plastic, all of which keeps usable materials out of the landfill.

Eco-Flooring

Consider carpet alternatives: tile, bamboo, cork, or wood flooring with throw rugs. Rugs can be made of natural materials such as hemp, jute, and sisal. Jute is a vegetable fiber that is also used to make burlap, and sisal is actually the fiber from the agave plant. (There are almost 200 species of agave, a native succulent from Central America. Certain species can be used for sweeteners, as well as to make tequila—very versatile plant!) One mainstream store that sells some rugs made of natural materials such as jute, sisal, and seagrass is Pottery Barn.

Companies like EarthWeave.com focus on creating furnishings that are less toxic. "Earth Weave is the premier North American manufacturer of all natural, nontoxic carpet, area rugs, and padding. Bio-Floor™ is quickly becoming the concerned consumer's floor-covering of choice. Our products are made using undyed, untreated wool on the face, along with hemp, cotton, jute, and natural rubber for the backing materials."In response to market demand, the Carpet and Rug Institute (CRI) has created a Green Label to "ensure that customers are purchasing the lowest emitting carpet, adhesive, and cushion products on the market."[23]

ECO-Renovation TIP: There are some green stores now that are competing with big-box hardware chain stores and carry paints, building supplies, and furnishings that are less toxic. Two examples are GreenDepot in Brooklyn, NY[24] and Eco Home

---

22   Greenguard Certification from UL Environment. www.greenguard.org. 2015.
23   The Carpet and Rug Institute, Inc. "Green Label Plus: A Higher Standard For Indoor Air Quality." Carpet-Rug.org: CRI Testing Programs. 2015.
24   Green Depot. http://www.greendepot.com/. 2013.

Improvement in Berkeley, CA.[25] While these products can sometimes cost a bit more, it is worth looking into, especially when renovating or furnishing children's rooms. For offices, look for carpet that comes in carpet tiles, so that only worn down or dirty sections need to be replaced instead of the whole carpet. This concept was pioneered by the carpet company Interface, which also takes used carpet back for recycling.[26]

So, while it may take a little more research, you do have the ability to complete your green wardrobe with at least "greener" furniture, bedding, and flooring as well. By doing this you are not only helping to reduce toxins brought into your bedroom and living space, but you are also encouraging sustainable practices to become mainstream industrywide.

25   Ecohome Improvement LLC. http://www.ecohomeimprovement.com/. 2015.
26   Interface, Inc. "Our Sustainability Journey – Mission Zero." InterfaceGlobal.com: Sustainability. 2008.

Conclusion

Awareness Trends and the Future of EcoFashion

I hope this book has provided a broad look at the promising growth of eco-friendly fabrics for apparel, as well as some greener, healthier options for personal care and houseware items.

There are many things needed for eco-fashion to move forward and take its rightful place in the mainstream norm. Here are some suggestions:

- There needs to be far more attention paid to the environmental impacts, the wearer's health, and garment workers' conditions by all involved in clothing—both from the supply and demand side. From producers to consumers, we must begin embracing a more planet-friendly and human rights ethic as an important part of the production of clothing. Mindsets need to change towards seeing items in a "cradle to cradle" context, meaning thinking about where a product comes from, how it will be produced and then used, and finally, where it will end up. Understandably, many manufacturers do not want to take the risk of using unconventional fabrics if they fear their extra efforts will be unappreciated by consumers. This is the reason for this book—education and inspiration! The Food and Agriculture (FAO) of the United Nations declared 2009 the "International Year of Natural Fibres" to help raise awareness.[1] One important way for change to happen is to educate future consumers about sustainability issues from early on in school, and to educate up-and-coming fashion professionals about issues of sustainability right from the start while they are studying in fashion school. Sustainability studies should be a mandatory aspect of fashion school curriculum. For example, Fashion Institute of Technology and Parsons Institute in NYC now offer classes in sustainability. The Brooklyn Fashion + Design

---

[1]   United Nations: Food and Agriculture Organization (UN FAO). "Welcome: International Year of Natural Fibres." NaturalFibres2009.org/en. 2009.

Accelerator[2] considers itself a hub for ethical fashion, and there is a Center for Sustainable Fashion in London.[3]

Though it is just starting, hopefully we will continue to see more coverage of sustainable fashion in popular fashion magazines like Vogue, Cosmopolitan, Glamour, and others. It is also helpful to have celebrity involvement from those who have shown interest in sustainability to keep associating green with glamour. Woody Harrelson has worn a hemp suit on multiple occasions over the past decade, including the Oscars in 2010.[4] In fact he is part-owner of a hemp-clothing company.[5] Jessica Alba has also become a spokesperson for chemical-free living. Making sustainability desirable is key. Companies will create more clothing with natural materials if they know customers will buy it.

- Awareness and promotion of standards should be increased. For example:

  o The Global Organic Textile Standard (GOTS), created by the England-based Soil Association. This standard guarantees that cotton is not grown with synthetic pesticides and fertilizers, is not processed with certain chemicals, and is not manufactured in sweatshops. The standards do not allow certain solvents, pentachlorophenol, formaldehyde, and certain heavy metals.[6] The number of facilities certified by GOTS in sixty-three countries is 4642.[7] As of 2011, twenty US companies were certified by GOTS,[8] and as of 2017 there are fifty.[9]

  o The Bluesign® standard is a Restricted Substances List (RSL) that excludes dyes and other substances that are potentially hazardous to the human health or the environment.[10] Many companies were

2   Brooklyn Fashion + Design Accelerator. http://bkaccelerator.com. 2016.
3   Center for Sustainable Fashion. http://sustainable-fashion.com. 2016.
4   US Weekly. "Woody Harrelson Wears Hemp Tux to the Oscars." USMagazine.com: News. March 7, 2010.
5   Notable Names Database (NNDB). "Woody Harrelson." NNDB.com. 2014.
6   Fletcher, Kate. Sustainable Fashion & Textiles: Design Journeys, 50. London: Earthscan, 2008.
7   Global Organic Textile Standard (GOTS) International Working Group. Global Organic Textile Standard: Ecology & Social Responsibility, Annual Report 2016." Global-Standard.org. 2017.
8   Carpenter, Susan. "Cotton That's Kinder to the Planet." Los Angeles Times, June 19, 2011.
9   The Organic Report. "Fifty U.S. companies certified to GOTS." organicreport.org. January 2017.
10   Bluesign Technologies AG. http://www.bluesign.com. 2013.

coming up with their own such lists but there was no one standard for the industry. So an independent Swiss company put together this web-based database to make it easier for companies to follow a greener supply chain, and if they adhere to the system the company is able to use the Bluesign label. The system is based on the principles of resource use, consumer safety, water and air emissions, and occupational health and safety. Some brand-name Bluesign partners include Eileen Fisher, Patagonia, Marmot, Nike, and Puma.[11]

o The International Organization for Standardization (ISO) has expressed interest in developing standards for a labeling system to identify garments that met criteria as environmentally friendly.[12]

o The European Union's Oeko-Tex Standard 100 is a chemical testing and certification program established in 1992 that gives the textile and clothing industry information on the potential harm of substances from raw materials to finished products.[13] By paying a verification fee for lab testing and audits, companies wishing to avoid harmful chemicals can have their products certified with Oeko-Tex's "Confidence in Textiles" label. Oeko-Tex also provides a list of already certified source materials and in 2015 launched The World Apparel & Footwear Life Cycle Assessment Database (WALDB).

The European Union (EU) in general is taking concrete steps towards more transparency—in 2015, they passed a resolution mandating textile reporting especially focused on trade with Bangladesh, and also supporting sustainable garment initiatives

---

11   Bluesign. "How to Find It." Bluesign.com: Consumer. 2013.
12   Claudio, Luz. "Waste Couture: Environmental Impact of the Clothing Industry." *Environmental Health Perspectives* 115. no. 9 (2007): 449-454.
13   OEKO-TEX Association. "OEKO-TEX Standard 100." Oeko-Tex.com: Manufacturers > Concept. 2015.

within several of its member countries.[14] It is also considering bans on some chemicals in textiles sold in the EU.

o Another European label is Eko-Skal.[15] Skal is an independent inspection body for organic production in the Netherlands that strives to ensure that organic products truly originate from an organic production process by means of inspection and certification.[16]

o Not specific to the textile industry, the US EPA has established principles of "Green Chemistry." The principles guide "the design of chemical products and processes that reduce or eliminate the use or generation of hazardous substances. Green chemistry applies across the life cycle of a chemical product, including its design, manufacture, and use."[17] So, if a company is not using organic cotton but adheres to Green Chemistry principles, at least the cotton that is produced will have fewer environmental impacts associated with it.

For the past nineteen years EPA's Office of Chemical Safety and Pollution Prevention has sponsored an annual Presidential Green Chemistry Challenge Awards. Several of the awardees have included companies that are creating either more eco-friendly fabrics or less hazardous substances to replace existing toxic chemicals that can be used in the fiber production process. For example, Novozymes North America won an award for producing enzymes that remove cotton wax. This is a much milder alternative to using sodium hydroxide, chelating agents, and acetic acid, as mentioned earlier in chapter 1.

• The Clean Clothes Campaign has also created an ethical clothing model code that focuses on living wages for workers, no child labor, and reasonable working

---

14   Mowbray, John. "EU resolution backs mandatory textile reporting." Ecotextile News. http://www.ecotextile.com/2015061221527/labels-legislation-news/eu-resolution-backs-mandatory-textile-reporting.html. June 12, 2015.
15   Skal Biocontrole. "About Skal." Skal.nl. 2015.
16   Organic Lifestyle. "Buy Smart When Going Green." OrganicLifeStyle.com: Articles. 2015.
17   US Environmental Protection Agency (EPA). "Green Chemistry." EPA.gov. July 10, 2015.

hours.[18] They are also urging brand name companies to be more transparent about in what conditions their apparel is manufactured.

- Designers buy fabrics without easily being able to know each item's impacts. To change this, there needs to be efforts made on systems of disclosure. This means keeping track, perhaps via a universal database program, of where items originate and where they go along the supply chain, since materials may pass through several hands before they reach the consumer. A design company may be in Italy, but the cotton was grown in India and treated in China. It is difficult to trace what a fabric or dye might be made of unless records are kept at each step. Designers, or owners and management of design teams, should be able to find out what chemicals are in the fabrics they are using so they can make good choices for their collections. Ideally, some basic information could be made available to the public, perhaps through a ranking system on the label or a smartphone app.

- Organically raised fibers should be identified on clothing labels sold in the US with a US Department of Agriculture (USDA) symbol if they indeed have been produced in a manner that satisfies US organic standards. A similar symbol used on organic foods could be used for clothing. Consumers should have a

18   Clean Clothes Campaign. "What We Believe In: The Principles of Clean Clothes Campaign's Work." CleanClothes.org: About. 2015.

right to know more about what they're buying and who is accountable. Write to the USDA and urge for this change.

- In addition to more production of sustainable fabrics, designers also need to know how and where to find them. Summer Rayne Oakes, an eco-model and author of "Style, Naturally," cofounded Source4Style (now Le Souk), a business that helps match green designers with suppliers of eco-textiles. Pickering International (picknatural.com), begun in San Francisco in 1992, is another great source of multiple eco-fabrics.

- We also must realize that the world is not perfect, so we may find fabrics that are plant-based but dyed with s, or made from polyester in a plant that at least was using renewable energy and recycles all its waste. There are certainly gradations of green, and we as consumers can and must do our best to make the best choices given all the varying, and sometimes confusing, factors. Whatever we do, we are voting with our dollars, so we must help drive the fashion industry in the right direction. When you see a company doing less than they could be, write to them. When you find a company striving to do things right, support them.

More organizations working to bring about change

- Textile Exchange:[19] Texas-based organization that holds international textile conferences, provides resources, helps develop markets for organic cotton farmers, and advocates for industry integrity. They offer an "Organic 100 Content Standard," a "Recycled 100 Claim Standard," and a "Responsible Down Standard." They issue an "Organic Cotton Report" and a "Preferred Fibers Market Report."

- Sustainable Apparel Coalition:[20] San Francisco-based coalition of global apparel and footwear companies seeking to address sustainability issues through broad adoption of the Higg Index, a measurement tool used by hundreds of companies to evaluate the environmental and social performance of apparel and footwear.

---

19   Textile Exchange. http://www.textileexchange.org. 2015.
20   Sustainable Apparel Coalition. "The Higg Index: Overview." ApparelCoalition.org. 2015.

- Zero Discharge of Hazardous Chemicals (ZDHC): [21] "In 2011, a group of major apparel and footwear brands and retailers made a shared commitment to help lead the industry towards zero discharge of hazardous chemicals by 2020." Members include Adidas, H&M, Esprit, Benetton, Gap, Marks & Spencer, Nike, and Puma.

- Sustainable Fashion Business Consortium (SFBC):[22] "A group of Hong Kong-based companies in the textile and apparel sector committed to promoting and increasing the use of sustainable practices across the fashion supply chain."

- RITE Group:[23] a British-based nonprofit organization dedicated to reducing the impact of textiles on the environment by increasing awareness across the global apparel supply chain. It organizes an annual conference and has a goal of developing clear ways of communicating 'green' information to consumers.

New Trends

Reducing, Reusing, Upcycling
In addition to choosing the eco-friendly fabrics described within, there are other creative choices we can make to green our wardrobe. Though it does require a shift in awareness since fast fashion has contributed to making inexpensive clothing so accessible, if we want to be "green wardrobers," any clothing that is in good condition should never be thrown in the garbage. If you can't fix things yourself, there is usually a tailor at your local dry cleaner. Whether clothing is made from natural or synthetic fibers, it has value and contains embodied energy and resources. This fact provides the underlying basis for a shift in attitude towards a willingness to reuse existing garments, either as-is or in new forms. Clothing cycling through thrift stores, consignment shops, vintage stores, and swapping programs help save resources.

On the production side, many companies are now also looking at how to reduce waste—15 percent of fabric is left on the cutting room floor and goes to waste.[24]

---

21   Zero Discharge of Hazardous Chemicals (ZDHC). http://www.roadmaptozero.com. 2015.
22   Sustainable Fashion Business Consortium (SFBC). http://www.sfbc.org.hk. 2015.
23   Reducing the Impact of Textiles on the Environment (RITE) Group. http://www.ritegroup.org. 2015.
24   Rosenbloom, Stephanie. "Fashion Tries on Zero Waste Design." *New York Times*, August 13, 2010, Fashion & Style sec.

Consignment/Thrift

Instead of just tossing a garment when we get bored with it, we can bring it to a consignment shop where they will sell it as long as it is in good condition and you get a small sum of money back. This is especially an option for higher-end clothing. Thrift stores tend to accept a wider range of clothing as long as it's in decent condition but these are for donation. Thrift shops can be great for people with children who outgrow clothing rapidly. It's always good to support local shops, but if you don't have a consignment shop or thrift store in your community, there are online options like eBay, Etsy, and Threadflip. If you're into vintage clothing, see rustyzipper.com or monstervintage.com — and both include menswear.

Leasing

For renting dresses, there is RenttheRunway.com, but what if we could lease clothing like we lease a car? Some companies are creating leasing programs so we can have a continual series of up-to-date clothing items, only this time you don't own them. Clothing is leased monthly for a certain period of time and then can either be returned or purchased. When an item becomes unusable, it is taken out of circulation, but may have served three, five, or ten people. This model could be used for anything from jeans to prom dresses. One example is Europe-based Mud jeans.[25]

Upcycling

The definition of "upcycling" is "the practice of taking something that would otherwise be disposed of and transforming it into something of greater use and value."[26] Like Julie Andrews showed us in the Sound of Music, curtains due to be tossed could become playclothes for seven children. A more modern example of this is Patty O Designs—she takes used blue jeans and mixes the denim with other fabrics to create tote bags.[27] Her popular original design bore the slogan "These are my ex's jeans.™" Several companies now repurpose billboards into tote bags, including Billboard Ecology[28] and Gorilla Sacks.[29]

25   MUD Jeans. http://www.mudjeans.eu. 2015.
26   Kane, Ashley. "Upcycling." About.com: About Style > Vintage Clothing > Glossary/FAQs. 2015.
27   Patricia Ordonez Sustainable Designs. http://www.pattyodesigns.com. 2009.
28   Billboard Ecology. http://www.billboardecology.com. 2015.
29   Gorilla Sacks. http://www.gorillasacks.com. 2015.

Other cool examples are:

- Looptworks: airplane seats into bags[30]
- Remade USA by Shannon South: leather jackets into handbags[31]
- Sword & Plough: employs veterans and makes bags from military surplus fabric[32]
- The Good Wardrobe: (UK) resource for upcyclers[33]
- The Reformation: factory where clothing is made clothes from sustainable materials, repurposed vintage clothing and rescued dead-stock fabric from fashion houses that overordered

Upcycling is a positive trend that is now the subject of many blog posts, books, posts on Pinterest, and even the focus of a nonprofit organization in New Mexico called Upcycled Fashion.[34]

Clothing Customization

What about out-of the box thinking whereby instead of consumers just buying what designers provide them in stores, they actually take an active role in creating their own clothes? For example, what if you saw a shirt you liked but didn't like the collar? Clothing stores could have areas set up in their stores whereby you could rent a sewing machine and alter it there and then. This way, the store still makes money and you get to be creative, customize your piece, and feel more connected to the clothing and how it is made without having to own your own sewing machine.

30   Looptworks. http://www.looptworks.com. 2015.
31   Remade USA By Shannon South. http://remadeusa.shannonsouth.com. 2013.
32   Sword & Plough, LLC. http://www.swordandplough.com. 2015.
33   The Good Wardrobe. http://www.thegoodwardrobe.com. 2015.
34   Upcycled Fashion and Accessories. http://www.upcycledfashion.com. 2015.

These sewing areas could also provide places to repair clothing if it gets torn, and become social areas too whereby you can share creative ideas with others. The green aspect of this, is that you are less likely to just throw away a piece of clothing that you tailored yourself, and also a bit slower to devalue an item that doesn't fit anymore or becomes damaged—you might think about fixing it instead of throwing it away.

Clothing Swaps

Clothing swapping is becoming a popular trend among those who want to keep their wardrobes fresh but also don't want to spend a lot on new items that they only wear once or twice. Businesses have formed around this concept of trading clothing with others in on city or even beyond. Some swaps are done in person so are a way of socializing with others, and other swaps are carried out online.

Some examples of clothing swaps are:

- Swap Style: (global) longest running and features high quality and vintage items—http://www.swapstyle.com
- Clothing Swap: (San Francisco) arranges organized in-person clothing swaps and donates unclaimed items to local charities. Their tagline: "Be good. Be green. Be glam!" – http://www.clothingswap.com

A great resource to find out if there are local swaps happening near where you live is clothing swap "Meetup" (http://www.meetup.com) groups. As of early 2015, the clothing swap Meetups website had ninety-four groups and 13,300 members in seventy-five cities in fourteen countries. More than half of the Meetup groups are in the United States. If you don't see one near where you live, host one! This is a fun way to give your clothing a second life and meet other people interested in fashion.

A Word on Clothing Donation

Some nonprofits such as the Salvation Army, Goodwill, and other social justice organizations may have clothing donation bins set up around your community for clothing that is good quality and still in wearable condition. Some of this clothing goes to the organization's thrift store, which helps keeps clothing out of landfills longer and helps support people in need of affordable clothing. However, not all of donated clothing makes the cut, and much of it gets tossed. A recent problem is the existence of large stockpiles of discarded fast fashion that isn't good enough quality to resell.

There definitely needs to be a better distribution system to get usable donated clothing to those in need.

Textile Recycling

Clothing that is not in good enough condition to donate or repair has started to become a solid waste problem for municipalities. So, some towns and cities offer textile-recycling programs. Some retailers also are starting to accept textiles for recycling, such as H&M.[35] New York City's Grow NYC program states,"5.7% of NYCs residential waste stream consists of textiles like clothing and towels. All told, New Yorkers discard 193,000 tons of textiles every year in NYC, at a cost to taxpayers and our environment."[36] As a result, the city has made it easier for people to recycle their fabrics and put landfills "on a diet." Textiles including clothing and bedding, shoes, handbags, and belts can be dropped off weekly at several Greenmarkets around New York City, and the locations are listed online. Materials are sorted and then sold for direct reuse or to recycling markets that turn materials into wiping rags, or fiber for car seats and insulation. It doesn't get much better than that, and in this case donations are tax deductible.

ॐ ॐ ॐ ॐ

We live in exciting times where information is more readily at our fingertips via the internet, so I think people will start questioning more and more how products are made and where they end up. For example, for the first few years of computer technology no one thought about how computers were made or where they ended up. Now, most people are aware that computers and cell phones can contain toxins and heavy metals, and many municipalities provide "e-cycling" programs to facilitate proper disposal of electronic devices. I think that, like knowing the farmer who produced your food, there is a satisfaction and a different relationship with a clothing item once you know how it was produced, with what fabric and dyes, and in what type of conditions.

So, though ecofashion may have a ways to go in terms of being more convenient and affordable, the main obstacle to its broader acceptance in the market is awareness. But, thankfully, that is starting to change.

---

35   H&M Hennes & Mauritz AB. "H&M Conscious." HM.com. 2015.
36   GrowNYC. "Clothing is Not Garbage: Greenmarket Clothing Collection." GrowNYC.org: Recycling > Recycling Resources. 2015.

I hope that those who read this book will share what they've read with others and collectively, over time, spread the message that, just like what you eat and what you drive matters, what you wear matters to human health and our environment, too. As I write, we have exceeded a human population of 7 billion. Eventually as we all continue to use the earth's resources, some more than others, the environment may force the necessity for fashion to be more eco-friendly rather than just be a cool thing to do for those who care. Let's do what we can now so it never gets to that point. Let's instead create a world of closets filled with eco-friendly clothing made by fairly paid workers, without toxins in our environment.

Stay current by reading these ecofashion blogs:

- Ecouterre[37] (Jill Fehrenbacher and Jasmin Malik Chua, editors)
- Eco-chick.com[38] (Starre Vartan, editor)
- Eco Fashion World[39] (Magaly Fuentes, editor)
- MCL Global's EcoTextile News (e-newsletter and www.ecotextile.com)

---

37   Ecouterre. http://www.Ecouterre.com. 2016.
38   Ecochick. http://eco-chick.com. 2016.
39   Ecofashion World. http://www.EcofashionWorld.com. 2016.

Interview: Jasmin Malik Chua, Editor, Ecouterre

1)   What in your background led you to get into this movement? What drew you to want to promote sustainable fabrics and eco-fashion?

I have a bachelor's degree in animal biology and a master's degree in biomedical journalism. My passion for wildlife conservation, science, and medicine led me to TreeHugger, where I was first exposed to some of the issues plaguing the fashion industry. At the time—this was eight, nine years ago—they weren't problems that were widely known and certainly news to me. My interest was piqued and I took it upon myself to learn more and share what I knew.

2)   Tell us about Ecouterre—what is its purpose and mission?

We're the leading website on sustainable fashion, particularly in the United States. Our goal is to shine a light on some of the more unsavory aspects of the fashion industry and imbue the consumer with a sense of empowerment that what they choose to buy (or not buy) can make a difference. Our audience also includes fashion designers and other influencers in that space, so we also dive into discoveries that might be helpful, such as a cool, new eco-fabric or a new transparency labeling system. We'd also like to be more carrot than stick, so we showcase labels that are out there swimming against the tide with responsibility as one of their chief aims.

3)   What do you think is the most important thing the fashion world needs to keep in mind as we move into the future? Where do you see the ecofashion/ sustainable clothing movement going in the future?

I think all the recycling technology in the world won't help us if we're not doing anything about our consumption. It's simply untenable and if I had my druthers, the slow-fashion movement that we're glimpsing will become the norm.

4)   What would sustain the ecofashion movement and help it grow? What must people/consumers and/or designers and manufacturers do to ensure ecofashion's success?

Transparency and innovation are both key. Transparency to open up the supply chains and uproot endemic problems like child and forced labor and opaque environmental policies, and innovation to create ways of doing things better, whether it's reconstituting waste materials into good-as-virgin fibers or wastewater treatment to clean up factory effluent.

5)   Should it scale up and become more affordable—that is, be available at Wal-Mart?

While I believe that fashion should be attainable, mass-produced, cheap wares, no matter how sustainably made, will still trap us in a cycle of consumption and disposal. We need to buy less, invest in quality, and love what we own. A quality $60 shoe, for instance will stand us in better stead than six cheaply made $10 shoes and, in the long run, cost us less to maintain and replace.

6)   What have you found are some of the most exciting things happening in the world of ecofashion—for example, new fabrics, novel ideas, new policies?

Many fashion companies are talking about "closing the loop" and developing "circular economies." We need to take a cradle-to-cradle approach with product design, rather than cradle to grave, i.e. landfill.

7)   Who are some of your favorite people involved in ecofashion—designers, activists, or otherwise—that you think deserve more recognition?

I'm a big fan of the scrappy outfits that may not have the scale of an H&M or Levi's but are pushing the dial forward in their own way. A lot of the best works I've seen are from fashion students—they haven't had limits placed on them and they're willing to expand beyond typical parameters. These are the people who use bacteria to dye silk or make jewelry out of smog particles. You definitely wouldn't see that at your local Gap.

8)   Anything else you would like to share with readers?

No matter your budget, buy the best quality you can afford so that your garment will last you for years to come. Less is definitely more.

EcoFashion Store List

The main question I get asked when I tell people I'm wearing eco-friendly clothing is, "Where do you get it?" Within this book we have mentioned some of the larger retailers who are now carrying natural fiber clothing and bedding. But until ecofashion becomes even more mainstream (and hopefully one day becomes the norm), the following is a nationwide listing (alphabetical by state, in the US) of both "brick and mortar" shops, as well as web-based outlets that have made it a priority to feature clothing made from natural fabrics. Some stores are exclusively organic or natural.

A main purpose of this book is to help people locate retailers that sell eco-friendlier clothing. While I have made every attempt to make this list comprehensive, there may be new stores emerging that have been unintentionally missed. This list has already changed in the course of researching, so I hope this list soon becomes outdated, because there are so many more to add to it!

*Listings marked with ** are among my Top Ten favorite ecofashion stores in the US!*

My Top 10 Favorite Eco Fashion Stores
(in alphabetical order)

★ Amour Vert, San Francisco, CA
★ Cariloha, HQ in Utah (nationwide)
★ Clothing Matters, Grand Rapids, MI
★ Ecotopia in Encinitas, CA
★ Fed by Threads, Tucson, AZ
★ Green Serene, New Orleans, LA
★ Of the Earth Eco-Boutique, Eugene, OR
★ Patagonia, Washington DC (nationwide)
★ Reformation, New York, NY (also Hamptons & CA)
★ Spiritex, Asheville, NC

UNITED STATES

ALABAMA

Alabama Chanin
www.alabamachanin.com
High-end, couture organic cotton styles for women.
Available online.
  Corporate office:
  462 Lane Drive
  Florence, AL 35630
  Phone: (256) 760-1090
  orders@alabamachanin.com

Earth Creations
www.earthcreations.net
Natural clay dyes; hemp and organic cotton casual
wear for men, women, and kids. To find retailers,
search on website.
  Corporate office:
  3056 Mountainview Way
  Bessemer, AL 35020
  Phone:1-800-792-9868
  Email form: www.earthcreations.net/
  index.php?main_page=contact_us

Zkano
www.zkano.com
Organic cotton socks
1715 Airport Road
Fort Payne, Alabama 35968

ALASKA

Shtumpa Shop
www.shtumpa.com/wordpress
Organic custom printed tees. Available online.
  Corporate office:
  PO Box 508
  Haines, AK 99827
  Phone: 406-600-9802
  eric@shtumpa.com

ARIZONA

Fed By Threads**
www.fedbythreads.com
Sustainable, organic fabric clothing, made in USA,
for women, men, and children.
  Storefront location:
  345 E. Congress Street
  Tucson, AZ 85701

Phone: (520) 396-4304
info@fedbythreads.com

ARKANSAS

Good Things Boutique
Good-Things-Boutique.shoptiques.com
Organic cotton clothing for women.
  Storefront location:
  108 N. Block Ave.
  Fayetteville, AR 72701
  Phone: (479) 442-3689
  info@goodthingsboutique.com

The Green Corner Store
www.thegreencornerstore.com
clothing for men, women and children made with
natural fibers, organic materials, and low-impact
dyes
  Storefront location:
  1423 Main Street, Suite D
  Little Rock, AR 72202
  Phone: 501-374-1111

CALIFORNIA

Amour Vert**
amourvert.com
Stylish Tencel, modal, organic cotton, linen, and
recycled polyester fashions for women; nontoxic
dyes.
  Storefront location:
  437 Hayes Street
  San Francisco, CA 94107
  Phone: (415) 800-8576
  hello@amourvert.com

The Bamboo Home Store
bamboohomestore.com
Bamboo clothing and housewares for women,
men, and children.
  Storefront location:
  Bamboo Home Store
  130 Mill St.
  Grass Valley CA 95945
  Phone: (530) 272-0303
  bamboohomestore@yahoo.com

Bamboosa
www.bamboosa.com
Bamboo clothing; available online and at stores
throughout the country. Search website for
locations.

Corporate office:
9808 Venice Blvd Suite 706
Culver City, CA 90232
Phone: (310) 425-9932
info@bamboosa.com

Bambu Batu
bambubatu.com
Bamboo and fair trade clothing for men and women, bedding and home décor.
> *Storefront location:*
> 1023 Broad Street
> San Luis Obispo, CA 93401
> Phone: (805) 788-0806
> mail@bambubatu.com

Bead & Reel
www.beadandreel.com
Los Angeles-based organic, fair trade, vegan clothing for women and babies. Available online.
> Phone: (323) 389-7091
> hello@beadandreel.com

Beaumonde Organics
beaumondeorganics.com
Los Angeles-based, organic cotton scarves, eco-friendly dyes. Available online.
> Phone: (818) 781-5607
> Email form: beaumondeorganics.com/
> customer-care-assistance-or-inquiries

BGreen
www.bgreen.com
Organic, fair trade loungewear and intimates for men and women.
> *Corporate Office:*
> 3097 East Ana Street
> Rancho Dominguez, CA 90221
> Phone: (310) 667-9023
> Email form: www.bgreen.com/contact-us

Blue Canoe
www.bluecanoe.com/index.asp
Organic cotton intimates and loungewear. Available online or see website for retailers.
> *Corporate office:*
> 1900 Oakdale Avenue
> San Francisco, CA 94124
> Phone: (888) 923-1373
> info@bluecanoe.com

Cottonique
www.cottonique.com
Organic cotton intimates for women, men, and children. Available online.
> *Corporate office:*
> 1857 Lombard St. 1st floor
> San Francisco CA, 94123
> Phone: (888) 902-6886
> customerservice@cottonique.com

Dash Hemp Santa Cruz
www.dashhemp.com
Hemp clothing for men and women.
> *Storefront location:*
> The Old Sashmill
> 303 Potrero Street, Unit 47-101
> Santa Cruz, CA 95060
> Phone: (831) 446-1824
> sales@dashhemp.com

Ecoland
www.ecolandinc.com
Organic cotton socks and underwear for men, women, and children. Available online.
> *Corporate office:*
> 5825 Lincoln Ave,
> Buena Park, CA 90620
> Phone: (714) 523-8860
> Email form: www.ecolandinc.com/store/
> contact-us.html

Ecoconscious
www.econscious.net
Organic cotton casual clothing for men and women. Available online.
> *Corporate office:*
> 2180 South McDowell Blvd.
> Petaluma, CA 94954
> Phone: (877) 326-6660
> Email form: www.econscious.net/crm.
> asp?action=contactus

Eco Goods
www.ecogoods.com
Sustainable, organic clothing and accessories for women, men, and children.
> *Storefront location:*
> 1130 Pacific Ave
> Santa Cruz, CA 95060
> Phone: (831) 429-5758
> ecogoodssc@gmail.com

Ecotopiia**
www.ecotopiia.com
Sustainable, organic clothing and accessories for

213

women, men, and children.
Storefront location:
543 S. Coast Hwy 101
Encinitas, CA 92024
Phone: (760) 753-7420
Email form: www.ecotopiia.com/contact-us

Ecozuzu
www.ecozuzu.com
Organic cotton and recyled basics for men, women and children. Available online.
Corporate office:
319 E. Anapamu Street #6
Santa Barbara, CA 93101
Phone: (805) 689-5380
info@ecozuzu.com

Ecofabrik
ecofabrik.myshopify.com
California based. Organic cotton, hemp, and bamboo clothng for men and women. Available online.

Ethical Clothing
www.ethicalclothing-petaluma.com
Sustainable and natural fabric clothing and acessories for women.
Storefront location:
122 Kentucky St.
Petaluma, CA 94952
Phone: (707) 769-8564
Email: www.ethicalclothing-petaluma.com/contact

Farm Fresh Clothing Co.
www.farmfreshclothingco.com
Organic cotton t-shirts for men and women. Available online.
Corporate office:
7190 Keating Ave.
Sebastopol, CA 95472
Phone: (707) 634-7053
sales@farmfreshclothingco.com

Green Apple
www.greenappleactive.com
Bamboo athletic wear for women. Available online and at Marshall's locations.
Corporate office:
1511 Aviation Blvd.
Rodondo Beach, CA 90278

Phone: (866) 516-3180
info@greenappleactive.com

Green Woman Store
www.greenwomanstore.com
Organic cotton and modal clothing for women and children. Available online.
Corporate office:
P.O. Box 234173
Leucadia, CA 92023
Phone: 800 479 4439
Email form: www.greenwomanstore.com/contact.html

Groceries Apparel
www.groceriesapparel.com
Organic and recycled cotton, recycled plastic, hemp, and vegetable dyes. Available online or see website for retailers.
Corporate office:
5510 Soto St. Unit A
Vernon, CA 90058
Phone: (213) 488-1002
hello@groceriesapparel.com

Hae Now
www.haenow.com
Wholesale, customizable organic cotton t-shirts for men and women, aprons, and bags.
Corporate office:
654 Alfred Nobel Dr.
Hercules, CA 94547
Phone: (888) 423-6698
Email form: www.haenow.com/content/about-us/contact-us

Indigenous Designs
www.indigenous.com
Organic cotton, fair trade, clothing for men and women made with low-impact dyes.
Corporate office:
6780 Depot Street, Suite 210
Sebastopol, California 95472
Phone: 707-861-9719
service@indigenous.com

Kasper Organics
www.kasperorganics.com
Vendor of several brands of organic cotton and hemp bedding and clothing for men, women, and children. Available online.
Corporate office:
6500 Hazeltine Ave

Van Nuys, CA 91401
Phone: (818) 988-3924

Kristinit
www.kristinit.com
Sustainable fabric clothing for women.
Storefront locations:
Bryan Lee
802 State St.
Santa Barbara, CA
Phone: (805) 936-0206
service@kristinit.com
Fred Segal Emphatic
500 Broadway

Santa Monica, CA 90401
Phone: (310) 458-9940
service@kristinit.com

Larkspur
larkspurla.com
Organic cotton, modal, and upcycled fabric lingerie
for women. Available online and several boutiques.
Corporate office:
651 Clover Street
Los Angeles, CA, 90031
Phone: (559) 790-4693
info@larkspurla.com

Mendocino Twist
www.mendocinotwist.com
Organic cotton, hemp, upcycled, clothing for
women, men, and children.
Storefront location:
45140 Main St.
Mendocino, CA 95460
Phone: (707) 937-1717
info@mendocinotwist.com

Natural High Lifestyle
www.naturalhighlifestyle.com
Organic cotton and hemp clothing and accessories
for women and men; sustainable bedding.
Storefront location:
2510 Main Street #217
Santa Monica, CA 90405
Phone: (323) 691-1827
sales@naturalhighlifestyle.com

Recycleatee
www.recycleatee.com
Organic cotton basics for men, women, and
children. Available online.

Corporate office:
2607 Brighton Avenue
Los Angeles, CA 90018
Phone: (323) 643-4390
contact@recycleatee.com

Reformation
www.thereformation.com
Tencel and vintage clothing for women.
Storefront location:
West Hollywood
8253 Melrose Avenue
Los Angeles, California 90046
Phone: (323) 852-0005
customerlove@thereformation.com

Seabags
www.seabags.com
*Bags made of upcycled boat sails. Available
online.*
Corporate office:
2240 Shelter Island Drive, Ste. 202
San Diego, CA 92106
Phone: (207) 415-5104
christa@seabags.com

Synergy Organic Clothing
www.synergyclothing.com
Organic cotton clothing, made with low-impact
dyes, for women. Supports workers in Nepal.
Storefront locations:
Santa Cruz, Flagship
1229 Pacific Avenue
Santa Cruz, CA 95060
Phone: (831) 331-4014
pacificstore@synergyclothing.com

San Francisco, Mission
969 Valencia Street
San Francisco, CA 94110
Phone: (415) 539-0612
SFMission@synergyclothing.com

Santa Cruz, Outlet
1126 Soquel Avenue
Santa Cruz, CA 95062
Phone: (831) 427-9121
soquelstore@synergyclothing.com

Tara Luna
www.taraluna.com
Fair Trade, Organic & Green Gifts
Storefront Location:

17025 Casper Road
Weed, CA 96094
Phone: 877.325.9129

Tianello
www.tianello.com
Tencel clothing for women and men. Available in multiple retail locations in the US.
Corporate Office:
138 West 38th Street
Los Angeles CA 90037
Phone: (323) 231-0599
Email form: www.tianello.com/T/CS

Toad & Co.
www.toadandco.com
Organic cotton, Tencel, and modal casual and travel wear for men and women; available through retailers across the US.
Corporate Office:
2020 Alameda Padre Serra, Suite 125
Santa Barbara, CA 93103
Phone: (800) 865-TOAD
Email form: www.toadandco.com/service/contact-us.html

Topo Ranch
www.toporanch.com
Sustainable clothing for men and women.
Storefront location:
1219 Abbot Kinney Blvd
Venice CA 90291
Phone: (310) 392-8676
venicestore@toporanch.com

Vital Hemptations (Formerly Vital Hemptations)
www.vitalhemp.com
Hemp casual wear for men and women.
Storefront location:
2305 Main St.
Santa Monica, CA 90405
Phone: (310) 450.2260
hempinu@vitalhemp.com

COLORADO

Envirotextiles
www.envirotextile.com
Specialize in hemp fabric and a variety of sustainable textiles
Storefront Location:
3214 South Grand Ave
Glenwood Springs, CO 81601

Phone: (970) 945-5986
contact: info@envirotextile.com

Gaiam
www.gaiam.com
Organic cotton yoga clothing. Available online and in health food stores.
Corporate office:
833 W. South Boulder Road
Boulder, CO 80307
Phone: (877) 989-6321
customerservice@gaiam.com

Goddess Gear
goddessgear.net
Organic linen, organic cotton and hemp clothing for women. Available online.
Corporate office:
616 Terry Street
Longmont, CO 80501
Phone: (877) 447-4367
Email form: goddessgear.net/pages/contact

Jim Morris Environmental T-Shirts
www.jimmorris.com
Organic cotton printed t-shirts. Available online.
Corporate office:
PO Box 18270
Boulder, CO 80308
Phone: (303) 444-6430
wolf@jimmorris.com

Onno Textiles
www.onnotextiles.com or www.onnot-shirts.com
Organic cotton, hemp, bamboo t-shirts for men and women. Available online.
Corporate office:
1633 Pine Street
Boulder, CO 80302
Phone: (303) 928-7170
us@onnot-shirts.com

CONNECTICUT

Ban T-Shirts
www.bant-shirts.com
Organic cotton and hemp printed t-shirts. Available online.
Corporate office:
Southington, CT 06489
Duncan@bant-shirts.com

Our Green House
www.ourgreenhouse.com
Organic cotton items for babies and children,
loungewear for women and men. Available online.
> *Corporate office:*
> 83 S. Main St.
> Newtown, CT 06470
> Phone: (203) 270-3797
> willow02@aol.com

DELAWARE
N/A

FLORIDA

Under the Canopy
www.underthecanopy.com
Organic cotton clothing for women. Bedding
and towels available at Macy's and Bed, Bath &
Beyond.
> *Corporate Office:*
> 3601 N. Dixie Hwy, #1
> Boca Raton, FL 33431
> Phone: (888) 226-6799
> info@underthecanopy.com

Sassis
www.sassiscollections.com
Socially responsible, eco-friendly, organic clothing
for women and children.
> *Storefront location:* (available by
> appointment)
> 2068 J and C Blvd
> Naples, FL 34109
> Phone: (239) 449-8417
> info@sassiscollections.com

GEORGIA

Body Sense
www.bodysenseonline.com
Spa that sells organic cotton and other natural
fabric clothing for women.
> *Storefront location:*
> 2226 Ridge Crest Circle
> Hiawassee, GA 30546
> Phone: (706) 896-6457
> bodysense@windstream.net

Earth Lover
www.earthlovershopping.com
Hemp, recycled, and fair trade bags and
accessories.

> *Storefront location:*
> 114 S Broad Street
> Thomasville, GA 31792
> Phone: 229-236-5141
> customerservice@earthlovershopping.com

HAWAII

Lily Lotus
lilylotus.com
Organic cotton yoga clothing.
> *Storefront locations:*
> 609 Kailua Road Suite 102
> Kailua, HI 96734
> Telephone: (808) 888-3564
>
> 3632 Waialae Avenue
> Honolulu, HI 96816
> Telephone: (808) 277-1724

Yoganics
www.yoganicshawaii.com
Bamboo, hemp, organic cotton, recycled materials,
yoga clothing for women.
> *Storefront location:*
> 79-7401 Suite B. Mamalahoa Hwy.
> Kainaliu, HI 96750
> Phone: (808) 322-0714
> yoganics@gmail.com

IDAHO
www.etsy.com/shop/louderthanwords
Hemp, organic, upcycled adventure gear.
Available online.
> *Corporate office:*
> McCall, Idaho 83638
> bluecloudgoods@yahoo.com

ILLINOIS

Global Hemp
www.globalhemp.com
Online retailer of different companies' hemp items
and clothing. Available online.
> *Corporate office:*
> PO Box 5124
> Peoria, IL 61601
> Phone: (309) 686-9000
> Email form: store.globalhemp.com/
> contact-us-a/131.htm

Greenheart Shop

greenheartshop.org
Fair trade and some organic clothing and housewares.

> *Storefront location:*
> 1714 N Wells St.
> Chicago, IL 60614
> Phone: (312) 264-1625
> info@greenheartshop.org

Oops! (Outstanding Organic Products)

oopsnormal.com
Organic cotton, hemp, bamboo, and Tencel clothing for men, women, and babies, plus towels and eco-friendly housewares.

> *Storefront location:*
> 1520 E College Ave
> Normal, IL 61761
> Phone: (309) 862-3121

INDIANA

Eden Outfitters

edenoutfitters.wix.com
Organic cotton, hemp, bamboo clothing for men and women.

> *Storefront location:*
> 60 North Van Buren St.
> Nashville, IN 47448
> Phone: (812) 988-8800
> Email form: edenoutfitters.wix.com/eden#!contact-us

IOWA

Blue Fish Clothing

www.bluefishclothing.com
"Wearable art" using some organic cotton, linen.

> *Storefront location:*
> 58 S. Main Street
> Fairfield, IA 52556
> Phone: (641) 209-3920
> service@bluefishclothing.com

KANSAS

4 All Humanity

www.4allhumanity.com
Fair trade, upcycled clothing and bags made from cortes, part of the traditional Mayan dress worn in Guatemala.

> *Corporate office:*
> 3216 Northwestern A

Hutcinson KS 67502
info@4allhumanity.com

Janay-A Eco Bridal

www.janay-a.com/wordpress
Silk, hemp blend, organic cotton and vintage fabrics wedding gowns.

> Storefront location:
> 5939 Woodson Road
> Mission, KS 66202
> Phone: (866) 900-6565
> Email form: janay-a.com/wordpress/about/contact-form

KENTUCKY

RebirthRecycling

www.etsy.com/shop/RebirthRecycling
Upcycled textiles and recycled material clothing. Available online.

> *Corporate office:*
> Frankfort, Kentucky 40601

LOUISIANA

Green Serene**

www.greenserenenola.com/default.html
Sells various lines featuring organic cotton, hemp, bamboo, recycled, Tencel.

> *Storefront location:*
> 2041 Magazine St.
> New Orleans, LA 70130
> Phone: (504) 252-9861
> greenserenellc@cox.net

Tasc Performance

www.tascperformance.com
Bamboo sportswear for men and women. Available online.

> *Corporate office:*
> 4308 Firestone Road
> Metairie, LA 70001
> Phone: (504) 731-2989
> Email form: www.tascperformance.com/contacts

MAINE

Seabags

www.seabags.com
Upcycled bags made from boat sails. Several New England storefront locations, from Maine to New Jersey.

Corporate office:
25 Custom House Wharf
Portland, ME 04101
Phone: (888) 210-4244
contact@seabags.com

MARYLAND

Live Life Organics
www.livelifeorganics.com
Organic cotton casual wear for men, women, and children. Available online.
Corporate office:
P.O. Box 15
Glyndon, MD 21071
us@livelifeorganics.com

Nest
www.nestnaturalhome.com
Organic cotton, hemp, and recycled polyester clothing and eco-housewares.
Storefront location:
5809 Clarksville Square Dr.
Clarksville, MD 21029
Phone: (443) 535-0212
info@nestnaturalhome.com

MASSACHUSETTS

Conscious Elegance
consciouselegance.com
Massachusetts-based wedding attire for women.
Studio (By Appointment)
23 Flint Avenue
Stoneham, MA 02180
Phone: (781) 752-3039
Email: consciouselegance.com/contact

Fisherman's Daughter
fishermansdaughtermarket.com
Organic cotton and recycled polyester clothing and accessories for women.
Storefront location:
402 Main Street
Chatham, MA 02633
Phone: (508) 292-5463
fishermansdaughter@gmail.com

Green Goods
www.buygreengoods.com/index.html
Organic cotton casual clothing for women, children, and men. Available online.

Corporate office:
104 Wyman Rd.
Groton, MA 01450
Phone: (978) 302-8543
info@buygreengoods.com

Hempest
www.hempest.com
Hemp clothing and accessories for men and women. Available online.
Corporate office:
207 Newbury Street
Boston, MA 02116
Phone: (617) 421-9944
Email: www.hempest.com/contact-us

MICHIGAN

Clothing Matters**
www.clothingmatters.net
Organic cotton, hemp, bamboo, Tencel, soy, and recycled fabric clothing for men, women, and children.
Storefront location:
141 Diamond Avenue Southeast
Grand Rapids, MI 49506
Phone: (616) 742-2818
info@clothingmatters.net

Maggie's Organics
www.maggiesorganics.com
One of the pioneer organic, fair trade clothing companies; socks and acessories widely available at health food stores.
Corporate office:
306 W. Cross St.
Ypsilanti, MI 48197
Phone:(734) 482-4000
maggies@organicclothes.com

Our Greentopia
www.ourgreentopia.com
Organic cotton clothing for men, women, and children.
Storefront location:
3165 West 12 Mile Rd.
Berkley, Michigan 48072
Phone: (248) 268-2123
info@ourgreentopia.com

MINNESOTA

Moss Envy
www.mossenvy.com
Eco-products like mattresses, bedding, furniture,home decor, gifts, jewelry, bath and body, baby gear, and more.
> *Storefront Location:*
> 3056 Excelsior Boulevard
> Minneapolis, MN 55416
> Phone: (612) 374-4581
> info@mossenvy.com

Tees 4 Trees
www.tees4treesminneapolis.com
Organic cotton recycled polyester t-shirts; plants a tree for each tee purchased.
> *Corporate office:*
> Minneapolis, MN
> Phone: (952) 857-9879
> tees4treesminneapolis@gmail.com

MISSISSIPPI

Eco Fashionista Consignment
ecofashionistaconsig.wix.com/
ecofashionistaconsignment#!
Consignment vintage fashion.
> *Storefront location:*
> 1308 North Lamar Boulevard, Suite 1
> Oxford, MS 38655
> Phone: (662) 380-1648
> Email form: ecofashionistaconsig.wix.
> com/ecofashionistaconsignment#!contact

MISSOURI

Mid-Missouri Peaceworks
blog.midmopeaceworks.org
> *Storefront Location:*
> 804-C East Broadway
> Columbia, MO 65201
> Phone: 573-875-0539
> mail@midmopeaceworks.org

Yes It's Organic
www.yesitsorganic.com
Organic cotton, bamboo, and Tencel clothing for men, women, and children, and bedding. Available online.
> *Corporate location:*
> St. Louis, MS 63132
> Phone: (800) 455-4508

Email form: www.yesitsorganic.com/
contact.html#axzz3aGGodMoc

MONTANA

Ethos Paris Eco Designers Boutique
www.ethosecofashions.com
Organic cotton, fair trade clothing, and accessories for men and women.
> *Storefront location:*
> 26 Scullers Way
> Whitefish, Montana 59937
> Phone: (406) 333-0388
> studioleroux@cyberport.net

The Green Light
www.greenlightmt.com
> *Storefront Location:*
> 301 North Higgins Ave.
> Missoula, MT 59802
> Phone: 406-541-0080

Hermans Eco Inc.
www.greenecoshow.com
www.mensecofashion.com
www.repurposed.us
www.slowecofashion.com
Organic cotton, hemp, and upcycled clothing for men and women. Available online.
> *Corporate office:*
> 519 4th Street
> Deer Lodge, MT 59722
> Phone: (406) 645-1252
> herman@mensecofashion.com or info@slowecofashion.com

Jeanette Rankin Peace Center Fair Trade Store
www.jrpc.org
> *Storefront Location:*
> 519 S. Higgins St.
> Missoula, MT 59801
> Phone: (406) 543.3955

NEBRASKA
N/A

NEVADA

Aventura Clothing
www.aventuraclothing.com
Stylish organic cotton, hemp, bamboo, Tencel, and recycled polyester clothing for men and women. Available online and at boutiques around the US.

Corporate office:
1415 Greg Street, Suite 101
Sparks, Nevada 89431
Phone: (800) 921-1655
Email form: www.aventuraclothing.com/
contact-us

Hemp Blue
www.hempblue.com
Hemp clothing for men and women. Available online.

> *Corporate office:*
> 4262 Blue Diamond Rd
> Las Vegas, Nevada 89139
> hello@hempbluedenim.com

NEW HAMPSHIRE
N/A

NEW JERSEY

a.d.o. (anjelika dreams organic)
shop.adoclothing.com/main.sc
Organic cotton clothing for women.
> *Corporate office:*
> 1 Harborside Place, #155
> Jersey City, NJ 07311
> Email form: shop.adoclothing.com/
> contactus.sc

Blue Fish Clothing
www.bluefishclothing.com
"Wearable art" using some organic cotton, linen.
> *Storefront location:*
> 62 Trenton Avenue
> Frenchtown, NJ 08825
> Phone: (908) 996-3720
> service@bluefishclothing.com

Hemp Fair
www.hempfair.com
Hemp clothing and accessories for men, women, and children. Available online.
> *Corporate Office:*
> 8301 4th Avenue, Ste. 304
> North Bergen, NJ 07047
> Phone: (201) 982-3698

Sustainable Threads
www.sustainablethreads.com
Peace silk and organic cotton scarves for men and women, and other fair trade accessories.

Corporate Office:
84 Riverbend Drive
North Brunswick, NJ 08902
Phone: (732) 940-7487
info@sustainablethreads.com

NEW MEXICO
N/A

NEW YORK

Are Naturals
www.arenaturals.com
Organic bedding and housewares. Available online.
> *Corporate Office:*
> 61 Eastern Parkway Unit 1C
> Brooklyn, NY 11238
> Phone: (888) 330-6979
> customersupport@arenaturals.com

Catherine H.
www.catherineh.com
More than ten eco designers, including Linda Loudermilk.
> *Storefront location:*
> 18-24 Parkway
> Katonah, NY 10536
> Phone: (914) 232-2010
> info@catherineh.com

Hyde Yoga
yogahyde.com
Organic yoga clothing for women.
> *Storefront location:*
> 85 N. 3rd St.
> Brooklyn, NY 11211
> Phone: (646) 330-4646
> grace@yogahyde.com

Kaight
www.kaightshop.com
Stylish organic cotton, hemp, bamboo, Tencel, and sustainable fashions for women.
> *Storefront location:*
> 382 Atlantic Avenue
> Brooklyn, NY 11217
> Phone: (718) 858-4737
> info@kaightnyc.com

Prancing Leopard
www.prancingleopard.com
Organic cotton yoga wear for women and men.

Available online.

>Corporate office:
>481 Van Brunt Street #7C-1
>Brooklyn, NY 11231
>Phone: (800) 692-8110
>admin@prancingleopard.com

Reformation**

www.thereformation.com

Tencel and vintage clothing for women.

>Storefront locations:
>SOHO
>23 Howard Street
>New York, New York 10013
>Phone: (212) 510-8455
>customerlove@thereformation.com
>
>Downtown
>156 Ludlow Street
>New York, New York 10013
>Phone: (646) 448-4925

Royal Apparel

www.royalapparel.net

Organic cotton, hemp, bamboo, and recycled polyester casualwear for women, men, and children. Available online.

>Corporate office:
>65 Commerce Drive
>Hauppauge, NY 11788
>Phone: (866) 769-2517
>retail@royalapparel.net

Study NY

www.study-ny.com

>Storefront Location:
>630 Flushing Ave, Suite 704
>Brooklyn, NY, 11206
>info@study-ny.com

NORTH CAROLINA

Cape Fear

www.capefearapparel.com

Organic cotton, hemp, and bamboo clothing for men and women. Available via catalog.

>Corporate office:
>310 N. Front St. Suite 4-160
>Wilmington, NC 28401
>Phone: (910) 352-8835
>mail@capefearapparel.com

Gaia Conceptions

www.gaiaconceptions.com

Organic cotton, hemp blends, and low-impact dyes for women and children. Made to order. Available online.

>Corporate office:
>504 Guilford Ave,
>Greensboro, NC 27401
>Phone: (336) 617-6598
>Email form: www.gaiaconceptions.com/contact

Green Goods

greengoodsshop.com

organic products such as soaps, make-up, perfume, organic bamboo clothing, organic baby products, and much more.

>Storefront Location:
>220 NW Broad St.
>Southern Pines, NC 28387
>Phone: (910) 692-2511
>denise@greengoodsshop.com

Green Mother Goods

www.greenmothergoods.com

Organic cotton clothing for women.

>Storefront location:
>67 Biltmore Ave.
>Asheville, NC 28801 (formerly in Boone)
>Phone: (828) 263-7010
>Email form: www.greenmothergoods.com/contact-us

Organicality

www.organicality.com

Organic cotton clothing for women and children. Available online.

>Corporate office:
>PO Box 467
>Morrisville, NC 27560
>(919) 678-8100

Spiritex**

www.spiritex.net

Organic cotton clothing grown and sewn in NC, as well as Tencel and recycled polyester clothing for men, women, and kids.

>Storefront location:
>14 Haywood St.
>Asheville, NC 28801
>Phone: (828) 254-3375
>sales@spiritex.net

NORTH DAKOTA

Revolver
www.fargorevolver.wix.com/online
Organic cotton, bamboo and vintage clothing for women.
Storefront location:
627 1st Avenue North
Fargo, ND 58102
Phone: (701) 235-2883
fargorevolver@gmail.com

OHIO

Esperanza Threads
www.esperanzathreads.com
Organic cotton clothing for women and children.
Storefront location:
1370 W. 69th St.
Cleveland, Ohio 44102
Phone: (216) 961-9009
customerservice@esperanzathreads.com

LUR
lurapparel.com
Recycled cotton and recycled polyester, low-impact dye process, supports workers in Guatemala.
Corporate office:
1646 Hoffner St.
Cincinnati, OH 45223
Phone: (513) 873-5657
mark@lurapparel.com

OKLAHOMA

Kynd Clothing Inc.www.kyndclothing.com
Bamboo causal wear for men and women.
Available online.
Corporate office:
1622 Wind Hill Road
Norman, OK 73071
kynd@kyndclothing.com

OREGON

Cathy's Organic Superstore
www.cathysorganicsuperstore.com
Organic cotton and bamboo clothing for men, women, and children. Available online.
Corporate office:
2629 Bratton Lane
Bend, Oregon 97701
Phone: (877) 893-6447
sales@cathysorganicsuperstore.com

EcoVibe
www.ecovibeapparel.com
Stylish clothes for women made of modal, Tencel, bamboo and recycled fabric blends.
Storefront location:
904 NW 23rd Avenue
Portland, OR 97210
Phone: (503) 360-1163
info@ecovibeapparel.com

Faerie's Dance
www.faeriesdance.com
Large online retailer of multiple brands of organic, hemp, and bamboo clothing.
Corporate office:
12400 S.E. Crest Drive
Happy Valley, OR 97086
Phone: (971) 255-0752
Email form: www.faeriesdance.com/contact_us.php

Hemporium
www.facebook.com/Hemporium-Sustainable-Solutions-Earth-Friendly-Fashion
Hemp clothing and accessories for men and women.
296 E Main St
Ashland, OR 97520
(541) 488-4367

Of the Earth**
oftheearth.com
Stylish clothes for women, men, and children made of organic cotton, hemp, modal, Tencel, bamboo, and recycled fabric blends with low-impact dyes.
Storefront location:
Of the Earth's Eco-Boutique
Sweet Skins
782 Blair Blvd
Eugene, OR 97402
Phone: (541) 543-7195
OfTheEarth@gmail.com

Xylem
xylemclothing.com
Organic cotton, hemp, and soy clothing for men, women and children. Available online.

Corporate office:
3085 Whitbeck Blvd.
Eugene OR 97405
Phone: (541) 953-7799
info@xylemclothing.com

Yala

www.yaladesigns.com
Bamboo and organic cotton bedding, and clothing for women, kids, and men, sold at boutiques around the country.
Corporate Office:
255 Helman Street, Suite 1
Ashland, OR 97520
Phone: (877) 578-1730
care@yaladesigns.com

PENNSYLVANIA

Naturally Yours, The Organic Shop

Organic cotton clothing for women, men, and children.
Storefront location:
103 Broadway
Jim Thorpe, PA 18229
Phone: (570) 325-8209

United By Blue

www.unitedbyblue.com
Casual outdoor wear for men and women made with organic cotton, Tencel, and recycled polyester. For every product sold, removes one pound of trash from the oceans.
Three storefront locations in PA, one in Asbury Park, NJ, and one in NYC.
Flagship location:
144 North 2nd Street
Philadelphia, PA 19106
Phone: (215) 278-7746
blue@unitedbyblue.com

RHODE ISLAND

Simply Chickie

www.simplychickieclothing.com
Organic cotton baby onesies and women's t-shirts. Available online.
Corporate office:
PO Box 514
Newport, RI 02840
Phone: (401) 855-9504
Email form: www.simplychickieclothing.com/pages/contact

Simply Natural

www.simplynaturalandmore.com
Organic, fair trade accessories.
Storefront location:
24A Pier Market Place
Narragansett, RI 02882
Phone: (401) 782-3400
simplynaturalandmore@gmail.com

Touched by Green

www.touchedbygreen.com
Natural dyed scarves and eco-friendly accessories.
Storefront location:
271 South Main St.
Providence, RI 02903
Phone: (401) 223-4420
admin@touchedbygreen.com

Ure Outfitters

ureoutfitters.com
Sells several outdoor brands (see below) and Prana.
Storefront location:
1009 Main St.
Hope Valley, RI 02832
Phone: (401) 539-4050
ureoutfitters@hotmail.com

SOUTH CAROLINA
N/A

SOUTH DAKOTA

Granite Sports

www.granitesports.biz
Sells Patagonia and Prana eco-friendly and organic outdoor clothing.
Storefront location:
201 Main Street
(P.O. Box 1002)
Hill City, SD 55745
Phone: (605) 574-2121
gssales@hills.net

TENNESSEE

Bambooya

www.bambooya.com
Bamboo clothing for women, men, and children. Available online.

Corporate office:
6746 Lane Rd
College Grove, TN 37046
Phone: (615) 591-9565
katie@bambooya.com

TEXAS

Eco-Wise
www.ecowise.com
Organic bedding and baby supplies.
> *Storefront location:*
> 110 West Elizabeth Street
> Austin TX 78704
> Phone: (512) 326-4474
> ecowise512@gmail.com

Green Living Every Day
www.greenlivingeveryday.com
Organic cotton t-shirts and robes for men and women. Available online.
> *Corporate office:*
> PO Box 69
> Dripping Springs, Texas 78620
> Phone: (512) 607-6411
> info@greenlivingeveryday.com

Raven and Lily
www.ravenandlily.com
Eco-friendly, fair trade garments made by women world-wide
> *Austin, TX storefronts:*
> 11601 Rock Rose Ave Ste 110
> Austin, TX 78758
> 737.209.1072
> domain@ravenandlily.com
> &
> 2406 Manor Road, Suite C
> Austin, TX 78722
> 512.236.1378
> manor@ravenandlily.com

SOS from Texas
www.sosfromtexas.com
Printed organic cotton t-shirts for men, women, and children. Available online.
> *Corporate office:*
> 15781 FM 1036
> Samnorwood, TX 79077
> Phone: (806) 256-2033
> go@sosfromtexas.com

Wildflower Organics
www.wildflowerorganics.com
Home linens.
> *Storefront Location:*
> 524 North Lamar Blvd.
> Austin, TX 78703
> Phone: 512-360-0449
> info@wildflowerorganics.com

UTAH

Cariloha**
www.cariloha.com
Bamboo clothing and accessories for men and women. Multuple storefront locations around the US and Carribbean.
> *Corporate office:*
> 280 West 10200 South
> Sandy, UT 84070
> Phone: (801) 562-3001
> onlineservice@cariloha.com

Earth Linens
www.earthlinens.com
Organic cotton, bamboo bedding, and clothing for women, men, and children. Available online.
> *Storefront Location:*
> 1405 S 1020 W, I-8
> Orem, UT 84058
> Phone: (801) 923-3332
> support@earthlinens.com

VERMONT

Burton
www.burton.com
Outdoor travel clothing and gear using no chemicals on restricted substance lists. Available online.
> *Corporate office:*
> 80 Industrial Parkway
> Burlington, VT 05401
> Phone: (800) 881-3138
> info@burton.com

VIRGINIA

Fair Trade Winds
www.fairtradewinds.net
family-run retail store with six locations across the country. We exclusively offer fair trade products that support hard-working, talented artisans and farmers around the world.

Headquarters:
2905 District Ave. Suite 125
Fairfax, VA 22031

Green Label

greenlabelorganic.com
100 Percent Certified Organic t-shirts for men, women, and children, made with low-impact dyes and no *polyvinyl chloride* (PVC) in prints.
Storefront location:
210 W. Oxford Street
Floyd, VA 24091
Phone: (540) 745-6161
Email form: greenlabelorganic.com/contact-us

WASHINGTON

Bootyland

www.bootylandkids.com
Organic cotton and hemp clothing for kids, women, and men. PVC-free rain gear.
Storefront location:
1815 N. 45th St #208
Seattle, WA 98103
Phone (206) 328-0636
info@bootylandkids.com

Intertwined Designs

www.intertwineddesigns.com
Handmade hemp and soy casualwear for women and men. Available online.
Corporate office:
PO Box 187
Winthrop, WA 98862
Phone: (360) 319-0342
betsy@intertwineddesigns.com

Naked Clothing

nakedclothing.com
Organic cotton, hemp, bamboo clothing for women and men.
Storefront location:
1912 W. Highway 20
Sedro Woolley, WA 98284
Phone: (360) 746-9916
Email form: nakedclothing.com/pages/contact

Natural Clothing Company

www.naturalclothingcompany.com
Organic cotton, linen, hemp, and bamboo casual and intimates for men and women. Available online.
Corporate Address:
PO Box 69
Snohomish, WA 98291
Phone: (877) 800-8878
info@NaturalClothingCompany.com

Prairie Underground

www.prairieunderground.com
Stylish organic cotton clothing for women.
Corporate office:
940 South Harney Street
Seattle, WA 98108
info@prairieunderground.com

Rawganique

www.rawganique.com
Pioneer ecofashion brand; organic cotton, hemp, and organic linen clothing for men, women, and children; bedding and curtains; chemical-free manufacturing. Also located in Washington state, US. Available online and through multiple US retailers.
Corporate office:
1469 Gulf Road Ste. 102
Point Roberts, WA 98281
Phone: (250) 335-0050 or (877) 729-4367
info@rawganique.com

Texture

www.textureclothing.com
Organic cotton, hemp, soy, and Tencel clothing for women.
Storefront location:
1425 North State St.
Bellingham, WA 98225
(360) 733-3351
teresa@textureclothing.com

Wayi Clothing

www.wayiclothing.com
Bamboo and natural fabric clothing for men, women, and children, free of toxic *azo dyes*, available in some west coast Whole Foods Markets.
Storefront location:
513 North 36th Street, Suite F
Seattle, Washington 98103
Phone: (202) 632-9294
info@wayiclothing.com

WEST VIRGINIA

Winkin' Sun Hemp
www.winkinsunhemp.com
Hemp clothing for men and women.
> *Storefront location:*
> 111 Cracraft Avenue
> Wheeling, WV 26003
> Phone: (304) 281-3183
> wsh@winkinsunhemp.com

WISCONSIN

Duluth Trading Company
www.duluthtrading.com
Casual and outdoor clothing, some made of organic cotton and hemp.
> *Corporate Office:*
> Duluth Trading Company
> P.O. Box 200
> Belleville, WI 53508
> Phone: (866) 300-9719
> customerservice@duluthtrading.com

Fair Indigo
www.fairindigo.com
Available online. Fair trade, sustainable, vegan recycled clothing, and accessories for men, women, and kids.
> *Corporate Office:*
> 579 Donofrio Dr, Ste 104
> Madison, WI 53719
> Phone: (800) 520-1806
> service@fairindigo.com

Green 3
www.green3apparel.com
Organic cotton, recycled cotton, and pre- and post-consumer reclaimed fabric clothing for men, women, and kids; PVC-free, nontoxic dyes.
> *Storefront location:*
> 523 W. Water Street
> Princeton, WI 54968
> Phone: (920) 235-1288 x2
> info@green3apparel.com

Lillie's
www.lilliesgoods.com
Organic cotton, hemp, fair trade and recycled clothing for women, men, and children.
> *Storefront location:*
> W62 N553 Washington Avenue
> Cedarburg, Wisconsin 53012

Phone: (262) 377-7047
info@lilliesgoods.com
* Second storefront located in Boulder, Colorado.

Satara Home
www.satarahome.com
Natural mattress & organic bedding store
> *Storefront Location:*
> 6333 University Avenue
> Middleton, WI 53562
> Phone: (608) 251-4905
> info@satara-inc.com

SERRV
www.SERRV.org
> Outlet store:
>
> 500 Main Street
> New Windsor, MD 21776
> Phone: (410)635-8711
>
> Storefront locations:
>
> 2701 Monroe Street (in Knickerbocker Place)
> Madison, WI 53711
> Phone: (608) 233.4438
>
> 224 State Street (across from the Overture Center)
> Madison, WI 53703
> (608) 251.2370

WYOMING

Aion
www.aionmfg.com
Sweatshop-free, hip casualwear for men and women, some organic cotton and bamboo.
> *Storefront location:*
> 34 S. Glenwood St.
> Jackson, WY 83001
> Phone: (307) 743-7900
> info@aionheadwear.com

THE GREEN WARDROBE GUIDE

CANADA

Echo Verde
echoverde.com
Eco-friendly and organic clothing for women, ethical business practices. Sold in shops in US.
Corporate Office:
Vancouver, Canada
sales@echoverde.com

Eco Handbags
eco-handbags.ca
Bags made of organic cotton, hemp, and multiple recycled materials. Available online.
Corporate Office:
3551 Boulevard St-Charles, Suite 213
Kirkland, Quebec Canada H9H 3C4
Phone: (888) 223-4018
contact@eco-handbags.ca

Hemp and Company
www.hempandcompany.com
Hemp and bamboo clothing for men and women.
Storefront location:
1312 Government Street
Victoria, British Columbia, V8W 1Y2
Phone: (866) 383-4367
info@hempandcompany.com

Hemp Tent
hemptent.com
Hemp, bamboo, and soy fair trade clothing for men, women, and children.
Storefront location:
8A Bay St
Parry Sound ON
705.746.1549
sales@hemptent.com

Still Eagle
www.stilleagle.com
Organic cotton, hemp, bamboo, and recycled clothing for men, women, and children.
Storefront Location:
476 Baker Street
Nelson, British Columbia, V1L 4H8
Phone: (250) 352-3844
orders@stilleagle.com

ONLINE RETAILERS

ASOS Green Room
www.us.asos.com
Eco-friendly sustainable fashion, accessories, and beauty products

A Boy Named Sue
www.aboynamedsue.co
"Cool clothes with a conscience"

EcoMall
www.ecomall.com
Online retailer of different companies' eco-items and clothing.

EENVOUD
eenvoudny.com
Minimalist + sustainably conscious womenswear made in Brooklyn

Forest & Fin
www.forestandfin.com
Environmentally inspired sustainable apparel.

Green People
www.greenpeople.org
Large listing of sustainable clothing sellers for adults and children.

Shop Ethica
www.shopethica.com
Collective of sustainable, vegan, and ethical labor start-up designers.

Maiden Nation
www.maidennation.com
"Empowering women through ethical fashion"

Modavanti
modavanti.com
Seller of various sustainable-oriented brands.

Two Owls
www.shoptwoowls.com
Clothing and accessories for women, children and babies
805-617-4252
info@shoptwoowls.com

Yoxygen
www.yoox.com
"A green world of eco-friendly fashion and design"

SOME BRANDS/DESIGNERS TO LOOK FOR

- **Alternative Earth**: www.alternativeapparel.com
- **Angelrox**: angelrox.com
- **Bamboo Clothes**: www.bambooclothes.com
- **Deux Amies Sleepwear**: www.etsy.com/shop/DeuxAmiesSleepwear
- **Earth Yoga**: www.earthyogaclothing.com
- **Ecoskin**: www.ecoskincollections.com
- **Elsa and Me**: elsaandme.com
- **GreenSource**: www.greensource.com
- **Hemp Authority**: hempauthority.com
- **Hemp Couture**: www.hempcouture.ca
- **John Patrick**: www.organicbyjohnpatrick.com
- **Lila Organics**: lilaorganics.com
- **Loomstate**: www.loomstate.org
- **Midori**: www.midoristyles.com
- **Minawear**: minawear.com
- **Nudie Jeans**: www.nudiejeans.com
- **Organic Attire**: www.organicattire.com
- **PACT**: wearpact.com (Carried by health food stores)
- **Popomomo**: popomomo.com
- **Prana**: www.prana.com
- **Raw Earth Wild Sky**: www.rawearthwildsky.com
- **Revival Ink**: revivalink.com (low-impact dyes)
- **Sita**: sitacouture.com
- **SPUN**: www.choosespun.com
- **Stella Carakasi**: www.stellacarakasi.com
- **SVILU**: www.SVILU.com
- **Synergy**: www.synergyclothing.com
- **Tianello**: www.tianello.com
- **Titania Inglis**: www.titaniainglis.com
- **Themis and Thread**: themisandthread.ecrater.com
- **Threads for Thought**: www.threadsforthought.com (Carried by Whole Foods)
- **Two Star Dog**: www.twostardog.com
- **Vaute Couture**: vautecouture.com
- **Veja** (shoes): www.veja-store.com/en
- **Wabi Sabi Eco Concept**: wabisabiecofashionconcept.com
- **Yana Dee**: www.etsy.com/shop/yanadee
- **Zady**: www.zady.com

... And numerous other designers/brands are becoming available all the time! :) ...

HIGH END/LUXE ECO

- **Deborah Lindquist**: www.deborahlindquist.com
- **Edun**: edun.com
- **Eileen Fisher**: www.eileenfisher.com
- **Rêve En Vert**: www.revenvert.com
- **Stella McCartney**: www.stellamccartney.com

OUTDOOR/SPORTSWEAR

- **Eastern Mountain Sports**: www.ems.com
- **Gramicci**: www.gramicci.com
- **Nau**: www.nau.com
- **Patagonia****: www.patagonia.com (Beautiful storefront in Washington D.C.)
- **REI**: www.rei.com

BEDDING

- **Heart of Vermont**: heartofvermont.com (based in Vermont)
- **Nature's Crib**: www.naturescrib.com (based in upstate New York)
- **Wildflower Organics**: www.wildflowerorganics.com (based in Texas)

ORGANIC AND NATURAL FABRICS/MATERIAL

- **Eden Fabrics**: edenfabrics.com/organic-fabric
- **Pick Natural**: picknatural.com
- **Organic Cotton Plus**: organiccottonplus.com
- **Aurora Silk**: www.aurorasilk.com

Eco-Baby Stuff

Most parents do their best to protect their children from any type of known harm such as fire and busy street traffic. However, there is a risk of harm from unseen chemical actors that can accumulate over time starting the first day of birth and even in the womb.

Babies and small children are uniquely susceptible to the effects of toxic chemicals for three main reasons. One is because their detoxification systems such as livers and kidneys are not fully developed, so chemicals can stay in the body longer, doing more damage.

Secondly, from a size standpoint, exposure to even a small amount of chemical has a proportionally larger impact on a baby's body versus the effect on an adult. In other words, if a petite person drinks one alcoholic drink, it has more of an effect than it would on a large bodybuilder twice their weight.

Infants and toddlers can often be exposed to chemicals through their super-soft skin, and because of the tendency to put things in their mouths. For example, babies often put blankets in their mouths. Some clothing such as raincoats and rain boots are often made with PVC (polyvinyl chloride), a plastic that can contain hormone disrupting phthalates, such as DEHP (di-2-ethylhexyl phthalate).

Flame Retardants in Your Baby's Pajamas and Bed

In the 1970's, the U.S. Consumer Product Safety Commission (CPSC) required baby's pajamas to be resistant to flame. This is a laudable goal, but unfortunately, the chemicals used to achieve this goal could potentially cause health problems. "[S]cientists have found evidence suggesting that chemicals designed to prevent fires are getting into your children's blood and rewiring their brains, leading to attention deficit disorder, hyperactivity, hearing problems, slow mental development and, possibly, cancer."[1]

---

1   Kaplan, Sheila. "The poison crib: When protective chemicals harm." *Salon*. www.salon.com2010/06/10/dangers_flame_retardants. June 10, 2010.

Thankfully, some of the fire retardants have been phased out. However, "While flame retardant chemicals like chlorinated TRIS and PBDE have been phased out due to toxicity concerns, others remain, like tetrakis (hydroxymethyl) phosphonium chloride (THPC), aka "Proban" or "Securest." This popular treatment has been linked to a variety of health effects including genetic changes, cancer promotion, and liver and nervous system damage."[2] In the 1990s standards were changed to also allow for snug-fitting baby clothes to not be treated since it is the loose-fitting variety that tended to pose the most risk of catching fire.

Baby mattresses and changing mats containing foam may also contain fire retardants.[3] "Chemical flame retardants...are used in everything from computers to upholstery, including nursing pillows, cribs, strollers and fleece baby carriers."[4]

Organic cotton baby apparel by
Cherub's Blanket

Where do I find the safest options for my kids?

Fortunately many entrepreneurs, often parents themselves, have realized the need for safer baby items and have worked to fill the need. Below you will find a listing of websites to help you find organic cotton clothing, bedding and other products, such as organic cotton stuffed toys for children and babies, which are free of chemicals.

Another sensible option is to seek out previously owned baby items. The risk of chemicals residues declines with washing so maybe secondhand is not so bad; it can save money as well.

The Mount Sinai School of Medicine's Children's Environmental Health Center (CEHC) in New York City is a great resource for more information on how to protect children from all sorts of environmental health hazards such as pesticides, plastics, lead, and air pollution (see ribbet.org). Also see the Children's Environmental Health Network (www.cehn.org).

---

2   "Flame-Retardant Dangers," *Connors Clinic.* May 8, 2015. http://www.connersclinic.com/flame-retardant-dangers.
3   Green Science Policy Institute. greensciencepolicy.org/faq. 2013.
4   Kaplan, Sheila. "The poison crib: When protective chemicals harm." *Salon.* June 10, 2010. www.salon.com2010/06/10/dangers_flame_retardants.

Sources of Organic and Natural Clothing Stores for Babies and Kids

STOREFRONTS

ALABAMA

Swaddle
swaddleonline.com
2825 18th Street South
Homewood, AL 35209
(205) 870-3503

ALASKA

Betula Baby
780 Snodgrass Dr.
Palmer, Alaska 99645
(907) 745-2229

ARKANSAS

Terra Tots
www.store.terra-tots.com
15 S. Block Ave.
Suite 102
Fayetteville, AR 72701
(479) 587-8687

CALIFORNIA

Bambu Batu: The House of Bamboo
bambubatu.com
1023 Broad St.
San Luis Obispo, CA 93401
(805) 788.0806

Bonnetfriend
www.bonnetfriend.com
3579 E Foothill Blvd. #288
Pasadena, CA 91107
(626) 625-1175

Caro Bambino
carobambino.com
2710 Main St.
Santa Monica, CA
(310) 399-7971

Earthsake
www.earthsake.com
1772 Fourth St.
Berkeley, CA 94710
(510) 559-8440

Eco Bambino
www.shopecobambino.com
863 Monterey St.
San Luis Obispo, CA 93401
(805) 540-7222

Eco Goods
www.ecogoods.com
1130 Pacific Ave.
Santa Cruz, CA 95060
(831) 429-5758
ecogoodssc@gmail.com

La Jolla Bamboo
lajollabamboo.com
789 West Harbor Dr. Suite 146
San Diego, California 92101
(858) 366-5471
lajollabambooboutique@gmail.com

Lil Baby Sprouts
lilbabysprouts.com
1280 Bison Ave. Unit B9
Newport Beach, CA 92660
(949) 721-1077
info@lilbabysprouts.com

Sprout San Francisco
www.sproutsanfrancisco.com
1828 Union Street
San Francisco, CA 94123
(415) 359-9205

COLORADO

Snug Organics
snugorganics.com
484 S. Emerson St.
Denver, CO 80209
info@snugorganics.com

CONNECTICUT

Baby CZ
www.babyCZ.com
360 Greenwich Ave.
Greenwich, CT 06830
(203) 340-9932

Duck Duck Goose
duckduckgoosect.com
43 River St.
Milford, CT
(203) 874-6206

FLORIDA

Seedlings Baby & Children's Store
www.seedlings.com
1530 South Dale Mabry Hwy
Tampa, Florida 33629
(813) 251-5111

GEORGIA

Seed Factory
seedfactoryatlanta.com
1100 Howell Mill Rd.
Atlanta, GA 30318
(404) 335-2043

HAWAII

Bamboo Works Inc.
bambooworks.com
4-1388 Kuhio Highway #C-109
Kapaa, Hawaii 96746
(808) 821-8688
info@bambooworks.com

ILLINOIS

Monica + Andy
www.monicaandandy.com
2038 North Halsted St.
Chicago, IL 60614

INDIANA

The Natural Way
www.thenaturalway.org
U.P Mall
6501 Grape Rd. Unit 170
Mishawaka, IN 46545
(574) 807-8797

MASSACHUSETTS

Baby Koo
www.baby-koo.com
188 Needham Street
Newton, MA 02464
(617) 467-5860

Hatched Boston
www.hatchedboston.com
668 Centre St.
Jamaica Plain, MA
(617) 524-5402

UrthChild
www.urthchild.com
860 Bow Wow Road
Sheffield, MA 01257
(413) 248-1123

MICHIGAN

Modern Natural Baby
www.modernnaturalbaby.com
200 W 9 Mile Rd. Suite B
Ferndale, MI 48220
(248) 629-6306
contact@modernnaturalbaby.com

Our Greentopia
www.ourgreentopia.com
3165 West 12 Mile Rd.
Berkley, Michigan 48072
(248) 268-2123
info@ourgreentopia.com

MINNESOTA

Bambino Land
www.bambinoland.com
761 E. 8th Street
Winona, MN
(888) 415-5825
service@bambinoland.com

Pacifier
pacifier.me
Multiple locations in St. Paul,
Minneapolis, and Edina. See
website for details.
(888) 623-8123

MISSOURI

Cotton Babies
www.cottonbabies.com
1200 Town and Country
Crossing Dr.
Chesterfield, MO

NEW HAMPSHIRE

Bona Fide Green Goods
www.bonafidegreengoods.com
35 South Main St.
Concord, NH 03301
(603)224-9700

Stork Organic Baby Boutique
www.storkorganicbaby.com
273 Union Square, On The Oval
Milford, New Hampshire 03055
(603) 673-5381

NEW JERSEY

Hazel Baby & Kids
www.hazelbaby.com
199 Montgomery St.
Jersey City, NJ 07302
(201) 369-1999

NEW YORK

The Baby's Den
www.babysden.com/organic.html
3015 Ave J
Brooklyn, NY 11210
(718) 676-1748
thebabysden@gmail.com

Green Babies
greenbabies.com
28 Spring St.
Tarrytown, NY 10591
(800) 603-7508
mail@greenbabies.com

Little Hippie
www.littlehippie.com
107 W 68th St
New York, NY 10023
(917) 873-0404

NORTH CAROLINA

GreenPea Baby & Child
www.greenpeababystore.com
316 Colonades Way
Waverly Place
Cary, NC 27518
(919) 851-4000

OHIO

Adooka Organics
www.adooka.com
13005 Larchmere Blvd.
Shaker Heights, OH 44120
(216) 920-7570

Cherub's Blanket
www.cherubsblanket.com
530 Euclid Ave. Suite 14
Cleveland, OH 44115
(877) 902-2292

Two Crows for Joy
www.twocrowsforjoy.com
13005 Larchmere Blvd.
Shaker Heights, OH 44120
(216) 920-7570

OREGON

Baby Wit
www.babywit.com
1315 N. Shaver St.
Portland, OR 97227
(503) 284-2283

TENNESSEE

Arcade
arcadenashville.com
2106-B Acklen Ave.
Nashville, TN 37212
(615) 928-7660
hello@arcadenashville.com

TEXAS

Sloomb
www.sloomb.com
403 E. Stan Schleuter Loop
Suite 303
Killeen, TX 76542

ONLINE

Aquarian Dreams
www.aquariandreams.com

Baby, Go Green
www.shopbabygogreen.com
Based in Houston, TX

Baby Naturopathics
www.babynaturopathics.com

Baby's Enchanted Garden
www.babysenchantedgarden.
com

BabySoyUSA
www.babysoyusa.com

Burt's Bees Baby
www.burtsbeesbaby.com
Based in Fairfield, CT

Colored Organics
www.coloredorganics.com
Based in St. Paul, MN

Curly Monkey
shop.curlymonkey.com
Based in Marina Del Rey, CA

Danish Woolen Delight
www.danishwool.com
Based in Westford, VT

Dash Hemp
www.dashhemp.com
Based in Santa Cruz, CA

Dwell Smart
www.dwellsmart.com/Products/
Babies-and-Kids
Based in Charleston, SC

Earth Creations
www.earthcreations.net
Based in Bessemer, AL

Eartheasy
www.eartheasy.com

Ecomall
www.ecomall.com

Ever Simplicity
eversimplicity.com
Based in Tustin, CA

Fairies Dance
www.faeriesdance.com
Based in Happy Valley, OR

Finn and Emma
www.finnandemma.com
Also in department stores

Frugi
www.welovefrugi.com
Based in England

Funkoos
www.funkoos.com
Based in Danbury, CT

Garden Kids Organic Clothing
www.gardenkidsclothing.com
Clothing made in Oregon

Green Apple
www.greenappleactive.com
Based in CA

Green Envy
www.greenenvyshop.com

Green Pixie Baby
www.greenpixiebaby.com
Retail location in **The Shop
Around the Corner**
117 Third Avenue
N. Franklin, TN 37064
(615) 542-4338
greenpixiebaby@live.com

Hanna Anderson
www.hannaandersson.com
Based in Louisville, KY

Imagine GreenWear
stores.imaginegreenwear.com
Based in Fairfax, VA

Ittikid
www.ittikid.com
Based in Santa Rosa, CA

Kate Quinn Organics
www.katequinnorganics.com

Kook Wear
matthewmorey.com/kook-wear

Lady Bug Baby Organics
ladybugbabyorganics.com
ladybugbabyorganics@yahoo.
com
(866) 491-8883
Based in Comstock Park, MI

Le Petit Organic
www.lepetitorganic.com
Based in Valley Stream, NY

Levana Naturals
www.levananaturals.com

Lina and Mickey
www.linaandmickey.com

Little Animals
www.littleanimals.com
Based in Marlton, NJ

Little Spruce Organics
www.littlespruceorganics.com
Based in Denver, CO

Maple Grace
maplegrace.com
Based in Marin County, CA

Mini Apple Tree
www.miniappletree.com
Based in Portland, OR

MomKidsBiz
www.momkidsbiz.com
Based in San Diego, CA

The Natural Baby
www.naturalbabyhome.com
(330) 244-9518
Based in North Canton, OH

Nature's Crib
www.naturescrib.com
Based in Glen Spey, NY

Nature's Organic Market
naturesorganicmarket.com
Based in Gilbert, AZ

New Jammies
newjammies.com
Based in Carbondale, CO

Nico Nico Clothing
niconicoclothing.com
Based in Los Angeles, CA

Nirvana Mama
www.nirvanamamas.com
Based in Sebastian, FL

Oeuf
www.oeufnyc.com
Based in Brooklyn, NY

Omunky
www.omunky.com
Based in Norwalk, CT

Orange Rhino (Etsy shop)
orangerhinokids.com
Based in Minneapolis, MN

Organically Baby
www.organicallybaby.com
(323) 696-1644
Based in Austin, TX

Our Green House
www.ourgreenhouse.com
willow02@aol.com
Based in Sandy Hook, CT

Penguin Organics
www.penguinorganics.com
Based in San Francisco, CA

Repair the World
www.repairtheworldnow.com
(513) 873-5657

Serendipity Organics
serendipity-organics.com
Based in Denmark

Simple Family Living
www.simplefamilyliving.com
Based in Portland, OR

Simply Chickie
simplychickieclothing.com
Based in Newport, RI

Solmate Socks
www.socklady.com

SOS From Texas
www.sosfromtexas.com
Based in TX

Teres Kids
tereskids.com
Based in Santa Fe, NM

Under the Nile
underthenile.com

Vyssan Lull
www.vyssanlull.com
(646) 234-9505

Wild Dill
www.wilddill.com
Based in CA

Whole Foods
wholefoods.com
Numerous cities across the U.S.

Winter Water Factory
www.winterwaterfactory.com
Based in Brooklyn, NY

Cloth vs Disposable

I think most of us know by now that disposable diapers, which are the most commonly used, are not the best for the environment because they end up creating a lot of waste. According to the EPA, an estimated 3.6 million tons of disposable diapers were generated in 2013 alone, or 1.4 percent of total municipal solid waste generation.[1] So imagine that number occurring each year. There is a large debate about what is more convenient, cheaper, and what is better for your baby's skin. I'll leave that debate for the blogosphere, but I will point out that cloth diapers are not so low-tech anymore. Some brands come with waterproof covers to lock in moisture, cloth pad inserts to increase absorbency, and flushable liners that help contain the mess so you don't need to rinse the whole diaper before depositing them in a diaper pail for later washing.[2] And you can find them in organic cotton/hemp.

Here are just a few sources of cloth diapers:

- www.bumgenius.com
- www.bummis.com
- www.loveybums.com
- www.greenmountaindiapers.com
- www.happyheiny.com
- www.kissaluvs.com

---

1   Environmental Protection Agency. *Advancing Sustainabe Materials Management: Facts and Figures 2013.* June 2015. https://www.epa.gov/sites/production/files/2015-09/documents/2013_advncng_smm_rpt.pdf
2   Consumer Reports. *Diaper Buying Guide.* May 2016. http://www.consumerreports.org/cro/diapers/buying-guide

All About the Guys
Brands Focusing on Eco-Menswear

Cariloha

Criquet Shirts (www.criquet-shirts.com)
Texas-based organic cotton polo shirts for men and boys.

Dirtball Fashion (www.dirtballfashion.com)
Eco-friendly (recycled water bottles and recycled cotton). Hundred percent made in the USA. Water conservation practices in manufacturing.

Fanmail (www.fanmail-us.com)
Clothing made with plant-based fabrics and fair-trade labor.

Indie Peace (www.indiepeace.com)
Georgia-based, organic cotton men's t-shirts.

La Paz (www.lapaz.pt)
Ethical treatment of workers, cleanly sourced materials.

Outerknown (www.outerknown.com)
Fair trade, Bluesign certified (no toxins in manufacturing process).

Parallel Revolution (www.pararev.com)
California-based company, hemp and organic cotton-collared shirts.

Solosso (www.solosso.com)
Swiss-led Singaporean company, specializing in dress shirts.

Apolis (www.apolisglobal.com)
Clothing and accessories all ethically manufactured.

Archival (www.archivalclothing.com)
Clothing and accessories made in the USA. All materials manufactured by family businesses in the USA.

Arthur & Henry (www.arthurandhenry.com)
United Kingdom-based company. Fair trade, certified organic menswear made in India.

Brave Gentleman (www.bravegentleman.com)
NY-based vegan and sustainable clothing, shoes, cologne.

Cash Crop Clothing
(www.cashcropclothing.com)
Nevada-based organic cotton and recycled wool shirts and jackets.

Cock and Bull
(cockandbullmenswear.co.uk)
United Kingdom company uses sustainable fabrics and textiles.

Collared Greens
(www.collaredgreens.com)
Offers organic cotton tees and hats for men and boys. Storefront in Richmond, VA.

Cariloha

Svengali (svengalivesture.com)
Organic fair-trade cotton t-shirts and accessories for men.

Tuckerman & Co
(www.tuckerman.co)
Organic cotton men's dress shirts made in Connecticut.

We Three Leaves
(www.wethreeleaves.com)
Organic cotton and ethical wool, based in Brooklyn.

Index

CPSIA information can be obtained
at www.ICGtesting.com
Printed in the USA
FSHW02n1131260518
48528FS